EUROPEAN WELFARE PRODUCTION

Institutional Configuration and Distributional Outcome

Edited by

JOACHIM VOGEL

University of Umeå, Stockholm, Sweden

With Contributions by

TÖRES THEORELL, STEFAN SVALLFORS,
HEINZ-HERBERT NOLL and BERNARD CHRISTOPH

Reprinted from *Social Indicators Research*, Volume 64, No. 3 (December 2003)

KLUWER ACADEMIC PUBLISHERS
DORDRECHT / BOSTON / LONDON

Social Indicators Research Series

Volume 18

This new series aims to provide a public forum for single treatises and collections of papers on social indicators research that are too long to be published in our journal *Social Indicators Research*. Like the journal, the book series deals with statistical assessments of the quality of life from a broad perspective. It welcomes the research on a wide variety of substantive areas, including health, crime, housing, education, family life, leisure activities, transportation, mobility, economics, work, religion and environmental issues. These areas of research will focus on the impact of key issues such as health on the overall quality of life and vice versa. An international review board, consisting of Ruut Veenhoven, Joachim Vogel, Ed Diener, Torbjorn Moum and Wolfgang Glatzer, will ensure the high quality of the series as a whole.

CONTENTS

A C.I.P. Catalogue record for this book is available from the Library of Congress.

ISBN 1-4020-1149-0

Published by Kluwer Academic Publishers,
P.O. Box 17, 3300 AA Dordrecht, The Netherlands.

Sold and distributed in North, Central and South America
by Kluwer Academic Publishers,
101 Philip Drive, Norwell, MA 02061, U.S.A.

In all other countries, sold and distributed
by Kluwer Academic Publishers,
P.O. Box 322, 3300 AH Dordrecht, The Netherlands.

Printed on acid-free paper

Printed and bound in the Netherlands.

PREFACE

The Europe of today faces a concurrence of developmental problems related to structural shifts in the global economy, global competition, changing regional labour markets, demographic change, and European integration. Economic crisis, decreasing industrial employment, the shift to a service economy, flexible and insecure jobs, and persistent mass unemployment exhaust the capacity of the welfare state institutions. Countermeasures by reductions in the transfer systems and public services challenge the basic assumptions underlying the Western European social policies as well as the legitimacy of European integration.

Concurrently we are facing a gradual destabilisation of social bonds. Household sizes are declining, the populations are greying, birth rates are declining, divorce rates are inclining, single adults and single parents are increasing in number, and the family forms are becoming more pluralized. The family as a welfare-supporting institution seems to deteriorate as well.

These changes are affecting the living conditions in most member states, at variant pace and intensity. They affect the social cohesion in the European Union. In fact, they also challenge the legitimacy of the Union: European unification fostering individual prosperity, a general convergence of living conditions, and union-wide norms for national policies. Instead, there is a new concern related to social exclusion and poverty, to permanent mass unemployment and growing inequalities.

There is an urgent need of knowledge of the basics of living conditions in the European Union, from two perspectives:

- First, the descriptive monitoring of living conditions and their differentiation within and between EU nations; and their convergence or divergence in Europe.
- Second, an understanding of the institutional background shaping the differentiation of living conditions, within as well as between nations.

While there is a rapid increase in the knowledge base concerning living conditions within member states as well as its variation between nations and groups, there is less consensus on the driving forces shaping the distributive structure in Europe. Some focus on the evolvement of exogenous globalisation rewriting the agenda for welfare production. Global competition, the liberalisation of financial markets, and the transition to the knowledge society requires adjustment of the labour market as well as the welfare state and the family. The last two decades have been a period of reorientation to meet these challenges. The liberal approach of adjustment by increased competitiveness through cost reduction, deregulation, flexibility and wage differentiation is the offensive way of market logic. It includes deliberation from political control, export of responsibility for the welfare of less productive labour, and it adds to the responsibilities of the welfare state to reduce social exclusion in all its variant forms. The principle is 'less welfare state', increased responsibility for the household sector and increased inequality.

This is the ultimate test for the welfare state logic of solidarity. Redistribution by taxes, transfers and services serves to correct for inequalities created at the labour market. With decreased employment, increased unemployment, larger wage differentials, and insecure income larger demands will be laid on the welfare state as well as the family. Hence, 'more welfare state' is required, and equally expected by the voters, while 'less welfare state' is enforced by economic realities. The crisis of the welfare state is financial as well as moral. Along with cutbacks goes an understanding of insecurity in the social protection net, the experience of lost values and trust in politics.

In consequence, we are facing a breakdown of the division of responsibility for welfare production between labour market (jobs, earnings), welfare state (transfers, services), and family (care, sharing of resources). A new compromise is required between competitiveness and equality, redefining the roles of the market, welfare state and family. The character of this welfare mix is not an inevitable, technical matter; it is an ideological choice between different values such as solidarity, equality, effectiveness, and valued life styles.

This is the theme of this book; to identify the choice of institutional configuration and distribution of responsibilities for welfare delivery, and the corresponding welfare outcome at the micro level. We are looking for variation in welfare regimes within the European union, and their respective distributive outcomes.

The research agenda of this report sets out from the tradition of the social indicator movement, focussing on the distribution of living conditions at micro level. With access to new comparative welfare surveys (ECHP and Nordic databases) the variation of living conditions within as well as between nations can be studied in more detail, and for a complete set of EU member states, and for some nations even in a longitudinal perspective. Likewise is recent *regime research* drawing on new comparative data on the institutional context behind individual living conditions. Combining these data on 'welfare production' provides insight into the way living conditions are monitored by the labour market, welfare state and family at national level, and on the combined 'welfare efficiency' of these institutions.

The new perspective in this report is an integrated approach. We have combined these two research traditions. First, we have explored the general character of national welfare production by integrating labour market, welfare state and family characteristics in the European union towards an integrated typology. Second, the corresponding distributive features have been identified, and included in the typology.

We have abandoned the tradition of using nations as single illustrations of idealtypical categories. Instead we use the new comparative databases to utilize the full set of EU-member states to explore the variation of institutional features and distributive outcomes. We have explored this link in a *comparative* perspective as well as *longitudinal* perspective. The comparative approach is aiming at the identification of similarities and dissimilarities between EU member states with respect to institutional configuration and corresponding distributive outcomes in the mid 1990s. The longitudinal approach follows the Swedish case over a period of some 35 years.

This research has been supported by a consultancy from the statistical office of the European union EUROSTAT, and the Swedish Social Research Council.

Joachim Vogel
Stockholm and Umeå, Sweden

JOACHIM VOGEL

INTRODUCTION

The Europe of today faces a concurrence of developmental problems related to structural shifts in the global economy, global competition, changing regional labour markets, demographic change, and European integration. Economic crisis, decreasing industrial employment, the shift to a service economy, flexible and insecure jobs, and persistent mass unemployment exhaust the capacity of the welfare state institutions. Countermeasures by reductions in the transfer systems and public services challenge the basic assumptions underlying the Western European social policies as well as the legitimacy of European integration.

These changes have a major impact on the standard of living and quality of life in Europe. Public policies designed to protect and insure for risks in the course of life related to employment, income, health, and family maintenance fail to deliver, as the number of beneficiaries grows. Compensation levels and periods have been reduced, and individual contributions expanded. Life became less predictable.

Concurrently we are facing a gradual destabilisation of social bonds. Household sizes are declining, the populations are greying, birth rates are declining, divorce rates are inclining, single adults and single parents are increasing in number, and the family forms are becoming more pluralized. The family as a welfare-supporting institution seems to deteriorate.

These changes are affecting the living conditions in most member states, at variant pace and intensity. They affect the social cohesion in the European Union. In fact, they also challenge the legitimacy of the Union: European unification fostering individual prosperity, a general convergence of living conditions, and union-wide norms for national policies. Instead, there is a new concern related to social exclusion and poverty, to permanent mass unemployment and

Social Indicators Research **64:** 329–347, 2003.

growing inequalities. Today's key discourse concerns the limits of social policy and the demands of the market:

- Can we afford the Welfare State?
- Is enhanced economic insecurity, flexibility and social exclusion a necessary prize for competitiveness?
- How are these forces to be balanced to preserve social cohesion and political legitimacy for the difficult task of European unification.

WELFARE RESEARCH PERSPECTIVES

There is an urgent need of knowledge of the basics of living conditions in the European Union from two perspectives:

- First, the descriptive monitoring of living conditions and their differentiation within and between nations; and their convergence or divergence in Europe.
- Second, an understanding of the institutional background shaping the differentiation of living conditions, within as well as between nations.

While there is a rapid increase in the knowledge base concerning living conditions within member states as well as its variation between nations and groups, there is less consensus on the driving forces shaping the distributive structure in Europe. Concurrently we see malfunctioning of the labour market as well as the welfare state and the family. The popular interpretations are related to the major ideological beliefs. There is considerable consensus on the profound changes over the past decades in the way welfare is produced, as well as the direction of this change. However, there is disagreement on the causes and desirability of this change. Some focus on the evolvement of exogenous globalisation rewriting the agenda for welfare production. Global competition, the liberalisation of financial markets, and the transition to the knowledge society requires adjustment of the labour market as well as the welfare state and the family. The last two decades have been a period of reorientation to meet these challenges. The liberal approach of adjustment by *increased competitiveness* through cost reduction, deregulation, flexibility and wage differentiation is the offensive way of market logic. It includes deliberation from political control, export of responsibility for the welfare of less productive labour, and it adds to the responsibilities of the welfare state to reduce social exclusion in all its variant forms. The principles are is 'less welfare state', increased responsibility for the household sector and increased inequality.

This is the ultimate test for the welfare state logic of solidarity. Redistribution by taxes, transfers and services serves to correct for inequalities created at the labour market. With deceased employment, increased unemployment, larger wage differentials, and insecure income larger demands will be laid on the welfare state; first, because of more recipients, and second, because of less resources delivered by tax income. Hence, 'more welfare state' is required, and equally expected by the voters; while 'less welfare state' is enforced by economic realities. The crisis of the welfare state is financial as well as moral. Along with cutbacks goes an understanding of insecurity in the social protection net, the ideological sense of lost values and trust in politics.

The crisis of the welfare state is primarily a consequence of the crisis of local and regional labour markets, under the pressure of global competition. In consequence, we are facing a breakdown of the division of responsibility for welfare production between labour market (jobs, earnings), welfare state (transfers, services), and family (care, sharing of resources). In the past two decades globalisation and the new economy demand a new compromise between competitiveness and equality, redefining the roles of the market, welfare state and family. The character of this welfare mix is not an inevitable, technical matter, it is an ideological choice between different values such as solidarity, equality, effectiveness, and valued life styles.

This is the theme of this book; to identify the choice of institutional configuration and distribution of responsibilities, and the corresponding welfare consequences at the micro level. We are looking for variation in welfare regimes within the European union, and their respective distributive outcomes.

This research has been supported by the Swedish Social Research Council.

The Social Indicator Tradition

The social indicator tradition is our first entry to the comparative analysis of living conditions. Social indicators are our tool to measure the level and distribution of living conditions at micro level. Social indicators go beyond the merely descriptive or "bookkeeping" approach of traditional social statistics, and incorporate a potential for evaluation, prognosis and planning:

- They usually focus on ***individual well-being at micro level***, and they are typically ***output-related*** (e.g., state of health in contrast to health care expenditure).
- Normally, social indicators are disaggregated for subgroups of the population in order to permit analysis of the distribution of living conditions. They facilitate systematic ***comparisons between groups*** (degree of inequality) and ***over time*** (trends).
- Social indicators look ***beyond traditional global monetary indicators*** in order to chart social change. Non-monetary aspects such as social contacts, victimisation, political participation, the natural environment and health and are among the additional aspects introduced.
- There is also a strong interest in measuring '***system performance***', through comparisons between *regions* and *nations*. On a general level, social indicators are ***policy-related***, and therefore ***normative*** in character. They are usually regarded as an integral component of social programs.
- Ideally, social indicators form ***a user friendly and compact system of measures***, which also makes it possible to collect and analyse data on the main issues without exhausting available resources.

Much of the early thinking of the social indicator movement was influenced by the unity of economic statistics, as well as its success as a basis for planning. However, neither a unifying general social theory nor a corresponding linkage (such as money in economic statistics) is yet available.

Nowadays most national statistical offices and several international agencies produce standardised Social Reports. Social reporting refers to comprehensive presentations, ranging from relatively simple statistical compendia covering several fields, to extensive and elaborate attempts to give a comprehensive as well as analytical picture of living conditions, beyond a mere descriptive presentation of tables. The means employed are similar to those of social indicators: output-oriented and policy-related presentations of the well-being of individuals and households, including trends and systematic disaggregations for distribution analyses.

Social indicators and social reports are usually structured around a series of social domains, with the presentation organised under such chapter headings as:

- Population
- Family and household formation
- Education
- Social mobility
- Employment
- Working conditions
- Income and wealth
- Consumption
- Housing
- Leisure and culture
- Time use
- Transportation
- Natural environment
- Social contacts
- Victimisation
- Participation
- Health.

The experiences of the social indicator movement, and the national social reporting practices are further discussed in Vogel (1995). There appears to be a trend in national social reporting towards a convergence of domains, more comprehensive coverage, and growing similarity. Nowadays there is a variety of activities ranging from General Social Reports to specialised reports focusing on a special domain (e.g., Health Reports), or a special group of observation (e.g., Youth Reports, Regional Social Reports). A general overview of living conditions in the European union along these lines is given in a general social report for the union (Vogel, 1997). From this report we have retrieved statistics on the distributive structure with respect to income, material living standards, housing, family networks and health.

The Democratic Function of Social Indicators and Social Reporting

The primary use of European social indicators and social reporting is ***general enlightenment*** on living conditions, needed for public debate and monitoring of the social dimension of Europe. The experience from the national level indicates that important policy issues can be addressed at a general level. However, social reporting seldom aims directly at details of policy analysis.

One very important function is to ***focus public and political attention*** at social exclusion, at the distribution of living conditions, and at convergence or divergence of living conditions. Proper social reporting should therefore be institutionalised (systematic, regular), producing regular and authorative statistics on the national variation as well as regional variation of living conditions (within regions/nations as well as between). It should also deliver ***systematic information*** on the variation by major social cleavages, such as gender, age, social class, household type, ethnicity and by labour market participation. The ***convergence/divergence of living conditions*** among such entities as well as among Member States should be monitored by systematic trend analyses.

Social reporting performs an important function in the representative democracies of Europe. All actions bearing upon our living conditions – the formation of political opinion, voting, decision-making, etc. – should be based on objective information gathered by means of scientific methods, and that information should be available to everyone. Social indicators and social reporting, at both the national and international level, illuminate trends, comparative dissimilarities and patterns of inequality.

Data Collection: The Comprehensive Survey

At the national level, data sources often have not typically been developed for the kinds of purposes served by social indicators, with their output-related measurements, individual/household statistical units, and their focus on individual resources and well-being. Administrative registers have often been designed to serve administrative needs to count inputs, costs and activities. Existing registers are often unable to provide micro-data for disaggregations (individuals and households as statistical units; disaggregations by a coherent set of background variables). For all these reasons, in several countries new kinds of comprehensive surveys have been developed, which capture social indicator characteristics. Today, similar data are available in most countries, but they tend to be scattered about in many surveys conducted by various institutions, and at different points in time.

There are several advantages of a comparative and comprehensive survey of living conditions. Most important, a comprehensive survey provides simultaneous measurement, and hence integrated data regarding several areas of interest for the same sample of persons, and for the same period or point in time. This affords the opportunity for analyses of the co-variation, compensation and accumulation of living conditions, and for a better understanding of causal relationships. In particular, such surveys will provide the best basis for studies of the distribution of social indicators and living conditions in a wider sense. From a technical perspective, there is also better control of comparability and data quality, by reducing the effects of quality variation that may arise from the use of different sources, as well as by common procedures of implementation. Comprehensive surveys are flexible tools for tailored indicators, responding to policy issues and user demands. Conducting a comprehensive surveys on a regular basis also provides an opportunity to incorporate additional modules relating to special social domains, as well as in-depth enhancements of selected topics. Compared to previous methods of harmonising national data sources by ex post facto coordination, a co-ordinated European survey speeds up reporting considerably, since all data would be collected at the same time.

This report used data from the first genuine comparative database for the full set of 15 EU member states, which, in principle, has been coordinated ex ante to produce best comparability. This is the combined data set of ECHP and Nordic Social Surveys covering the situation of the mid 1990s (the ECHP/NSS database developed for this report).

Arenas and Resources

The second entry to this report places social indicators in its social context, the *arenas* where individuals act, where market forces, public intervention and social networks jointly contribute to the production of individual living conditions. Social indicators can be interpreted as *resources invested and achieved* on arenas, such as the labour market, the consumer market, the housing market, the political arena, the educational system, the neighbourhood, or the marriage market. Arenas represent the social and economic environment where resources such as education and competence, income, capital, health, status and social capital (connections) are utilised as well as produced. We can speak of a transformation of invested resources to final outcomes, as well as to new resources to be utilised in other arenas.

The productivity of available and invested resources is influenced by social intervention as well as social network support. Inequalities of living conditions are usually arranged in patterns, related to lack of initial resources (e.g., education) affecting secondary resources and outcomes on other arenas (employment, income from work). It is such chains of exclusion that public transfers, services and taxation are designed to influence. Public intervention expands available resources, or restricts their use in order to improve the general distribution of living conditions.

In the Scandinavian research tradition the focus of measurement is primarily on resources and factual information related to these. This tradition also dominates in the European Panel and ECHP/NSS database.

Social Exclusion

The third entry to the comparative analysis of living conditions is the classical sociological conflict perspective, looking at the social order and the distribution of living conditions as imposed by a set of hierarchical power relations. Social exclusion, and related concepts such as poverty, inequality and social exclusion reflect the interplay of group self interest and available power resources such as property, status, skill, political influence, ethnic group and social network support.

Social exclusion can be seen as a ***social relationship*** between the included and the excluded, as a ***dynamic process*** or as an ***identity*** of the excluded. Social exclusion is usually legitimised and institutionalised, sometimes creating near impermeable boundaries for the excluded. The 'included' enjoy access to scarce resources, and they share a common interest of preserving the social order. Hence there is a corresponding ideological value system to support the going distribution of resources, utilising concepts such as fairness, justice, and efficiency. There is as organised defence of the social order as well as attack on the social order, such as labour unions and employers organisations, and interest organisations focusing on gender, handicap, environment, immigrants, channelling group interest and serving as partners in the social dialogue.

In modern democracies, and in particular the European welfare states, social exclusion is usually regarded as a persistent remaining condition of an earlier period. However, over the last decade there is a new insight that social exclusion can also develop as a mode of adaptation in times of economic crisis: today we are facing twenty years of persistent mass unemployment and a 'new poverty'. It seems that the idea of a social citizenship, the growth of prosperity and welfare in all member states, and the levelling of disparities of living conditions within and between member states have not been fulfilled.

The intensity of social exclusion may vary between member states, and between the various types of social cleavages, following political history and traditional conflicts, power relations at national level, and the present economic situation. Social class, gender, generation, region, ethnicity and handicap represent the traditional cleavages common to most member states. Lately several 'new' cleavages can be added to the list recognised in political debate and social research, such as labour market position, family type and education. Some of the major subgroups included in a comparative screening of possible disadvantaged groups are:

- women
- young adults
- single mothers
- parents of 3+children
- manual workers

- unemployed
- part-time workers
- home workers
- old age pensioners
- pre-mature pensioners
- people living in poverty
- immigrants.

Welfare Delivery Institutions: Labour Market, Welfare State and Family

While the social indicator tradition is distinctly descriptive and micro level oriented, the arena perspective introduces a causal thinking, looking at individual behaviour and welfare outcomes in relation to institutional arrangements and power relations. Resources are the link between the micro level and institutional level.

A fourth entry to this report is recent social research focusing on the national level, identifying patterns of institutional configuration related to social protection, employment, gender issues and family arrangements, and the interactions between these in shaping the specific national environment, whose unique national outcome we can measure in terms of living conditions, or as social indicators.

In the tradition of Titmuss (1958) and Marshall (1975) several typologies of welfare state models have been developed by Esping-Andersen (1991, 1999), Castles and Mitchell (1992), Korpi and Palme (1994) and others. This line of thinking in terms of national characteristics identifies *welfare state regimes* as ideal types. The regimes tradition originally focussed on the relation between the labour market and welfare state, and in particular on the provisions of the welfare state. Research along these lines is expanding, exposing inconsistencies between these ideal types and empirical reality, and adding new dimensions. In the same vein models of *employment regimes, gender regimes and family regimes* have been developed (Lewis, 1992; Duncan, 1995; Hirdman, 1990 and others), adding new dimensions to the institutional background of the variation of living conditions. These new perspectives will be incorporated in a new typology integrating the contributions of the welfare state, labour market as well as the family, towards a typology of *European welfare production models* or *integrated welfare regimes*.

The approach chosen in this report is exploratory and empirical: to identify modalities of institutional configuration and distributive outcome, with nations as statistical units.

THE FOCUS OF THIS REPORT: WELFARE DELIVERY INSTITUTIONS AND DISTRIBUTIVE OUTCOME

The improvement of living conditions is the prime objective in social planning. The issue of distributive justice and social exclusion receives central attention in the public debate and policy-making in most developed nations. With increased access to general social surveys, comparative social indicators and social reporting we are slowly unfolding the distributive structure, at first within developed countries, then expanding social indicator research to comparative analysis, and adding to the field of observation more complete lists of domains and indicators. In addition, with increased insight into the distribution of living conditions within nations, the variation of distributive structure between nations is unfolded.

Recent comparative research focusing on the European union (Vogel, 1997, 1998, 2000a, 2000b) displays a clear clustering of nations concerning the national distribution of a wide range of welfare outcome indicators, e.g., income and poverty, housing conditions, consumption, assets, working conditions, education, participation, social networks, family formation, health, etc, along major social cleavages such as social class, gender, generation, family types, region and ethnicity. The major lesson from these studies is that there is a grouping of nations in clusters with similar *level* of inequality, as well as similar *structure* of distributive outcome. And there is a clear dissimilarity between these clusters in the distributive outcome.

The empirical base for theorising this variation of distributive outcome is growing with new tools such as the European Community Household Panel (ECHP) and equivalent comparative surveys in the Nordic countries. ECHP began 1994 and has then been followed up as a panel each year. The coordination of data collection has been carried out ex ante. Hence, during a few years in the mid 1990s we have a time window with good access to comparative data, which then is gradually closed as this panel loses its representativity due to panel attrition and member states terminating their original sample.

The new elements here is the access to coordinated data for a full set of member states, instead of single representatives of various welfare regimes which have been used as illustrative cases in primarily theoretical research. ECHP/NSS covers comparable data for a vast social indicator list.

Similar distributive outcome should reflect a similarity in institutional arrangements with impact on the level and distribution of living conditions. This is the focus of this report. We will explore the link between the institutional configuration and their distributive consequences. We will search for a parsimonious typology of *welfare production models* (or welfare regimes), not restricted to welfare state arrangements, but focused on the wider configuration between welfare state, labour market and family. Our first attention is focused at the labour market and its provision of jobs and earnings to a maximum fraction of the population at sufficient levels. Next we will look at the compensatory role of the welfare state vis-à-vis the labour market's entrapment and its logic of competence and competitiveness ('decommodification'). The same applies to correction of the dependency or even entrapment in the family ('defamilialization'), or alternatively the supportive role of the family. Here lies some of the major critique of the original typology of welfare state regime (Esping-Andersen, 1990), in relation to its gender blindness, neglect of the household economy and implicit neutrality to the single breadwinner model (later revised in Esping-Andersen, 1999). In summary, the analysis will explore the ways the welfare state redistributes resources (or social rights) to the individual, by deliberation from dependencies of the market and family.

It should be understood that this conception of the role of the welfare state is by no means uncontroversial. It collides with liberal thinking of the market's sovereignty, as well as the subsidiary principle of the primacy of the family. Nevertheless, social citizenship and social rights are well-established entities in political thinking of the welfare state. In fact, it is the reality manifested in the configuration of welfare institutions, their division of responsibilities, their real performance and malfunctions we wish to capture.

Our yardstick in this exercise will be the distributive outcome. In the second part of this book we will explore the corresponding structure of inequality within countries with similar institutional arrangements. In particular, the following questions will be pursued:

- Is there a closer correspondence between clusters of similar welfare production models and distributive outcome?
- How are the various welfare production models performing in minimising inequalities along social cleavages?
- Is the an 'optimal' model of welfare production with higher efficiency in reducing inequalities?
- Are there deviants from the dominant welfare mix of institutional configuration and distributive outcome? How can these be explained?

There is a wide variation of institutional forms between the European Union member states, which also should produce large variation in the distributive pattern of living conditions. In fact, the European Union can be seen as a natural laboratory for the institutional-individual link. Exploring this link in a ***comparative perspective*** is the first objective of this paper, aiming at the identification of similarities and dissimilarities between EU member states in institutional configuration and corresponding distributive outcomes. In short: can the degree and structure of inequality in member states be explained by the 'welfare mix', i.e., the national configuration of market, welfare state and family?

In addition, we will use Swedish case to study the link between the institutional configuration and distributive outcome in a ***longitudinal perspective***. Within Europe Sweden has earlier plaid a special role as a leader towards a general expansion of the welfare state, as well as towards the 'inclusive labour market', and towards a general breakdown of traditional family bonds. The 'Swedish model', or rather Nordic model, has been recognised for its egalitarian policies, and its special features in reducing poverty and class inequality, and for promoting equal opportunities for women and men. Furthermore, Sweden is a pioneer country for empirical research, with access to excellent time series data, which just recently are beginning to be built up in Europe. The second objective of this paper is therefore to adding a longitudinal perspective to this analysis by exploring the evolvement of the Swedish model of welfare production over the past 30 years concerning key indicators of institutional performance in Sweden and corresponding distributive outcomes. This will add a second dimension to the analysis of the link between institutions and distributive outcome.

THEORETICAL FRAMEWORK

Recent empirical studies of welfare production (Vogel, 1997, 1998, 1999) build on the regimes tradition (welfare state regimes, employment regimes, gender regimes, family regimes[1]), in search for similarities and dissimilarities between nations in the institutional preconditions shaping the distribution of general living conditions. The regimes perspective of this report is not restricted to any of the major welfare delivery institutions per se (labour market, welfare state, family), but focused on their configuration ('welfare mix'). The model of welfare production (see next page) summarises this perspective. This report explores the link between the welfare mix and various aspects of the distribution of living conditions within and between EU-member states, including inequality of disposable income (Gini-coefficients), poverty and affluence rates, and inequality of material living conditions along cleavages such as class, gender, generation, region, and family forms.

Welfare Model

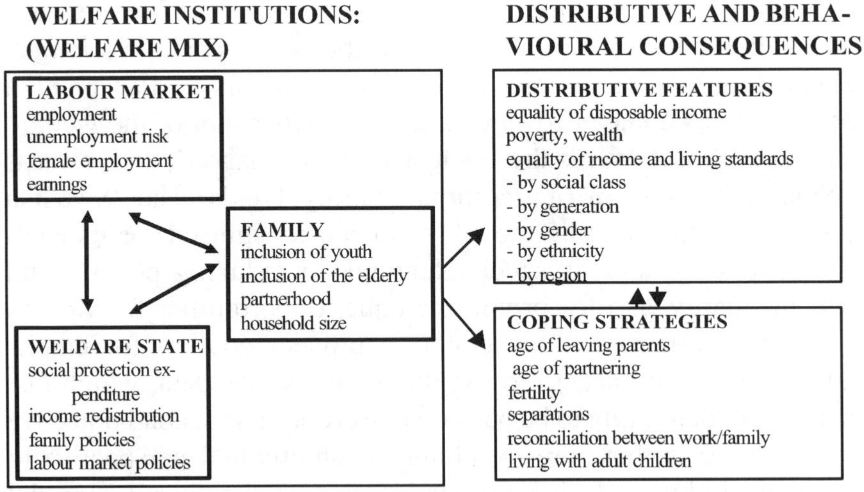

The distribution of living conditions is related to the institutional arrangements at national level. The objective of this paper is to explore the link between institutions and distributive outcome in a comparative as well as a longitudinal perspective; in short, can the degree and structure of inequality and social exclusion be empirically explained by the 'welfare mix', i.e., the national configuration of labour market, welfare state and family?

The basic assumptions of this approach are as follows:

- The three welfare delivery institutions represent a functional *division of responsibility for welfare delivery* between the labour market (employers), welfare state (politics) and family (social networks);
- The character of the distributive outcome (level of inequality and impact of social cleavages) will correspond to the welfare mix;
- The division of responsibility, as well as the provisions of each of the three institutions, can be evaluated with respect to its contribution or *efficiency* to distribute living conditions and reducing poverty, social exclusion and general inequality;
- In various proportion, the overall distributive structure displays the imprint of each of the three institutions, reflecting the distributive principles of the labour market (competition, competence), welfare state (collective solidarity) and family (reciprocity);
- The institutional configuration (the 'welfare mix') should be reduced to a limited number of logical combinations or welfare productions models;
- We should designate the major role to the labour market: Malfunctioning of the labour market will exhaust the welfare state as well as the family. Welfare state and family are two alternative correctives; 'efficient' labour markets (jobs, earnings) will relieve the welfare state as well as the family. In reverse, the generous welfare state requires an efficient labour market; and likewise, efficient labour markets promote emancipation from the family;
- The *driving forces* behind the current welfare mix are external and internal factors, such as global competition, national

resources, infrastructure, the historical and ideological tradition, power relations and ideological struggle;

- The 'welfare mix' will change over time and differs between nations. The welfare mix will accommodate to economic change, political cleavages and power relations;
- There is a variation of institutional forms between the EU-member states, which accordingly should produce a variation in the distributive pattern of living conditions. In fact, the European Union can be seen as a natural laboratory for analysing the institutional-individual link;
- At the micro level, people will adapt to the available options. *Coping behaviour* serves to avoid poverty and social exclusion and maximise general living conditions; it relates to the labour market (e.g., job seeking, training), welfare state (adjusting to available transfers and services), as well as the family (family formation including the age of leaving the parental home, partnering, child-bearing, and separations);
- Recent economic change involves major malfunctions of the welfare mix, related to the labour market (global competition, mass unemployment, job and wage flexibility), the welfare state (recovery policies), as well as the family (fragmentation), implying a changing institutional configuration as well as decreased overall institutional efficiency in providing good and equal living conditions.

The analysis will establish the link between the institutional configuration and its distributive outcome at the nation level. We will identify similarities and dissimilarities between 15 EU member states at the mid 1990s, as well as for Sweden in a longitudinal perspective for the past 30 years, with respect to the welfare mix as well as the distributive outcome.

The first part of this report gives a summary of the institutional arrangements and clusters of similar welfare mix among EU member states and Sweden, reducing this variation towards a typology of European welfare production models.[2] The second part of this report then gives the findings concerning distributive outcome, with comparative EU-data and longitudinal Swedish data. The concluding discussion then summarises these findings in the perspective of European welfare production models.

The typology presented in this report has been studied empirically in earlier reports (Vogel, 1998, 1999, 2000a, 2000b). In essence, this typology follows well the findings of earlier research. In this case, however, the elements included in its definition cover all three welfare institutions as well as a series of indicators of distributive outcome. The general structure does not deviate from the earlier typologies of the four (European) worlds of welfare capitalism (social democratic/Nordic; liberal/Anglo-Saxon; Continental/conservative; Mediterranean/family-oriented). The liberal world is not well captured, since data were restricted to the European union, where UK is the only clear representative. In order to facilitate reading and understanding of the clustering the three major clusters (Nordic; Southern; Central) are in most cases displayed in figures (black for Nordic cluster, grey for Southern cluster and striped for the intermediate central/islands cluster).

DATA

Living conditions are regularly measured by general social surveys and disseminated by general social reports. This paper draws on two recent General Social Reports published in 1997 concerning *Living conditions and Inequality in the European Union* (Vogel, 1997), and *Living conditions and inequality in Sweden: 1975–1995*, (Vogel and Häll (eds.), 1997). The European report is the first comparative general social report, based on micro data from co-ordinated comparative surveys in 15 countries, looking at the character of social exclusion, poverty and inequalities within and between the member states. The corresponding Swedish social report gives the corresponding Swedish trends for 1975–1995.

In 1994 the statistical office of the European Union, EUROSTAT, conducted the first comparative survey in the (then) twelve member states of 1994, collecting detailed information on income, employment, education, housing, material assets and selected indicators in several other social domains. This database from 1994 was used for the comparative analysis in this report (the European Community Household Survey, ECHP, first wave 1994). In addition three contemporary social surveys in the Nordic countries (Sweden, Finland and Norway) were integrated with this database. These 15 surveys have been harmonised ex post facto by the author to build a social indicator database for 15 countries (the 15 EU-countries less Austria, and including Norway). The total sample size of this comparative database is 143000 cases (adults 15–84 years of age). For short, this database is in this report labelled as ECHP/NSS.

Sample sizes and response rates for the comparative database are shown in Figures 1.1 and 2. The total sample size of the 15-nation database, 143000 interviews, makes this the largest survey ever conducted in this field. A complete set of systematic disaggregations for all indicators and nations are included in the comparative as well as Swedish social report.

In the case of Sweden there is an unbroken series of annual level of living surveys and social reporting since 1974 (Vogel et al., 1993; Vogel, 2000). The 1997 General Social Report published by Statistics Sweden (Vogel, J and Häll, L., editors, 1997) used 156000 interviews collected over these 20 years in repeated cross-sectional and panel surveys. This database is used for the trend analysis of the differentiation of Swedish living standards in this paper. The surveyed population is 16–74 years of age; the annual response rate is on the average around 80-85 percent.

In total the two survey systems utilised in this report amount to 300000 interviews.

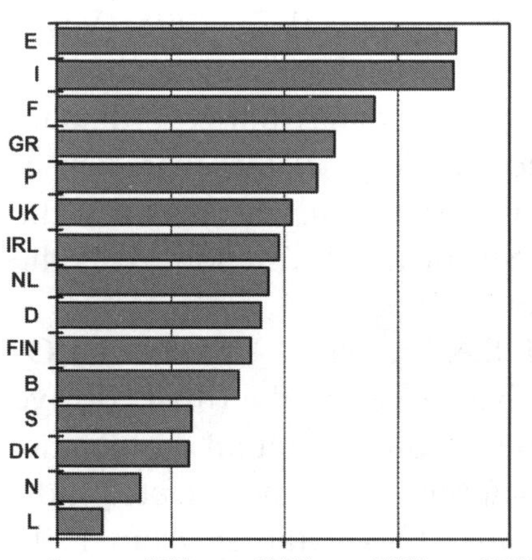

Figure 1.1 National sample size (persons). ECHP 1944 and Nordic surveys.

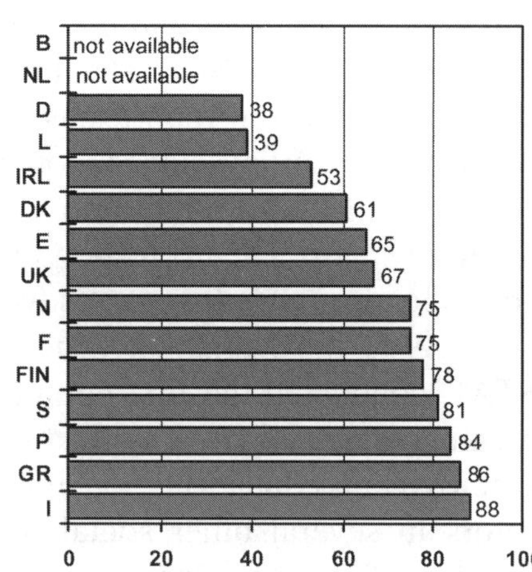

Figure 1.2 Response rates (persons). ECHP 1994/Nordic Surveys. Percent.

As can be seen from Figure 1.2 there are indications of large deficiencies in the general quality of data in several of the participating countries. For the Netherlands and Belgium already existing older panels were utilised. In these cases precise estimates of the response rates are not available, but can be estimated to be extremely low. The initial first-wave response rate of the Dutch and Belgium panels were approximately 50 percent. In the case of the Netherlands a ten-year old panel was used. The response rates in some of the countries are clearly problematic, as they fall well below 50 percent. The large *variation* in the national response rates (ranging from less than 38 to 88 percent) is in itself a major problem in comparative analysis, since non-response tends to be related to living conditions and social exclusion. Other quality problems are related to the conceptual comparability of data, which is not yet fully evaluated by Eurostat. Some of these methodological deficiencies explain outliers and unexpected findings in this report.

Additional data concerning the institutional level come from several national sources (Sweden) and international sources (OECD, Eurostat), such as the SNA, demographic databases, ESSPROS and the harmonised Labour Force Surveys.

NOTES

[1] E.g., Esping-Andersen (1990, 1991, 1999), Korpi and Palme (1994), Colbjörnsen and Esping-Andersen (1992), Castles and Mitchell (1992), Lewis (1992), Duncan (1995), Hirdman (1990), Rubery, Fagan and Smith (1995) and others; see also Vogel (1999) for a summary.

[2] Details are reported in Vogel 1997, 1999

SCB Statistics Sweden
Welfare Analysis Program
and
University of Umeå
PO Box 24300
10451 Stockholm
Sweden

JOACHIM VOGEL

THE LABOUR MARKET

The labour market is the major arena where the individual living conditions are determined. The performance of labour market is decisive for our general quality of life within as well as outside the work place. New personal resources are created on the labour market; first of all income, but also less tangible resources such as competence, identity, status and personal connections. Here are the individual resources acquired which then determine consumption and material living conditions in a wider sense. Earnings buys material goods as well as power and influence. Professional status and personal contacts established in the labour market open opportunities in most spheres of private life, such as social networks, family formation, culture and politics. Further, the lifelong working environment exposure impacts on health and life expectancy, with further consequences on the general quality of life.

Our interest is on the efficiency of the market in its role as a welfare delivery institution, and in particular, to which extent the population is offered opportunity to 'self-service welfare', i.e., by gainful employment. Opportunities offered on the labour market, and our personal performance influence outcomes on most other arenas. accordingly, the distribution of life chances created on the labour market also characterises social stratification in general. Such issues as inequality, poverty, and social exclusion are rooted on the labour market. Today's major political cleavages, such as general class conflict, equal opportunities for women, the generation gap, exclusion of the handicapped and non-nationals, and regional disadvantage, all relate to differential chances on the labour market.

EMPLOYMENT AND GENDER REGIMES

There is a wide variation in labour market performance between EU member states, and accordingly, a rather large variation in oppor-

Social Indicators Research **64:** 349–372, 2003.

tunity structures. Basic statistics and comparative surveys unfold a distinct variation and clustering of EU member states with respect to general employment rates and working hours, differences with respect to inclusion and exclusion (unemployment) of men and women (equal opportunities), the enrolment of youth (the transition from youth education to the labour market) and the elderly (retirement; age discrimination). The differences in labour market performance between member states go beyond inclusion and exclusion. They also concern qualitative aspects related to the work environment, and the social relations related to employment, such as influence and decision latitude, and union memberships. In this chapter we are in the search of the 'inclusive' labour market, which provides jobs earnings to maximally possible number of capable adults, as well as healthy and valued working conditions.

As a complementary and expansion of recent research on welfare *state* regimes (see chapter 3) several typologies focused at labour market performance have been proposed, with respect to employment. These models help to understand the national environment influencing distributive features and welfare outcomes such as income distribution, poverty and inequality by class, gender and generation. Kolberg and Esping-Andersen (1992) developed a model of three major *employment regimes* characterising developed nations. They identified a *Nordic model* with low levels of early exit, high levels of paid absence, and high rates of public employment. Their *Continental model* has high levels of early exit, moderate levels of paid absence, and low levels of public employment. The *Anglo-Saxon model* is characterised by low levels of paid absence and early exit, as well as public service employment, but high levels of private social service employment.

A second group of typologies are concerned with *gender regimes*, moving a gender perspective and gender-related issues such as female employment, unpaid work and role differentiation in families in a central position. These typologies are related to the labour market as well as to the family. One of these typologies distinguishes between strong, modified and weak breadwinner states (Lewis, 1992). In *strong (or male) breadwinner states* taxation and transfers is household related. Child raising allowances and unpaid leave encourage childcare in families and support low female employment rates. In the *weak (or two-) breadwinner states* taxation and transfers are related to individuals. Public childcare provisions, paid leave systems and opportunity to part-time work, support female employment.

Another typology follows the status of the *informal 'gender contract'*, the unique compromise between men and women defining gender roles, rights and duties. Gender contracts define the division of labour, power relations, legal arrangements, and the special character of female subordination. Gender contracts will vary over time and between nations. Hirdmann (1990) and Duncan (1995) discuss several types, starting with the original *Private Patriarchy* model (from which the southern countries presently are moving), towards a *Housewife Contract* (e.g., Germany), where the independent position of women in relation to marriage and domestic life is not yet established. Then follows a transitional stage towards a *Gender Equality Contract* (e.g., Sweden), where the independent role of women on the labour market is supported by legislation, public services and family transfers. A fifth model is the *Dual Role Contract* for women (e.g. France), varying over the life course and promoting paid work as well as unpaid work during child-rearing years.

In focusing on the special role of women and mothers on the labour market Rubery, Fagan and Smith (1995) identify three types of national patterns. Within a general European trend towards enhanced female employment rates they identify a *Continuous Pattern* (entering and staying on the labour market), a *Curtailed Pattern* (cutting down working hours temporarily), and an *Interrupted Pattern* (leaving the labour market to raise children).

The empirical indicators selected for this chapter are intended to cover these typologies. They are explored to test the feasibility of combining them into a single typology. In the next chapter we will then continue by adding welfare state characteristics, and finally, in chapter 4 follows a corresponding analysis of the family as a welfare delivery institution. Chapter 5 then adds the distributive structure to explore the variation of institutional performance.

22 indicators will be studied within 5 sub domains, with coverage of general enrolment, inclusion (employment rates), exclusion (unemployment), social and labour relations, and earnings:

General labour market enrolment

- Labour market participation
- Female enrolment: male minus female labour market participation
- Part-time employment

Inclusion (employment)

- Overall employment rate
- Female employment rate
- Youth employment rate
- Employment of elderly

Exclusion (unemployment)

- Overall unemployment rate
- Long-term unemployment rate
- Youth long-term unemployment
- Unemployment benefits

Social and labour relations

- Labour union membership
- Right to co-determination
- Discrimination of women, elderly and immigrants
- Training to improve skills and job prospects
- Instrumental/intrinsic work orientation

Earnings

- Inequality of earnings in the age group 20–64 years
- Inequality of earnings in the age group 20–84 years

The data have been extracted from the European System of Social Indicators (ZUMA). Detailed analyses of the variation between member state with respect to employment, unemployment, working hours and the quality of working environment are included in Vogel (1997).

LABOUR MARKET ENROLMENT

Overall Labour Market Participation

The first classification is concerned with the mobilisation of the potential labour force in the age group of 15–64 years. This indicator primarily reflects the opportunities available on the national labour market, but also employer's demands with respect to qualifications, support from the welfare state and family promoting employment (labour market and family policies), gender regimes, and health in later life. Lower participation rates also require higher welfare state support (elaborated transfer systems: pensions, unemployment allowances, training programs etc.) and/or family arrangements (support for non-active family members). Hence, lower employment levels demand solidarity by the active population (the generation and gender contracts), either by the electorate at large (welfare state arrangements) or by the nearest relatives (family support).

Figure 2.1 provides the *overall labour market participation rate for the age group 15–64 years in 1995*. There is a large variation between member states, with the highest levels in the Nordic countries. Sweden and Denmark have about 80 percent. In the Swedish and Finnish case the 1995 figures refer to an extremely deep recession. Both countries had much higher levels around 1990 and towards the end of the 1990s. Participation rates are the lowest in the Southern countries, with the exception of Portugal with recent increase, while Italy, Greece and Spain with low female participation rates and early retirement form the laggard cluster. Portugal leaves the southern cluster due to its higher female participation rates.

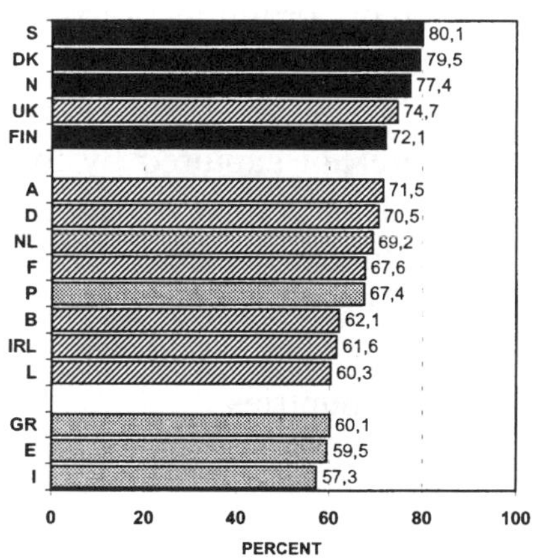

Figure 2.1 Labour force participation rate 1995. 15–64 years. Source: LFS.

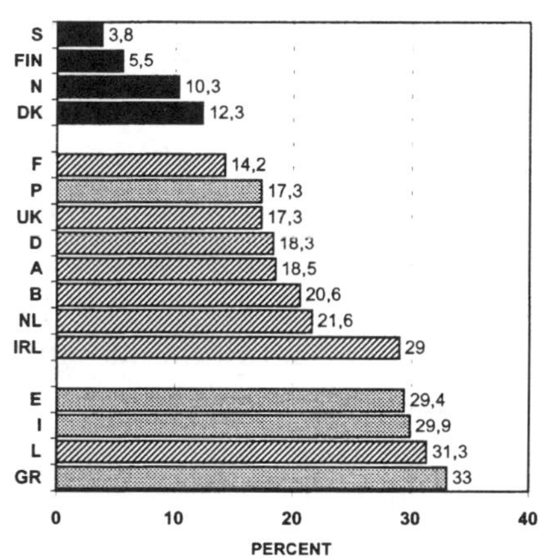

Figure 2.2 Male minus female labour force participation rate 1995. 15–64 years. Source: LFS.

In summary, Figure 2.1 shows that there is a clear North-South clustering in three groups of nations, with the central cluster falling at intermediate participation levels. These findings underline that the better performance of the labour market in the Nordic countries with respect to welfare efficiency, even in bad times with a deep recession (Sweden, Finland). The Nordic labour markets contribute better to welfare production, since the demographic burden is lower.

Female Enrolment

Next, we proceed to an assessment of gender differences in labour market participation, expressed as *the deviation of female participation rates (15–64 years; 1995) from male participation*. Female participation is the major factor improving equal opportunities for women and men, by offering economic independence as well as other personal openings to self-actualisation. Figure 2.2 shows the position of each nation between the male and two breadwinner models. In the North female participation is approaching the participation rates of men. A similar pattern is on the way in the other member states, however delayed by the long-lasting labour market crisis, and poor family policies (public child care facilities; paid parental leave). Figure 2.2 indicates again a clear distinction between the three clusters, with two exceptions. Portugal comes rather close to a Nordic level in recent years, which is primarily explained by increased female job opportunities; Luxembourg has a special participation structure related to foreign workers in EU-administration and services.

Many of the special national features are not captured by this classification. For instance there are special participation patterns related to childbirth and child-rearing (Rubery et alia, 1996). Finland and Portugal seem to join a tradition moulded by war-time female enrolment in the labour force. Another feature is the divers pension age for men and women in different countries.

A Longitudinal Assessment of the Swedish Case

The corresponding longitudinal data for Sweden 1975–1995 are given in more detail by displaying the labour force estimates by sex and age. From comparative statistics we already know that the participation rates are extremely high in Sweden for men as well as women, which was achieved during the 1970s and 80s. Figure 2.3 illustrates the rapid growth of female labour force participation up to about 1990, in particular in the public sector. This growth was especially strong among mid-age women and among the eldest age group (60–64 years). Concurrently, overall male participation declined slowly due to reduced formal pension age and liberal openings to premature retirement.

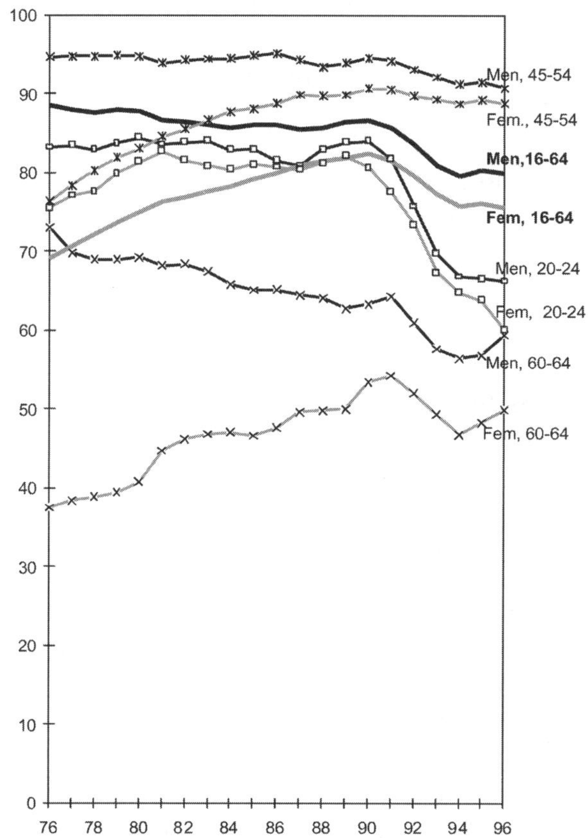

Figure 2.3 Labour force participation in Sweden 1976–95, by age and gender. Percent. Source: Swedish LFS.

After 1990 Sweden faced a new situation. A deep recession leads to a drop in participation among men as well as women, along with a rapid growth of unemployment. This also had severe consequences for the youngest men and women as well as immigrants (new entrants to the labour market). There was also a substantial decrease among the elderly (earlier exit), while prime age was better protected (insiders). However, in a period of stagnation in Western labour markets, with rather limited growth in female participation as well as permanent mass unemployment, Sweden managed to increase female participation, keep unemployment low, expand the public sector, and balance the public budgets. These policies came to an end around 1990 with new economic policies, and the coincidence of general deregulation, large non-financed tax reductions and a deep recession, followed by a sudden fourfold of unemployment and the corresponding exhaustion of the transfer systems. The Swedish case illustrates increased welfare efficiency in the period up to about 1990 with respect to job opportunities. The following chapter will show that during the same period there was an adjustment of welfare state provisions in the corresponding direction.

It should be noted, that throughout this period the Swedish labour market contributed more to the individual living standards than in all other EU member states. Today Sweden and the Nordic region still has the highest participation rates within the European union, and in consequence the most evenly distributed command over resources (earnings) relevant on other arenas as well.

Part-Time Employment

Our third indicator takes us towards the volume of employment, as indicated by part-time vs. full-time work (30- hours), which reflects access to full employment as well as coping behaviour with respect to demands from private life, or simply a choice of life style between work and leisure. These patterns also reflect family tradition and gender roles; as well as welfare state arrangements, such as family transfers and publicly financed childcare facilities. Figure 2.4 indicates a less distinct clustering of EU nations. Nations with higher labour market participation achieve this by larger (female) part-time employment. There are five country clusters identifiable by similar arrangements (Figure 2.5):

1. In Greece, Spain, Italy and Ireland female part-time work is of relative low frequency; employment rates for women are low, and if there are children the first option will not be part-time work but leaving the labour market.

2. Finland and Portugal form second cluster of high female employment and very low part-time levels for mothers. In both cases the high female employment rate has a historical background in the filling of ranks on the labour market during war-time economy. Portugal, in addition, has a recent record of good increase of employment rates
3. The Nordic countries Denmark and Sweden have rather high employment rates, and a lower part-time work rate among mothers. Generous family transfers and childcare facilities support this Nordic arrangement.
4. The highest part-time rates among mothers are found in the Netherlands, UK and Germany, with less supportive public arrangement. In the case of the Netherlands we can in fact identify a 'part-time work culture', with high part-time rates of free choice. Some 70 percent mention housework or satisfaction with part-time work as a reason for part-time (Vogel, 1997). Norway also belongs to this cluster.
5. France and Belgium have about the same female employment rates as the other central European countries, but relatively low part-time rates for mothers, supported by generous family transfers.

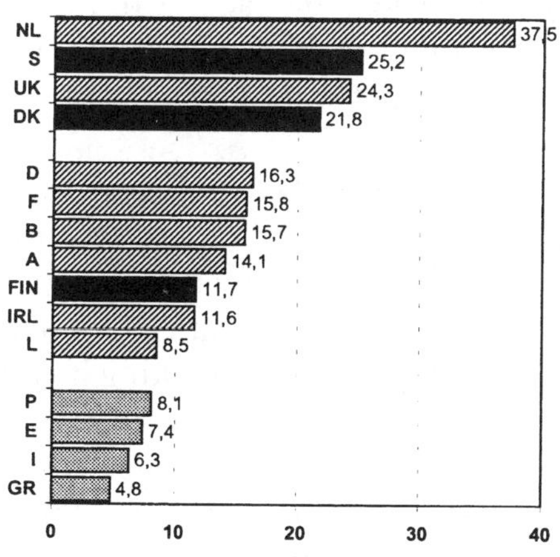

Figure 2.4 Part-time employment, as percent of total employment. 1995. Source: LFS.

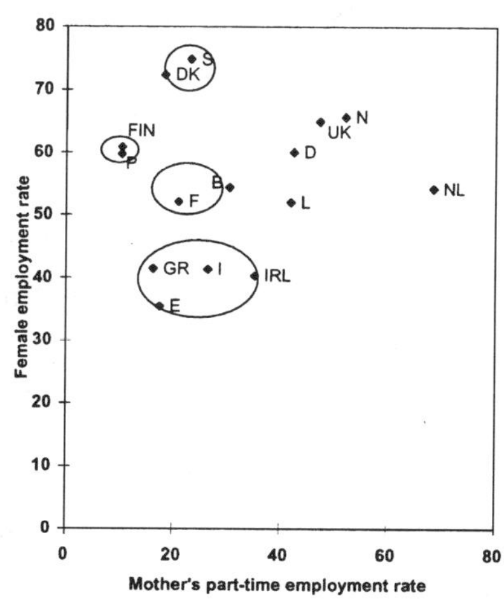

Figure 2.5 Female employment rates versus mother's rates. Percent. Source: ECHP/NSS.

Part-time jobs are also age related, and in different direction for men and women. Only a small proportion of men are working part-time, and when they do, this occurs in younger years during education. At the end of their working life, there is also a slightly enhanced part-time employment.

Part-time work as a mode of adaptation to family demands seems to be very frequent in central Europe (the Netherlands, Germany, UK, Norway), where 40–80 percent of mothers who stayed in the labour market work part-time. In this case the Southern and Northern countries (exc. Norway) reveal a similarity of rather moderate part-time rates of 10–20 percent of all employed mothers, but on very different levels of overall labour market participation. In the South the major pattern is leaving the labour market (or staying outside); in the North mothers are reducing their working hours. Portugal come close to this Nordic approach.

Some 12 percent of employed persons in employment (20–64 years) are presently working part-time, i.e., less than 30 hours per week (Vogel, 1997). This category was given a battery of questions concerning the reasons for their part-time work (ECHP/NSS). These responses again reflect the role conflict between employment and home and family life. In central Europe (Germany, Luxembourg, Belgium, the Netherlands and UK) the main reason for part-time work is in fact housework, for instance 66 percent in Germany. In the South these responses are much lower; instead the lack of full-time job was mentioned. In Denmark, Luxembourg the Netherlands and UK larger shares mentioned that they did not want longer working hours.

There are certainly very large differences between part-time working men and women. Women first of all mention housework, especially when they have children. Men instead mention occupational training, illness, and a lack of full-time opportunities. Women seem to be more satisfied than men with their present working hours (Vogel, 1997).

Training is of course mentioned mostly in young age, when education for economic reason is coupled with part-time working. In analogy, illness is a major reason for part-time towards the end of the working years just before retirement. This applies especially for men, in the sense that a larger proportion of the rather limited number of men working part-tome are doing so for health reasons, or during youth education and vocational training in younger age.

In summary, we have found that part-time work has divers reasons in various countries. Part-time work is primarily a consequence of job opportunities, gender roles, and family policies, and to some degree also a matter of choice and balance between work and leisure.

EMPLOYMENT RATES

Labour force participation includes the employed as well as the unemployed population, part-time workers, categories which are on (partial) leave for training, and persons on temporal contracts or other insecure job situations. In this section we continue by looking at the included population, i.e., the employed with respect to the margins of the labour force, i.e., youth (new entrants) and the elderly (in the exit process).

First, Figure 2.6 provides the *employment rates* corresponding to the labour force participation rates given in Figure 2.1. This figure also displays the Swedish and Finnish rates for 1991, before the recent deep recession when both countries lost more than one tenth of their employment. There is again a clear north-south clustering, with a large variation between member states. The following three figures (2.7–9) give the corresponding rates for three age groups. For the age where inclusion in the labour market is normally completed, and before the exit process takes over (25–54 years), we have a rather limited variation, especially between the Nordic and central clusters (Figure 2.7). The clusters are reasonably well separated, with Portugal as the exceptions. The major variation is in the youth generation (Figure 2.8; 15–24 years), where the employment rate is generally larger in the Nordic cluster, as ell as in UK and Austria; the transition into the labour market comes earlier in these countries. In this case is the clustering less distinct. In upper age where the transition to retirement again decreases employment levels (Figure 2.9), we again record large variation between member states, with higher employment rates in the North (except Finland), but no variation between the Southern and central clusters. Retirement comes later in the Nordic cluster.

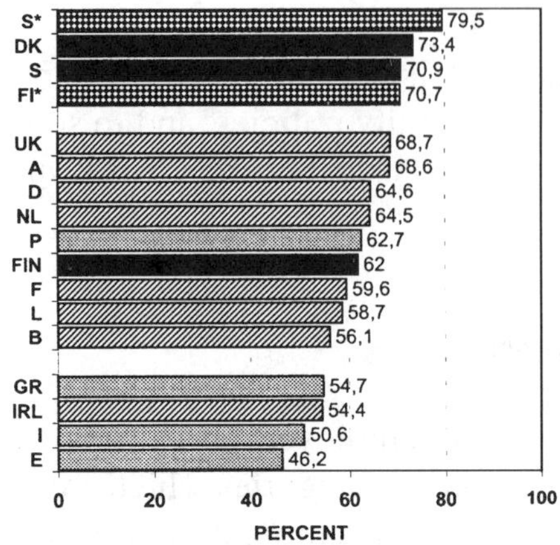

Figure 2.6 Employment rates 1995. 15–64 years. Source: LFS. (*=1991)

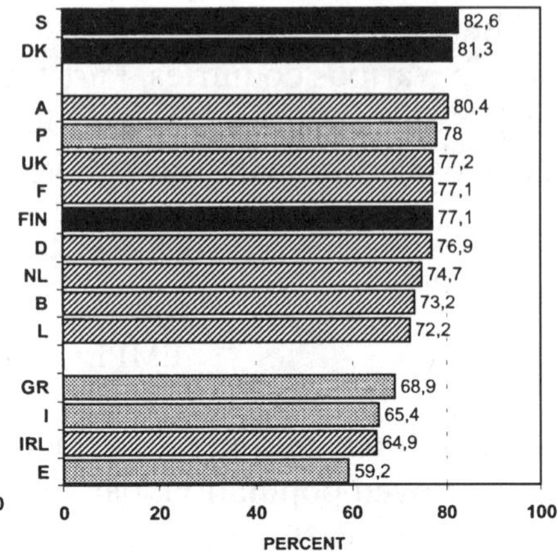

Figure 2.7 Employment rates for 25–54 years. 1995. Source: LFS.

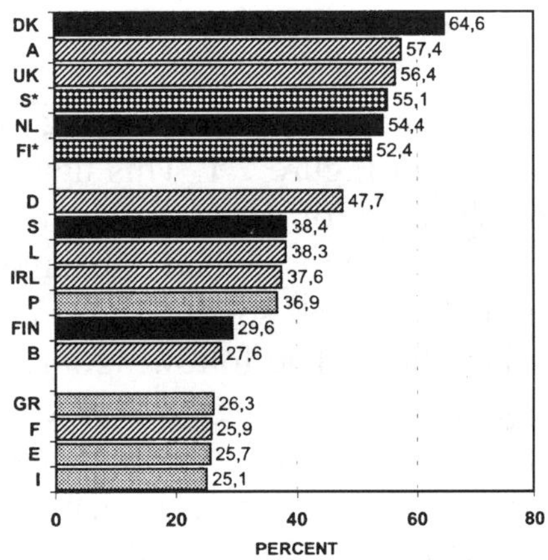

Figure 2.8 Employment rate for 15–24 years. 1995. Source: LFS.

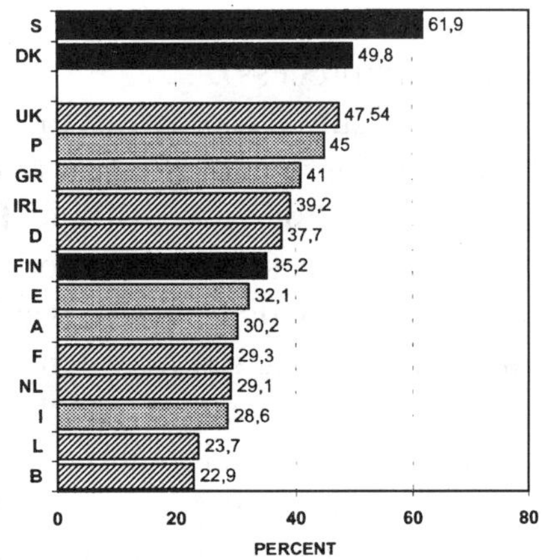

Figure 2.9 Employment rate for 55–64 years. 1995. Source: LFS.

UNEMPLOYMENT

Official labour force statistics is primarily measures registered and active job seekers. In addition there is a national pattern of unregistered inactivity, shaped by family tradition, youth education, and the national job creation performance. Hence, official statistic underestimates individual problems on the labour market.

The clustering with respect to overall unemployment rates is less distinct than previous indicators. Figure 2.10 indicates in particular the large increase in Sweden and Finland after 1991 (marked S∗ and FIN∗). The 1995 values are not representative for these countries in a longer perspective, which is also illustrated by the Swedish trends given in Figure 2.14. Unemployment follows business cycles, with larger increase for entrants to the labour market (youth and immigrants). The large increase in the early 1990s is extreme, but so was also the decline after the mid 1990s, which took Sweden down to about 4 percent in 2001.

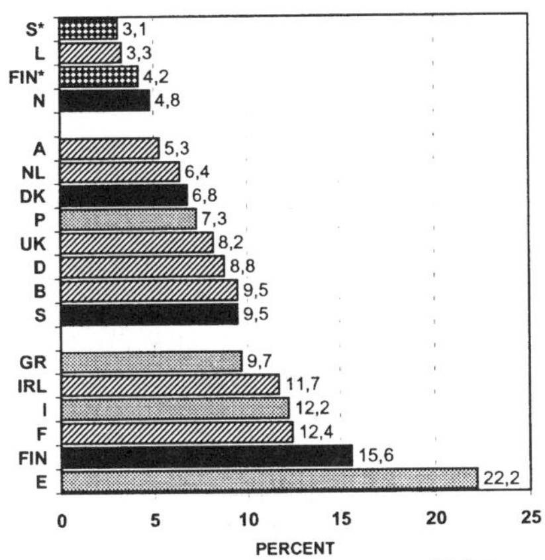

Figure 2.10 Unemployment rate 1996. Source: LFS. (*=1991)

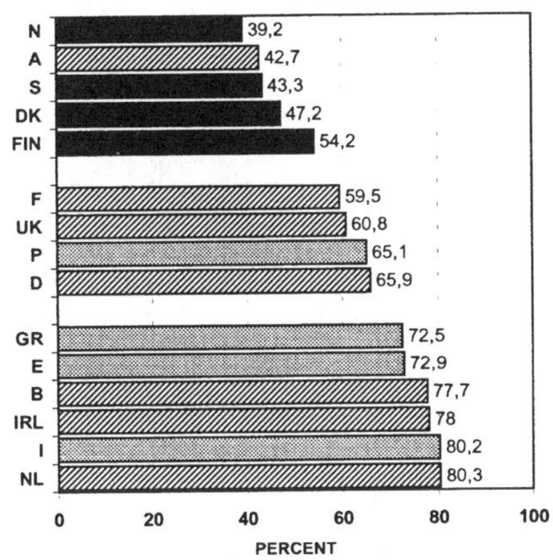

Figure 2.11 Long-term unemployed (6 months). Percent of all unemployed. 1995. Source: LFS.

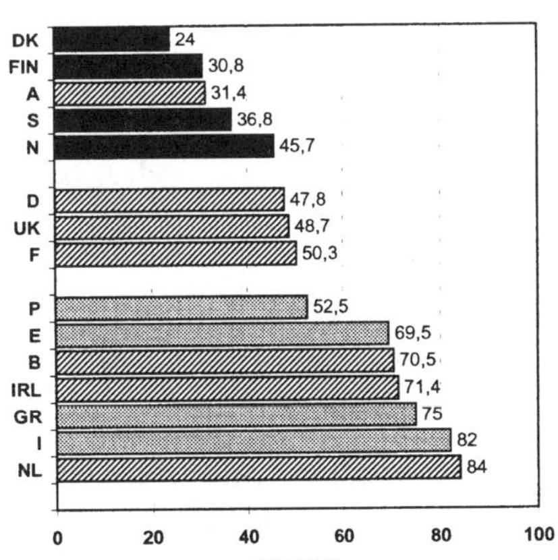

Figure 2.12 Long-term unemployed (>6 months), as percent of the labour force aged 15–24 years. 1995. Source: LFS.

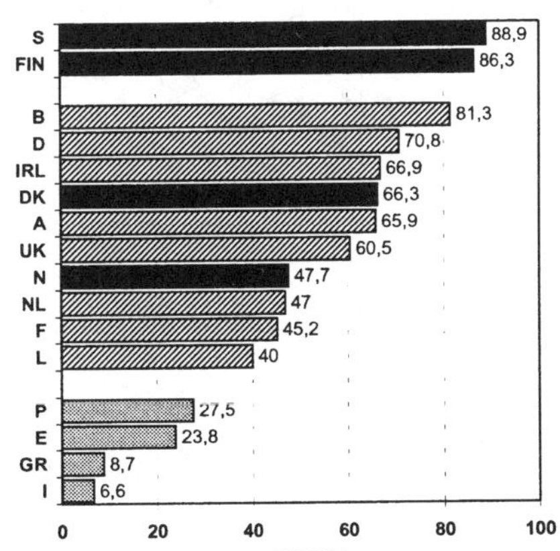

Figure 2.13 Unemployed persons who received unemployment benefits, as percent of all unemployed. 1995. Source: LFS.

Long-Term Unemployment

Unemployment could be temporary and short, or 'frictional' between jobs; or it may be long lasting. Figure 2.11 shows the long-term unemployment rate (6 months) as a percentage of all unemployed. Again, here we find a clear North-South clustering, with much lower rates in the Nordic cluster, even during the severe recession. The variation between the southern and central clusters is rather small.

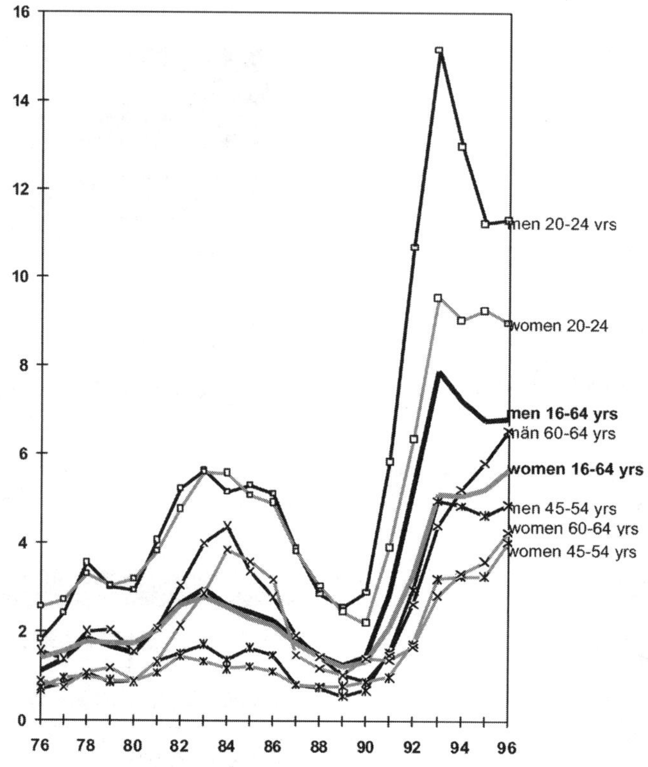

Figure 2.14 Unemployment rates for Sweden 1976–96. By sex and age. Percent. Source: Swedish LFS.

Sweden scores well, in spite of its intermediate unemployment levels in the mid 1990s. However, Sweden has a long history of extremely low unemployment rates, and the present intermediate level is of very recent nature. Therefore Sweden scores low on long-term unemployment, as well as on the excess unemployment of women and youth.

The variation in unemployment features between the three clusters is particularly clear when it comes to *long-term youth unemployment*, this time calculated as a percentage of the total labour force 15–24 years (Figure 2.12). The Nordic youth unemployment is much lower than the southern cluster, while the variation between the southern and central cluster is less distinct. The overall range between member states is 24 percent (Denmark) and 84 percent (Netherlands).

Income Compensation

We have seen that there is considerable variation in unemployment levels, and there is also a north south clustering, however less distinct as found for employment rates. The final indicator in this section measures *income compensation at unemployment* (Figure 2.13). When entitlements and compensation levels are generous, unemployment will have less serious individual economic consequences. With poor benefits poverty is soon unavoidable and social network support is required. This is illustrated by Figure 2.15, where the proportion of unemployed persons who have received unemployment benefits varies between 89 percent (Sweden) and 7 percent (Italy). Here we again find a very clear clustering with the Southern countries at the lower end, and Sweden and Finland in the lead; and in spite of the predicament in the mid 1990s, it might be added.

SOCIAL AND LABOUR RELATIONS

A job and regular income gives economic independency, and in a wider perspective personal resources to master the course of life and living conditions within other social domains. The job situation is and important aspect of the quality if life in itself, as well as a resource for other social domains. From a welfare perspective, the good work will provide safe, interesting and healthy working environment, expanding experiences and interests of the employed, security of employment, and social relations characterised by solidarity, co-operation, non-discrimination and democracy, which as an end-effect should contribute to personal involvement and overall positive assessment by the employed. Comparative studies of these aspects are rare, fragmented and scattered between many sources, but some key indicators are included in the major comparative surveys ECHP, ISSP, WVS and European survey of working conditions. This section selects eight social indicators, focusing on *democratic influence* (the right to co-determination, union membership), *cohesion* (non-discrimination against women, elderly and immigrants), *social capital* (participation in training), and job satisfaction (instrumental/intrinsic value orientation).

High levels of *labour union enrolment* is an indication of individual commitment and engagement in working conditions and decisions at the work place, as well as collective influence and cooperative labour relations. High levels of unionism also indicate there is a cultural tradition and forum of discussing job issues, demanding action, as well as providing a social network uniting and binding the workforce together, and offering social, economic and legal and support even beyond the mere workplace. In consequence, there should be higher levels of overall satisfaction with the work role and work place and higher levels of non-discriminatory labour relations, in summary: a stronger sense of commitment, belonging and work orientation.

Figure 2.15 provides some incomplete data on union enrolment for men around 1995. There is definitely a large much larger engagement in the Nordic cluster, while the two southern representatives fall at lower levels. There is also a North-South variation with respect to the proportion that reports to have *the right to co-determination*, while the central cluster exhibits a large variation at the lowest as well as highest levels (Figure 2.16).

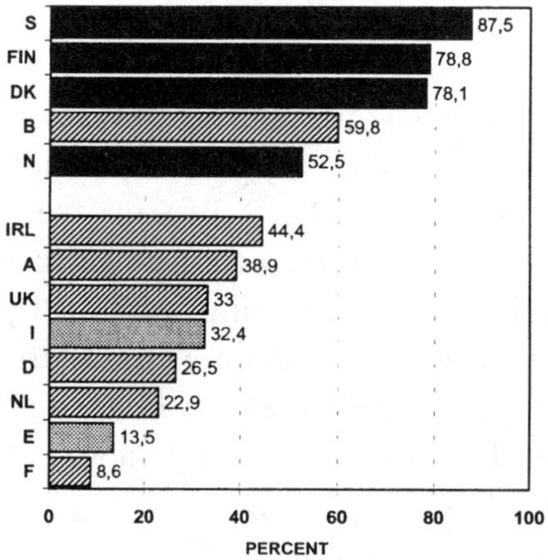

Figure 2.15 Labour union membership for men 1995. Source: Ebbinghaus, B./Visser, J., 2000.

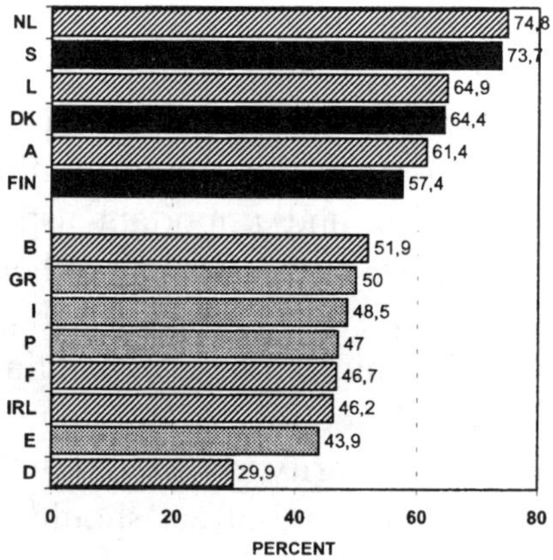

Figure 2.16 Employees with right to co-determination. 1997. Source: European Survey of Working conditions.

Discrimination of Marginal Groups in the labour market is a consequence of competition (related to unemployment levels), as well as lack of collective targeting of inequalities and focus on solidarity, in other words public opinion formation process through political organisations and labour unions. High employment rates, low unemployment levels (in normal times) and high level of union enrolment should support non-discriminatory attitudes in the Nordic cluster.

The World Value Survey has a battery on this issue (1990) including the following statements:

" . . . When jobs are scarce" . . .

- " . . . *men should have more rights to a job than women*"
- " . . . *older people should be forced to retire from work early*"
- " . . . *employers should give priority to national people over immigrants*".

The proportion of employed persons rejecting discrimination of women, older people and immigrants are given in Figure 2.17–19. Higher rates thus indicate higher levels of solidarity. The general structure of these results again points at a clear North-South divide, with a few exceptions. The Nordic labour force exhibits less discriminatory attitudes, along with the Netherlands. In the southern cluster, with lower employment and higher unemployment rates, as well as lower unionism, are in particular the elderly and immigrants less welcome.

Vocational Training

Participation in *vocational training to improve job skills and prospects* is an important element of a learning society, and in particular to support persons with poor qualifications, as well as to expand the general capacity of the work force. Training opportunities improve the competence, and in addition the sense of connectedness to the work role and work place. Figure 2.20 indicates a vast variation in the European union, again with a large gap between North and South. In Denmark and Sweden one third have had some work-related training during the last year, while Italy and Spain stay at 4–5 percent.

Socio-economic groups are clearly differing with respect to overall training as well as vocational training. Further analyses of the ECHP (Vogel, 1997) indicate that the distributive profile is much better in Denmark and Sweden: the proportion of manual worker receiving vocational training is about 5 times larger than in most other countries.

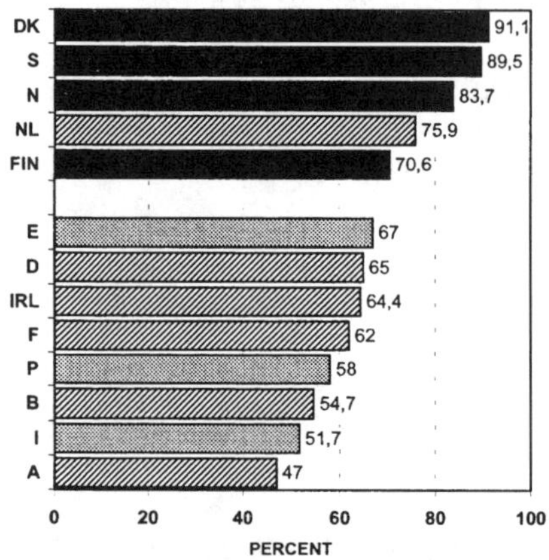

Figure 2.17 Rejects discrimination against women, 1995. Source: WVS.

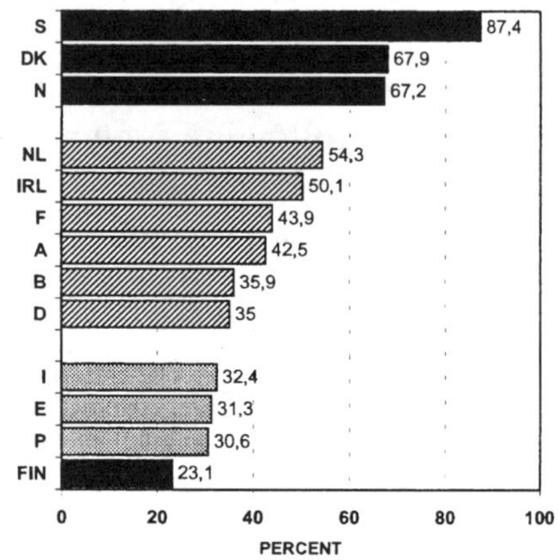

Figure 2.18 Rejects discrimination of the elderly. 1995. Source: WVS.

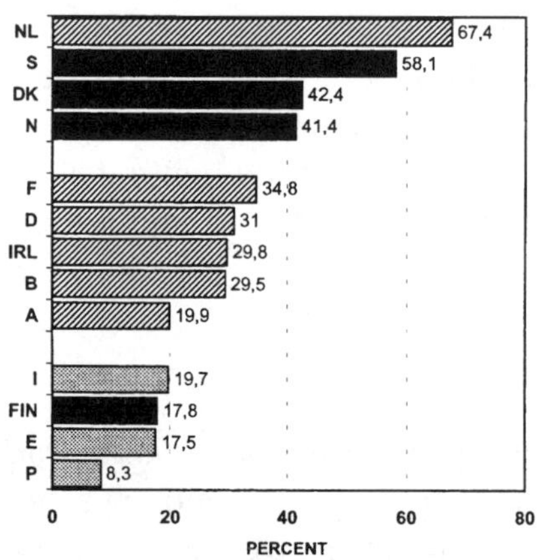

Figure 2.19 Rejects discrimination of immigrants. 1995. Source: WVS.

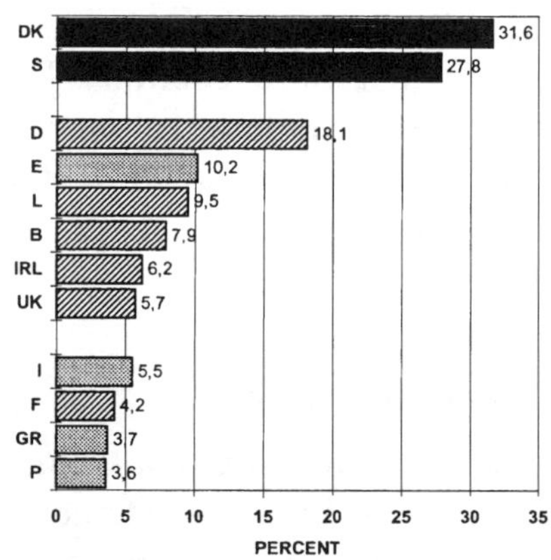

Figure 2.20 Course participation last year to improve skills and job prospects. 20–64 years. Source: ECHP/NSS.

To summarise this expose of social and labour market relation we provide two indicators of *work ethic* from two different sources (ISSP, 1997 and WVS, 1990), which focus on the dichotomy between *instrumental work orientation* ('work for pay') and *intrinsic work value orientation*. The variation between EU member states should reflect the objective environment as well as the 'systemic' quality imbedded in the work place with respect to social capital, job security, power relations, democratic co-determination, training opportunities and thrust. These indicators again reveal a clear clustering, in spite of the limited validity of such simple and overarching items. Figure 2.21 shows the proportion of employed persons who agree in the statement "a job is just a way of earning money" (ISSP, 1997). In the Nordic cluster and the Netherlands we find proportions between 10 and 21, while the Southern cluster falls between 24 and 46. The few representatives of the central cluster fall in intermediate position.

In order to corroborate this variation Figure 2.22 provides a picture of the opposite tail, i.e., persons mentioning that the 'job is interesting' as an important aspect of a job. This estimate, which is based on other measurement technique, another survey and sample, reveals the same North–South variation. Intrinsic work value is mentioned by 64–80 percent in the Nordic cluster, and between 47 and 58 percent in the Southern cluster. The central cluster tends to fall slightly lower than the Nordic cluster.

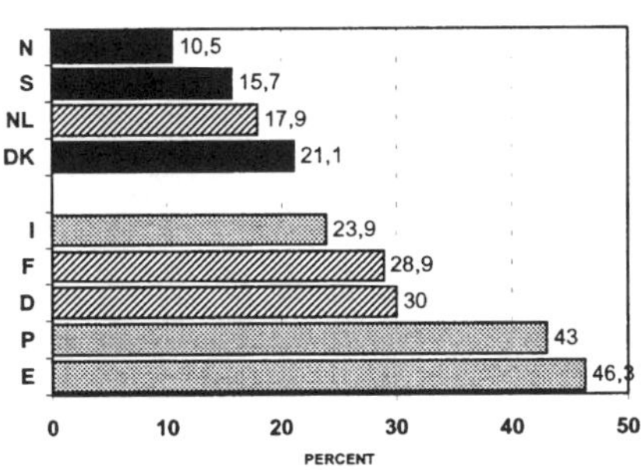

Figure 2.21 Instrumental work attitude. Percent. 1997. Source: ISSP.

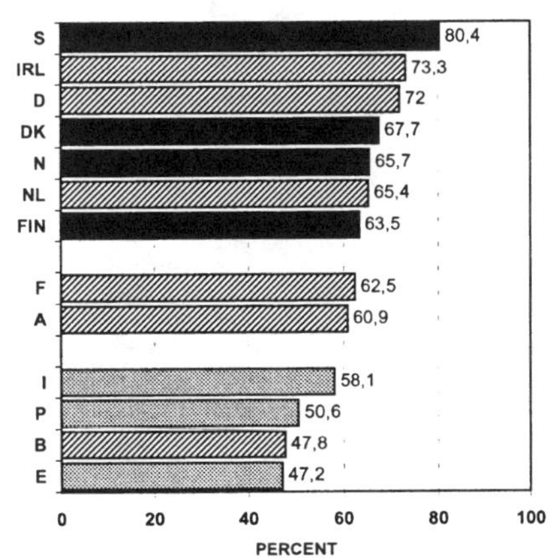

Figure 2.22 Intrinsic work orientation. 1990. Source: WVS.

Earnings

After this view on European employment features we turn to the economic resources achieved on the labour market, decisive for the material living conditions, i.e., personal earnings. Unfortunately the European Household Panel did not measure personal *gross* earnings, required to identify the (initial) distribution of resources created on the labour market separately. Only *net* earnings (post-tax) are available in the ECHP, and are presented here for the *total adult population aged 16–84 years* (Figure 2.24). Here are parts of the welfare state correctives (i.e., direct income taxes) already included, as well as (job-related) pensions. It is important to understand that the variation of intra-national distribution of earnings is primarily determined by the overall employment rates and the variation in working hours, in addition to the (hourly) wage structure in the active population.

Figure 2.24 again exhibit the same three country clusters, with perfect separation, indicating stronger market effects in the South. The ECHP database from 1994 shows for the Southern cluster much lower levels of earnings as well as higher levels of *inequality* of earnings (Gini-coefficients), primarily as a consequence of lower employment rates. The Nordic cluster again turns out to be less affected by market forces, with lower levels of inequality in earnings.

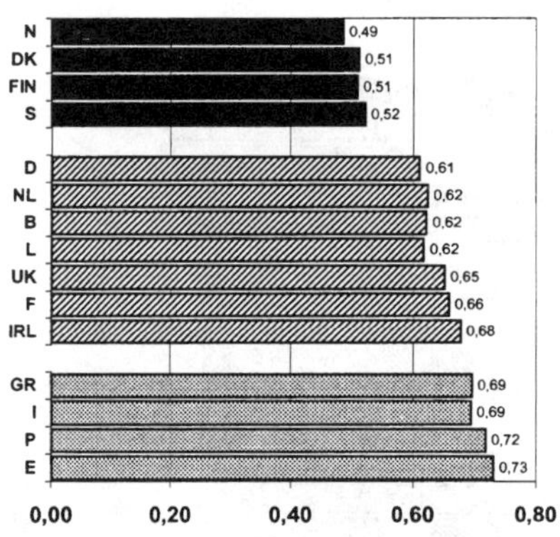

Figure 2.23 Gini-koefficient for net earnings 20–84 years. Source: ECHP/NSS.

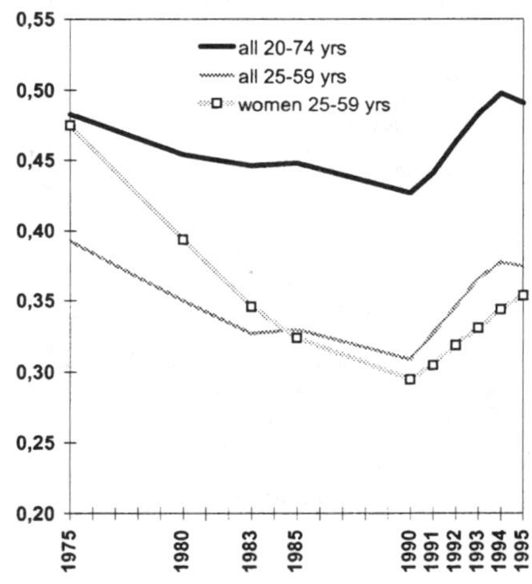

Figure 2.24 Inequality of gross earnings (Gini-coefficients). All persons in certain age/sex groups. Swedish trends 1975–95.

Corresponding data for Sweden 1975–95 are shown in 2.24, where the Gini-coefficients are calculated *pre-tax*. These findings of course correspond to the employment trends presented earlier.

Inequality in earnings for all adults 20–74 years declined up to about 1990, primarily due to the rapid growth in female employment. From 1990 this trend is sharply reversed as a consequence of the heavy decline in employment and growth of unemployment in the 90-ies. The effect of female employment growth up to 1990 is also indicated by the large decrease in Gini-coefficients for women. Here we also noticed that the Gini-coefficients for women deviate very little from the levels of men in recent years, reflecting the long-term change towards equal opportunities on the labour market.

Discussion

This chapter looks at the European labour markets from the perspective of their *welfare efficiency*, i.e., to what extent the labour market provides employment, income and working conditions that contribute to good living conditions in a wider sense. The key concept here is the 'inclusive' labour market: we are primarily concerned with the various resources which are achieved at the labour market, and their consequences for the distribution of living conditions in a wider sense an in other domains. The inclusive labour market offers job opportunities for all, with reasonably limited distribution of earnings, and it minimises income disparities, and exclusion from gainful employment. The labour market is the prime welfare institution; its welfare efficiency is the very precondition for the welfare state and family. Generous welfare state provisions require a large tax base based on high labour market enrolment and egalitarian structure of earnings. This combination is a sine qua non for equality of living conditions and lower levels of social exclusion. Without this winning combination the family has to take a larger responsibility for weaker members of the extended family.

The indicators studied in this chapter go beyond labour market enrolment, unemployment and earnings. They also include issues of exclusion and discrimination (women, youth, elderly, immigrants), the democratic and cooperative orientation at the work place, enhancement of human capital through training, and job satisfaction. The indicators capture the most pertinent current aspects of labour market performance, including the gender regime and equal opportunities (the male versus two breadwinner model), the transition to adulthood (youth enrolment), the democratisation of working life, and retraining. Many aspects are missing however, such as the lifelong exposure to working environment, and insecurity of employment, in the absence of good and comparable statistics.

We have explored these data to identify similarities and dissimilarities between EU member states with respect to labour market performance. By comparing many national cases (EU member state) we have identified three types of employment regimes, labelled by geographical location as the *Nordic model* (Sweden, Denmark, Finland and Norway), the *Southern model* (Greece, Italy, Spain, and in some aspects Portugal), and a remaining *intermediate central cluster* (Germany, France, Belgium, Netherlands, Luxembourg, UK and Ireland), in most aspects placed between the Nordic and Southern model. The representatives of these three clusters are in general terms ranking alike on most indicators (all indicators are positively correlated), indicating a logical interrelationship between the indicators, which underpins the rationale of the three models. The members of these three clusters of nations are not always distinctly separated, but there is substantive uniformity within clusters, and dissimilarity between clusters. There are two major explanations for the deviant cases from a more coherent clustering of nations, which we have encountered in this assessment of labour market characteristics at a fixed point in time (about 1995). There are some countries, which are on the move between models over the past decade; Portugal and recently Ireland are moving towards the central or even Nordic model with respect to employment, in Portugal in particular with respect to female employment. The second type of deviations is related to the economic cycles, which were very different for Finland and Sweden in 1995, as compared to the other member states. Both countries experienced a deep recession with a temporary loss of more than one tenth of their employment rates, in both cases triggered by unique national events, in the case of Finland the loss of the eastern market and in the Swedish case by a fundamental change in economic policies. However, both countries defend their position in the Nordic cluster in the early as well as the late 1990s, as indicated in some of the presentations.

With these comments in mind we might summarise that we have a rather distinct separation of the EU member states in three clusters. *The Nordic cluster* is characterised by high labour force participation, based on equal job opportunities for women and men, and a two breadwinner strategy, with consequences for the welfare state as well as the role of the family and family formation (see also chapter 3 and 4). The Nordic labour markets are also more inclusive, in the sense that they mobilise much larger proportions of youth and elderly (–25; 55+), unemployment benefits have better coverage, and they have lower rates of long-term unemployment. *The southern cluster* has much lower enrolment and consequently a larger demographic burden. Female employment is generally much lower, in the direction of the male breadwinner strategy. Youth transition to the labour market comes much later and youth unemployment is substantial, with larger responsibilities for the parental generation. The remaining central EU member states form an *intermediate cluster*, in some aspects close the Nordic model (Netherlands), and sometimes closer to the southern model (Germany: female employment).

Employment provides a variety of resources to be used in various ways on other arenas, including earnings, which determine the income distribution and material living standards. The national distribution of earnings is measured by Gini coefficients, which reflect two major factors, first, the distribution of gainful employment; and second, the relative market income in various occupations, where the major factor is the variation in labour market enrolment. The distribution of earnings determines the distribution of disposable income, as well as poverty and material deprivation. The inequality of earnings divides the European union in the same three clusters, perfectly separating the Nordic, central and southern countries. The Nordic countries have the lowest inequality of earnings, the southern cluster has the highest levels, and the central cluster falls at intermediate levels. This division is in various proportion influenced and reduced by welfare state and family arrangements. However, the initial clustering produced on the labour market is also found in the distribution of material standards and income (see chapter 5).

In addition, our data indicate there is a variation between the three clusters with respect to social and labour relations and job satisfaction, which, in a wider perspective, reflects what might be perceived as a variation in cultural and political concern with employment (job creation; labour market policies) and labour issues (labour protection, job security), and the going power relations between employers, labour unions and state. In the Nordic cluster we find much larger union membership rates, as well as co-determination at the work place, solidarity (rejection of discrimination of women, elderly and immigrants), retraining opportunities, and finally an intrinsic work value orientation (in contrast to instrumental work orientation, i.e., work for pay). The distance to the southern cluster is rather clear in all these aspects, but less to the central cluster, where Netherlands falls close to the Nordic cluster.

SCB Statistics Sweden
Welfare Analysis Program
and
University of Umeå
PO Box 24300
10451 Stockholm
Sweden

JOACHIM VOGEL

WELFARE STATE

The idea of the welfare state builds on a conception of social rights guaranteed to all citizens (Marshall, 1950). Social rights are an extension of democratic rights, defining welfare rights monitored on the political arena by collective decision-making. Social rights are usually expressed with explicit reference to equality and social inclusion. The issue has repeatedly entered public debate and social planning, promising a great leap forward as in Roosevelt's New Deal, Johnson's Great Society or the Swedish social democratic vision of the 'Folk Home'. The right to employment (supported by labour market policy), to safe working conditions (labour protection regulation), the right to education (tax-based mass schooling), poverty relief (transfers) and general public health care are all widely accepted in Europe in all political camps. However, there is less consensus on just how far social citizenship and the responsibilities of the welfare state should be reaching. This is the field of major political dispute between liberal, conservative and socialist ideology. Believers of the free market tend to see the welfare state, social rights and taxation as an obstacle to market efficiency. Competitiveness is often equated with fairness in the distribution of living conditions, and social rights as disincentives to work. Hence, there is a dual conception of social rights: most people take them for granted and inevitable, but just how comprehensive, residual or targeted they should be, and for what areas in life, is a matter of dispute.

The dominant power relation between these ideological positions is reflected in the way we choose to allocate the responsibilities of the welfare state. However, the actual role of the welfare state is also influenced by available options. Efficient labour markets producing high employment levels and low unemployment will facilitate generous welfare state intervention; and resourceful traditional families will reduce the need for welfare state intervention, or liberate resources for generosity in other areas. In the same vein,

Social Indicators Research **64:** 373–391, 2003.

malfunctioning labour markets and families will exhaust public resources and will limit the scope of social rights and equality.

The welfare state operates with two strategies, by *regulation* and by *redistribution*. By regulations it controls the distribution of resources at the labour market, as well as within and between families. Regulations include a large range of legislation as well as less formal ruling serving to produce welfare and equality 'at source', i.e., at the labour market or within the family, in order to minimize the inequality created on the labour market and by family networks. At the labour market labour rights are either regulated by law or negotiated between labour market parties with back up support from the political arena, or sometimes regulated by mixed approaches. At the family level we have extensive ruling of rights and duties of family members and the power balance between them. The other strategy is 'repairment' by redistribution, in other words by intervention through taxes, transfers and subsidised services. This strategy includes marginal income taxes and income substitutions (unemployment benefits, sickness benefits, old age pensions etc.) versus labour market risks; and family allowances, public care, and other services versus the family.

WELFARE STATE REGIMES

Several models of welfare *state* regimes have been proposed, identified by a range of different factors, such as the level of social expenditure, institutional arrangements of distribution (e.g., entitlements, compensation levels, the public/private mix of provisions), features of taxation, the initial need structure and the final distributive outcome, the historical tradition and actors, and present-day partisanships.

Esping-Anderson (1990) identified three distinctive welfare state regimes, representing different ways of 'decommodification' of labour in a capitalist economy, empirically measured by the replacement rates and contribution periods of benefits, and the financial arrangements. The *Liberal Welfare State Regime* is market-oriented in the distribution of resources and social protection benefits. Public provisions are typically modest, flat rate, and needs/means tested, producing a stigmatised and residual group of beneficiaries. The state encourages market solution by private welfare schemes. The decommodification effect is limited, and the distribution of living conditions is closer related to the stratification created by market forces. USA is the archetype in this category, as well as Canada and Australia. In Europe UK is moving in this direction.

The *Conservative Welfare State Regime*, rooted in corporatism and Catholic social policy, is identified by status-preserving intervention, supporting the market logic of distribution. Family and motherhood are supported, women encouraged to stay at home, and the one-breadwinner family is supported by benefits and taxation. Germany, France, Italy, Belgium and Austria belong to this category.

The third type is the *Social-democratic Welfare State Regime*, where social policy is encompassing, with high standards of material living conditions guaranteed, high levels of transfers as well as subsidised public service; hence also high levels of tax rates. The individual is the favoured unit instead of the family as in the conservative regime. Sweden is the archetype in this category, also including Finland, Denmark and Norway.

Several other welfare state regime typologies have been offered, some of them expanding the number categories, or renaming categories focusing on other core elements. A fourth missing type to be added to the threefold typology above would be the *Rudimentary Welfare State Regime*, found in countries where there is no history of full employment; but a recent history of authoritarian politics, where welfare politics is minimal and left to the household subsistence economy and a large informal sector. The southern countries (Greece, Spain, Portugal and southern Italy) fall into this category. Castles and Mitchell (1992) defined a similar fourfold typology, adding a fourth *radical* regime.

Korpi and Palme (1997) developed a typology of five types of institutional arrangements, focusing on features of the major social insurance programs, using the eligibility for benefits and the benefit levels as the major characteristics. In the order of their historical appearance these are labelled *the targeted, voluntary state subsidised, corporatist, basic security and encompassing* model. The major characteristics of this model are illustrated in Table 3.1.

The general idea of welfare state regimes is to understand variations in the distribution of material living conditions, or effects of

TABLE 3.1

Institutional types of social insurance programs

Type	Eligibility Principle	Benefit principle
Targeted	proved need	minimum
Voluntary	membership contributions	flat rate or income related
Corporatist	employment and occupation	income related
Basic security	citizenship	flat rate
Encompassing	citizenship and employment	flat rate and income related

'decommofication', in terms of income inequality, poverty, social exclusion and living standards in a wider sense. The different classifications of welfare state regimes relate to the social cleavages addressed earlier in unique ways. The liberal type (or basic security type) falls short of managing the class cleavage; hence, class conflict will continue to occupy political attention. The conservative (or corporatist) type creates a cleavage between insiders and outsiders not covered by social protection, including the new surplus population of unemployed. In the social democratic (or encompassing) model the gender conflict surfaces, corresponding to large female employment in the public sector, and the family's dependency on the public sector. Public services and equality by redistribution becomes a foremost female interest, moving the gender cleavage into the political arena.

Since the initial writings of Titmuss and Esping-Andersen regimes research has undergone profound expansion, moving from the welfare state focus as a market corrective ('decommodification') towards its impact in a wider sense, including the labour market as well as the family in their role as welfare producers. The increased interest in the interrelationship between the three institutions adds *defamilialisation* to the functions of the welfare state (Esping-Andersen, 1999), decreasing individual dependencies from market as well as family. In particular, the issue of gender roles, the two-breadwinner model and caring duties has been added and theorised in the context of welfare production (e.g., Lewis, Ostner).

Accordingly, in the search for a European typology of welfare production, our indicators have to address these new issues. Distinct empirical evidence of the complex web of welfare state arrangements along the lines of the theorised welfare state regimes do not come easily. Most countries display a mixed pattern with examples of all discussed principles of redistribution. Here we are not primarily concerned with these principles as such, but with their overall outcome in terms of equality. Hence, we need global indicators of the overall expenditure for redistribution, which are comparable between nations, plus indicators of special policies focused at the family, i.e., related to caring activities, and at the labour market policies. The following indicators have been selected:

- Total social protection expenditure (GDP-share and PPP/capita)
- Redistribution of market earnings (reduction in Gini-coefficients)
- Family policies (child care facilities, paid parental leave)
- Employment promotion expenditure

Global Indicators of Welfare State Provisions

Figure 3.1 displays the member states by the volume of social benefits as a percentage of GDP for 1994. As inn the previous chapter for employment, we find again that the Nordic countries (except Norway) are in the lead, ahead of central Europe, while the Southern cluster stays at considerably lower levels. It should be noted that the level of benefits again produces a clear distinction between the three clusters. The same applies to social protection expressed in purchasing power parities (PPP) per capita (Figure 3.2). Here we also see the effect of the general economic level, which places Luxembourg with the highest GDP level at the top. Finland and Sweden who experienced a heavy decline in their GDP in the mid 1990s step down in the country ranking, while Norway with booming economy advanced. But still, as a group the Nordic welfare states perform much better than the central cluster, and much better than the Southern cluster.

Finland as well as Sweden suffered rapid decrease in employment rates as well as GDP levels over the early 1990s, which was followed heavy reductions in their social protection expenditure, in absolute as well as in relative terms. Furthermore, in this period of unusual labour market crisis the need for social protection payments (unemployment compensation, social welfare payments) increased. Figure 3.3 shows the trends over the 1990s for the EU member states. Finland and Sweden display a step downwards decline after the early 1990 crisis. However the same applies to Denmark and Norway, and to some extent also to parts of the central cluster. Meanwhile most of the Southern cluster (except Spain) advanced, but slowly even aver mid 1990s. In summary, there was still some expansion of the welfare state in the early 1990s, but around 1993 this period came to an end. Then comes consolidation in the Centre and South, and decline in the North. The overall pattern seems to point at convergence.

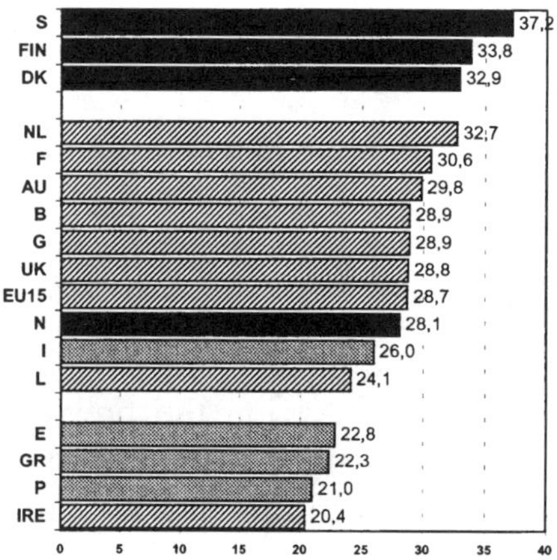

Figure 3.1 Total social protection expenditure 1994, as share of GDP. Source: Esspros.

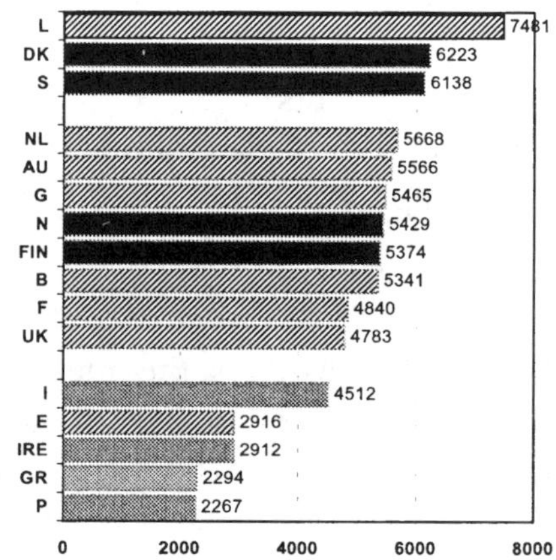

Figure 3.2 Total social protection expenditure 1994. PPS per capita. Source: Esspros.

This picture of stagnation or even reduction of the welfare state provisions seems disappointing. However, these trends are calculated in relative terms, as a percentage of the increasing GDP. If we look at social protection in absolute terms (Figure 3.4) then the picture is less distressing. There is considerable progress in all member states. However, there is no convergence between the South and the North and Centre. Furthermore, the distance between the central and Nordic cluster practically disappears. Around 1997 Sweden appears less extreme than is used to do in the 1980s. Again, the big spender is Luxembourg with extremely high GDP.

It has to be remembered that the expenditure data is not controlled for the national need structure, in terms of indicators such as poverty, unemployment or public health. In fact, there is much that indicates that the social expenditure is the lowest (in relative as well as absolute terms) where the needs are the greatest and the available resources (GDP) are the lowest.

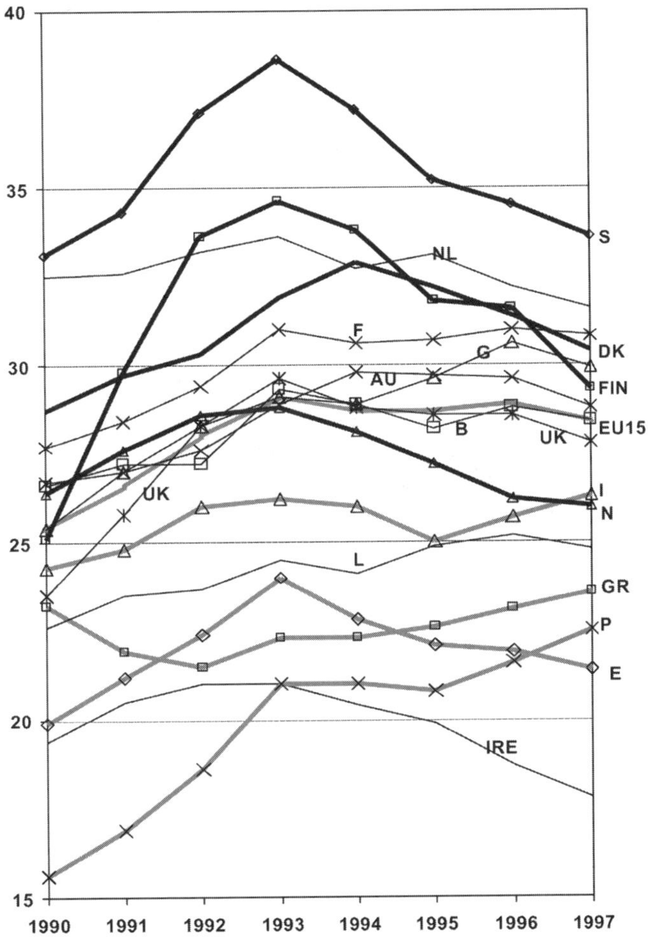

Figure 3.3 Total social protection expenditure 1990–1997. Percent of GDP.

Figure 3.5 demonstrates the link between the input and output side of the financing of the welfare state. Extensive social transfers and services will certainly demand high taxes and/or social contributions, as in the Nordic countries. On the other hand, this pays off in terms of lower levels of inequality in material living standards, concerning income inequality, lower poverty rates and lower levels of class inequality (see part 2). The southern cluster, with lower resources in terms of GDP, uses a lower share of its GDP for collective use in general as well as for redistribution in particular, by choosing lower tax levels. Lower levels of social protection as well as lower employment imply a larger burden on the family.

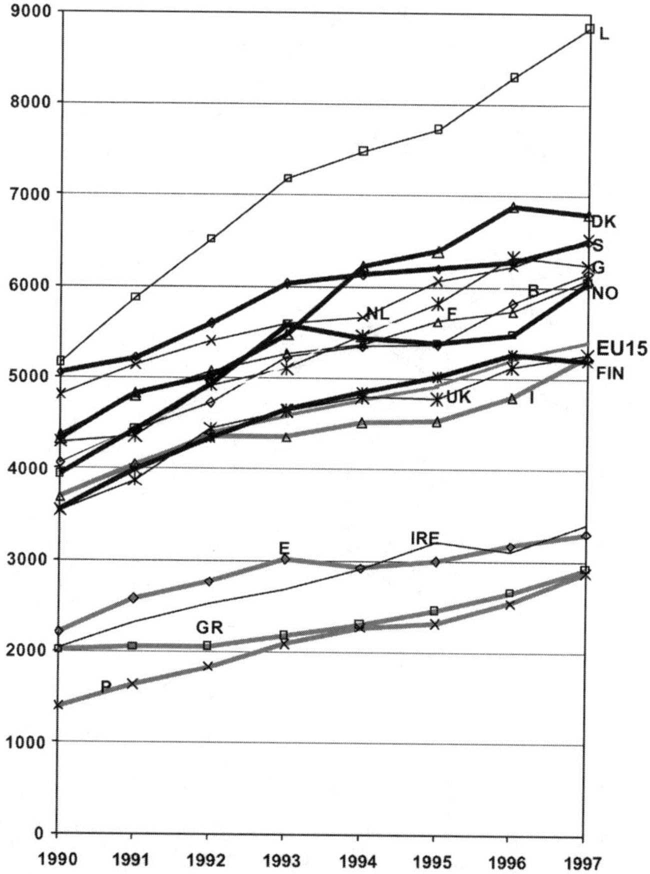

Figure 3.4 Total social protection expenditure 1990–1997. PPP per capita.

The long-term time series for the Swedish case, concerning social protection expenditure reaching back to 1960, will be commented later in conjunction with other institutional features in chapter 9.

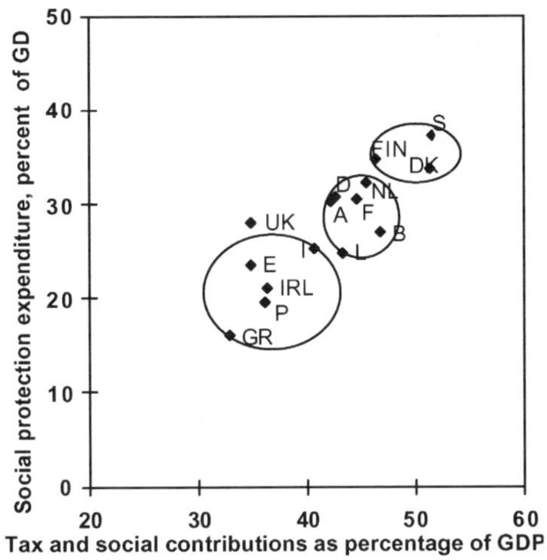

Figure 3.5 Social protection expenditure versus tax rates and social contributions. Source: Esspros 1995.

Income Redistribution

The second global indicator of the welfare state impact is based on the reduction of inequality of market income (earnings) by redistribution through taxes and transfers. Income inequality is usually measured by the Gini-coefficient. By comparing the change in Gini-coefficients from earnings to post tax/transfer disposable income the welfare state effect can be calculated as a percent reduction, which can be compared over time and between nations.

A recent study based on the Luxembourg Income Study (LIS) published by OECD (Burniaux et al., 1998) gives the following picture for an incomplete set of OECD-countries participating in the Luxembourg Income Study (Figure 3.6). This study again indicates that the Nordic countries (and Belgium) have the most re-distributive tax/transfer systems. Other representatives of the central cluster (Germany and the Netherlands), as well as Italy, the only Southern country included in this study, fall at a much lower level. USA and Japan are rated well behind all EU-member states in this study (UK was not included). Further analysis based on LIS indicates that nations with centralised bargaining (e.g., Germany, Sweden) display lower levels of inequality in earnings.

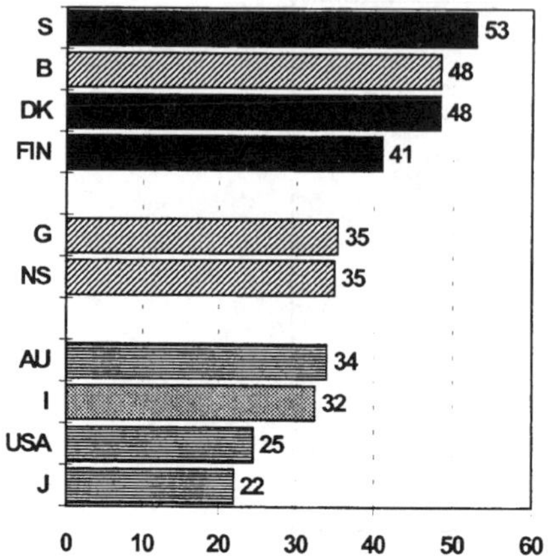

Figure 3.6 Percent reduction in income inequality (Gini-coefficient) by taxes/transfers. Mid 1990s. Source: Luxembourg Income Survey (Bumieau 1998).

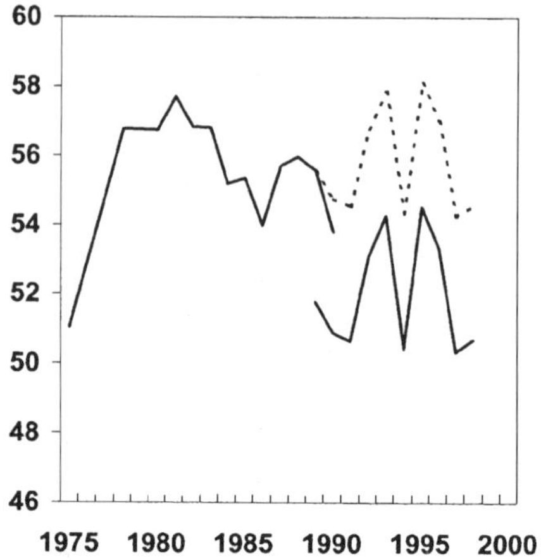

Figure 3.7 Redistribution by welfare transfers and taxes in Sweden 1975–98. Percent reduction of the Gini-coefficient for factor income.

Comparative trend data on redistribution are very incomplete (for countries as well as years of observation) and suffer from inadequate comparability. Very few countries have robust annual time series. In the Swedish case we can identify a clear increase in redistribution up to the early 1980s (Figure 3.7). From then on we record a decline in redistribution. In the 1990s followed a period of strong fluctuation in the aftermath of the 1991 tax reform, a decline employment of some 10 percent points, and further temporary changes in the tax system and reductions in the transfer system[1]. However, the general picture is clear: Sweden reached its peak in redistribution in the early 1980s, and thereafter followed a decline. The details of the redistributive features are discussed further in chapter 8.

Family-Related Public Expenditure

Family policies can be classified into two different categories; first, policies to *support* the family as a welfare institution, and second, to *substitute* the family as a welfare institution, by taking over responsibilities from the family. A second way of structuring family policies concerns *regulations* versus *redistribution*, as already applied to the welfare state-labour market relation in the previous chapter.

The traditional family can act as a powerful welfare institution within certain demarcations. This concerns above all the family's emotional support, which cannot be substituted by the welfare state.

Strengthening the family in this respect, by contributing to the support of social networks is a major objective in social planning in a wider sense. However, the family is also a welfare producer when it comes to material living conditions and requirements for care services. As a second function, can larger families share assets and utilise the economy of scale in pooling their income as well as coordinating their consumption. Larger household size then implies lower living costs. Thirdly, families can offer free care services to its member, including children, elderly and the handicapped. These three functions of the family form the basis of conservative priority of the family as the major responsible welfare institution. From there follows support of the male breadwinner model, tax rebates and child allowances for children, and meagre social supply of caring services usually assigned to the family. With the male breadwinner model follows non-activity on the labour market for women as well as lean pension rights. With poor care services and welfare state support of the family women tend to be entrapped in their families.

Recent demographic change point at a powerful trend away from the familiaristic welfare strategy, towards transferring the family's welfare duties to the welfare state. With the Nordic countries as a vanguard there is a drift towards increased female and maternal employment, underpinned by mass education and ambitions for a full career for men as well as for women. This trend leads to new demands on the welfare state to provide care services as well as paid leave. This seems to be a common ambition in all member states, but in reality welfare provisions have not yet adjusted to this model everywhere. Accordingly, we have two strategies with very different consequences, and we have several surprising findings with respect to family formation (see details in chapter 4):

- The Nordic cluster displays a success story: with generous public provision of care for children and the elderly, paid maternity and parental leave and other transfers related to dependents, female employment has expanded, family formation is supported (earlier partnering, increased fertility, increased gender equality in general terms);
- In the Southern countries we see a pattern of protest. Female careers are blocked by poor job opportunities as well as lack of public care and subsidised leave required to support employ-

ment. Accordingly, there is delayed partnering and fertility, as well as increased poverty.

Now turning to statistics on family-related expenditure, there is only limited access to harmonised overview data, due to the vast variation and complexity in types of arrangements and coverage. The best global indicator is the total expenditure for family/children benefits provided by Esspros. Family expenditure is required to promote employment for women, and in particular mothers. Again the EU-member states fall well separated into three clusters (Figure 3.8). It should be noted that family-related expenditure is the highest in the 'collectivistic' Nordic cluster, and the lowest in the familiaristic and catholic Southern cluster, including Ireland. It should be understood that the higher public support for the Nordic families serves to relieve the family, and in particular women, from caring duties, support female employment, and deliberate women from dependency on the patriarchy. In other words, family expenditure serves as a 'defamiliaristic' strategy. Lower family provisions, as in the Southern cluster tend to reinforce larger families, by leaving caring duties within the family.

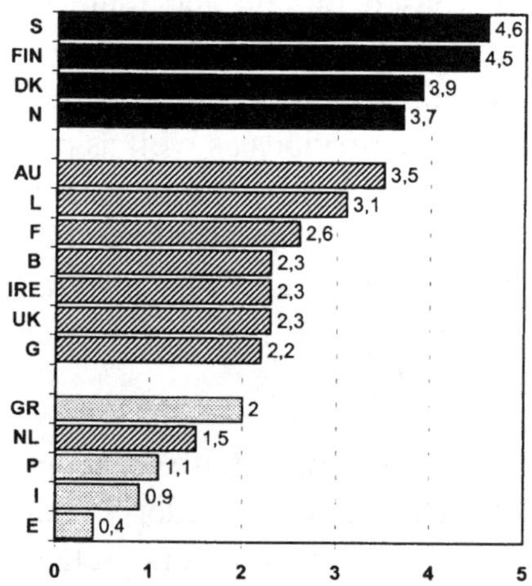

Figure 3.8 Social protection benefits for family/children 1994. Percent of GDP. Source: Esspros.

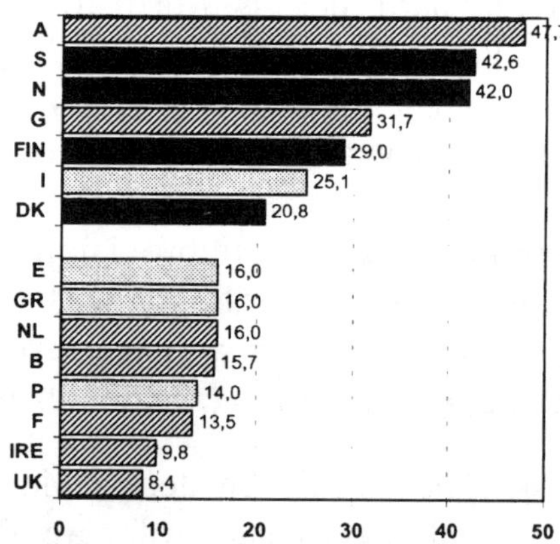

Figure 3.10 Weeks of maternity/parental leave with 100% pay of previous earnings (converted to equivalent weeks; applies to the first child and private sector). Source: European Commission/DG5 1998.

Figure 3.9 displays the available trend data for the 1990s, using the recent harmonised social expenditure statistics for the European union (Esspros). There is considerable change over the 1990s; in the first half we record an increase in the Nordic as well as the central cluster, towards a pattern of divergence. Then followed a clear decline in all of the Nordic countries. There is little change in the Southern cluster throughout the decade.

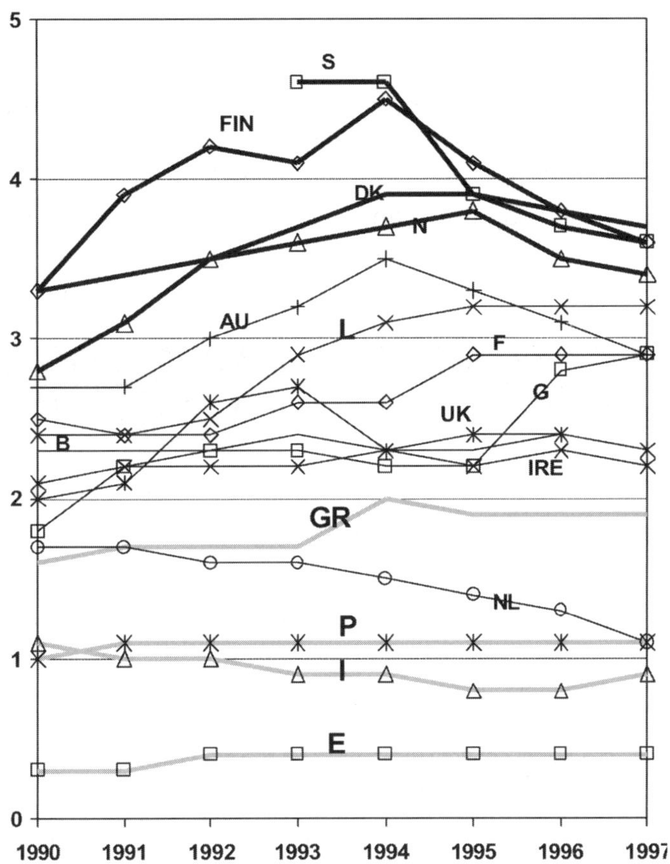

Figure 3.9 Social protection benefits for family/children 1990–1997. Percent of GDP.

Next, we proceed to welfare state characteristics relating directly to family formation and child-bearing by focusing on measures which support the reconciliation between work and family, and in particular the situation of women in this respect. A recent general overview in this direction by the European commission (DG5, 1998) gives a general picture of the public support in member states concerning the family's responsibilities in caring for children and elderly respectively, addressing:

- subsidised care services
- measures to enable workers to redistribute some of their time from the workplace to the home while retaining an employment contract ("time off")
- monetary benefits, including payments during leave, social security, social assistance, tax rebates.

The length of *paid* maternity plus parental leave (converted to equivalent weeks with 100% substitution) is best supported in the Nordic countries (Norway, Finland, Sweden, also Austria), while Greece, Spain, Portugal, Ireland and UK have the lowest provisions (Figure 3.10). This again places the Nordic cluster in the lead, but does not discriminate between the central and southern cluster.

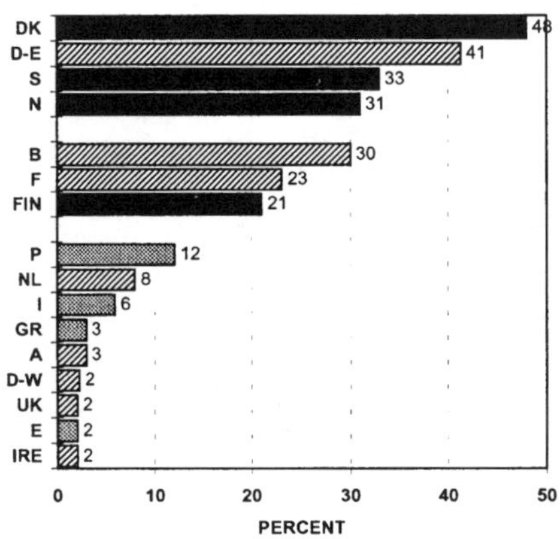

Figure 3.11 Percentage of children 0–3 years attending/places available in publicly funded services for children. Source: Deven, Inglis, Moss, Petri 1997.

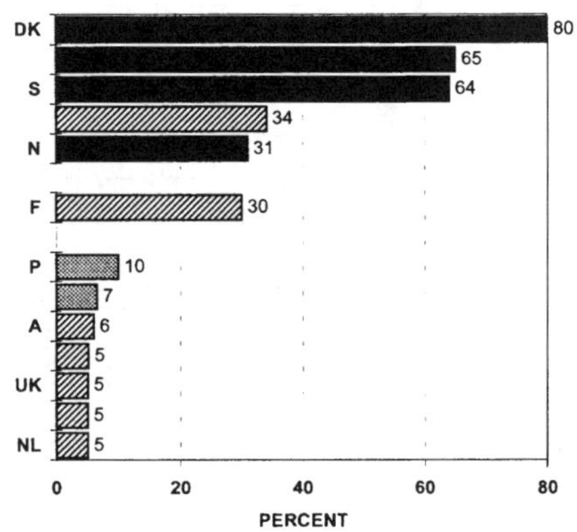

Figure 3.12 Percentage of children 6–20 years attending/places available in publicly funded services for children. Source: Deven, Inglis, Moss, Petri 1997.

The same applies to publicly funded care services for children; however, here the general pattern of three clusters is not equally consistent. Again the Nordic countries and the former East Germany are the best providers for children in the age of 0–3 years, followed by France and Belgium, while the Southern countries as well as some of the central countries (Germany-W, UK, Austria and the Netherlands) perform as poorly as the Southern countries (Figure 3.11). For children of higher age the variation is less pronounced (Figure 3.12). Notably, the Nordic countries are also good providers for school-age children 6–10 years. Again France is close to the Nordic countries, while most other central European countries unite with the Southern cluster. In summary, it is in this area the public sector should have a major impact in the Nordic countries to support child-bearing and parenthood.

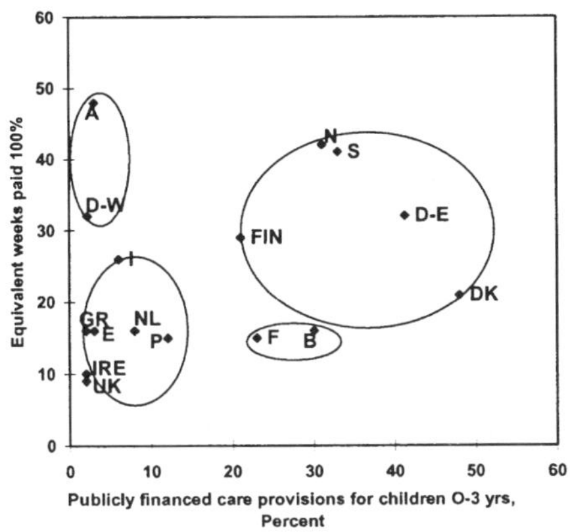

Figure 3.13 Public child care supported: Paid maternity/paternity leave (equivalent weeks paid 100%) and publicly funded child care provisions for the first child (percentage of children attending/available places).
Source: European commission 1998.

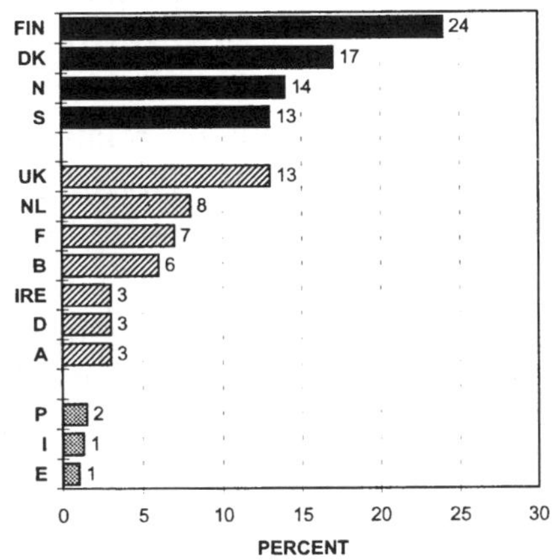

Figure 3.14 Percentage of older people receiving home care services.
Source: Deven, Inglis, Moss, Petri 1997.

In order to support the reconciliation between parenthood (or rather maternity) and gainful employment for women, *both* elements are required in public support of maternity. There is a need for child care facilities as well as provisions for time off, including the right to leave, and in particular the right to *paid* leave. A recent study has recalculated the full payment period (weeks with 100% pay, see Figure 3.10) from existing replacement rates and length of periods for the first child (European Commission/DGV, 1998). This indicator is in Figure 3.13 related to the available public care provisions for children aged 0–3 (based on Figure 3.11). *Both* conditions are of course necessary to support maternal engagement in the labour market, along with job opportunities. Here we again record a clear Scandinavian cluster (including East Germany) delivering both, and a Southern cluster rating low on both conditions. UK, Ireland and the Netherlands also belong to this group, with UK displaying the worst conditions in the European union. Germany-W and Austria have equally high financial provision as the Nordic countries, but fall short on childcare facilities. This will certainly reduce the employment levels of mother (which will be demonstrated in the second part of this report). France comes out lower than the Nordic countries on paid leave, which is calculated for the first child only. From the second child on these provisions are much better in France, which should affect female employment and earnings.

Concerning the care of elderly several countries support time off for care of ill adult relatives, with Sweden granting the longest duration. Notably the Nordic countries also have the largest proportion of elderly people receiving home care services (13–24 percent), while the Southern cluster falls at 1–2 percent, close to Germany (3 percent). Figure 3.14 again reproduces the already familiar three cluster of Northern, Southern and central European welfare production. The variation in institutional care of the older population is rather limited, but even here the Nordic countries are in the lead.

Labour Market Policy

While family policies serve to promote increased employment and equal opportunity, labour market policy is intended to do the same by influencing the demand of labour as well as the supply side. In this excursion we are primarily interested in what is usually called active labour market policies. We leave passive measures aside since these are difficult to identify in comparative measurement, because of the overlapping and variation of the various national programs. Active measures include training and job creation, youth measures inc. apprenticeships, subsidised employment, support to starting enterprises, and rehabilitation and work for the disabled. These measures are intended to mobilise the individual's resources to contribute to his/her personal welfare by gainful employment, by opening job opportunities, improve employability, stimulate job seeking, prevent depreciation of skill, and on a general level, prevent social exclusion. Labour market measures also have a central function on a societal level. They serve to minimise public expenditure, and relieve other urgent public expenditure. Hence, active labour market policies are an essential tool on the repertoire of the welfare state, since high employment levels are a prerequisite for a generous welfare state. Accordingly, the 'work line' and related concepts such as workfare and work incentives, are catchwords in most developed welfare states.

Figure 3.15 show that there is again a clear north-south clustering within the European union, with the Nordic countries in the lead, while the southern member states fall at much lower levels. However, expenditure for active measures should be corrected for the need for such intervention. Figure 3.16 shows a rough indicator linking the volume of expenditure to the (remaining) unemployment rate. Certainly should the preferred indicator be the initial unemployment rate, which however is not properly measurable. The proxy indicator in Figure 3.16 again confirms that the Nordic cluster is unique, and that Sweden, in particular, falls at very high levels. Since Finland as well as Sweden had dramatic rise in unemployment in the early 1990s (see chapter 2), the estimates for these countries from around 1990 are also displayed in Figure 3.16. At that time Sweden as well as Finland had much higher active labour market expenditure, in relation to its unemployment level.

The important message from these findings is that Sweden as well as Finland institutionalised active labour market measures, and had comparatively low unemployment levels (2–3 percent) while most other EU member states parked at much higher levels. Even after the Swedish/Finnish crisis Sweden kept its uniqueness.

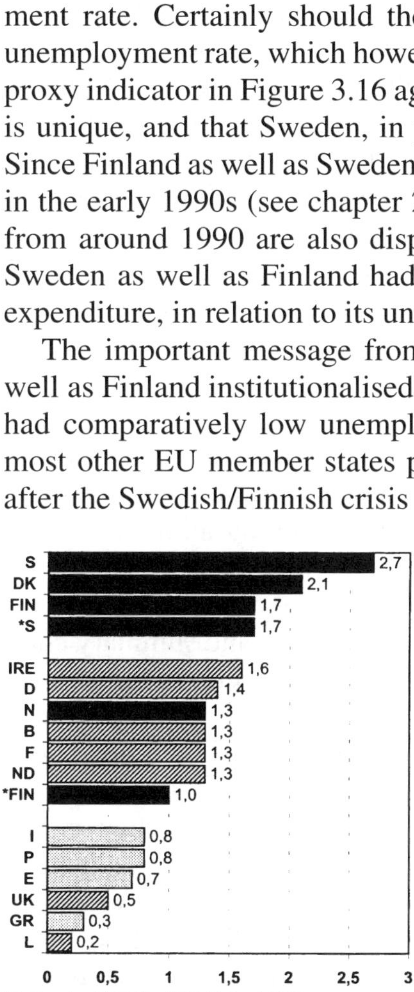

Figure 3.15 Expenditure on active labour market policies. Percent of GDP. 1993–95. Source: Hvinden 1999 and OECD.

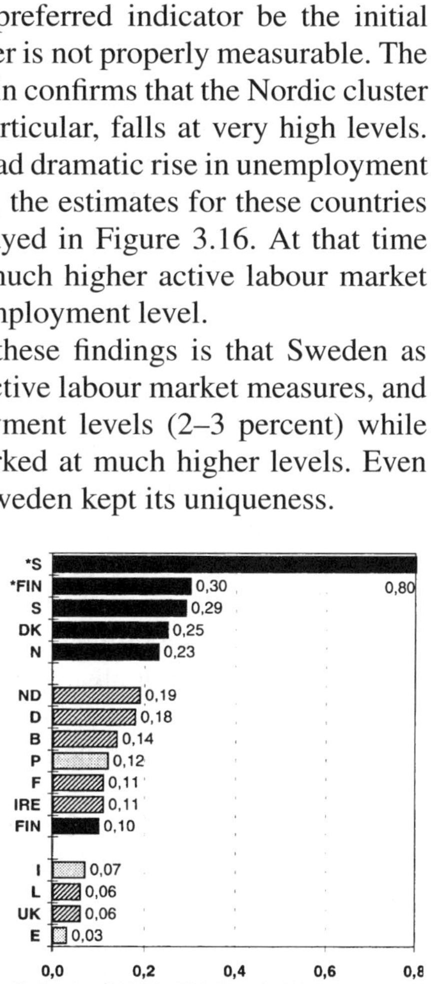

Figure 3.16 Expenditure on active labour market policies. Percent of GDP spent per percent of unemployment. Source: OECD 1997 and Hvinden 1999.

DISCUSSION

The findings in this chapter on the variation of welfare state provisions in the European union again demonstrate a clear grouping of EU member states into three rather distinct clusters, with three levels of general generosity. We have explored the general level of social protection expenditure, as well as welfare policies relating to the other two welfare institutions, i.e., labour market policies and family policies. In summary, the Nordic welfare states (Sweden, Denmark, Finland and Norway) are most interventionist in their general social expenditure and redistribution strategies through taxes and transfers, as well as in regulating the other welfare institutions, i.e., the family and the labour market, as compared to the southern and central cluster. The southern member states (Italy, Portugal, Greece and Spain) have the least interventionist and generous policies. The central member states (Germany, France, Belgium, Netherlands, Luxembourg, UK, Ireland) again form an intermediate cluster.

However, as compared with the findings on labour market and family characteristics (chapters 2 and 4) the clustering is less distinct, with several exceptions. It should also be mentioned that the choice of indicators is restricted by the variation in institutional forms and by the access to comparable data for the entire set of EU member states. As for labour market characteristics in the previous chapter, we utilise indicators of global and summary character, which might not always capture the specificity of all national welfare state strategies.

The clustering of EU member states by welfare state provisions is highly correlated with labour market characteristics: Inclusive labour markets, signified by high employment rates, low unemployment levels and lower inequality in earnings, have in general larger social protection expenditure, as well as extensive labour market policies and family policies supporting high employment. The Nordic countries come out as forerunners towards activation policies, by much larger expenditure in active labour market expenditure. The logic between this positive correlation is further discussed in final chapter.

Further, in the next chapter we will demonstrate that we have an equally clear negative correlation between welfare state provisions and family characteristics in EU member states: regions with poor labour markets and lean welfare state arrangements have to adapt by inclusive family networks.

The large variation in public provisions and labour market performance in Europe explains the very different family structure in the Southern countries as compared to the Nordic and central clusters. A whole range of indicators on the 'traditional family' tells us that the age of exit from the parent's home and partnering comes much later, and fertility is lower in the South and higher in the Nordic countries. Recent trends also indicate that these differences have been increasing. The explanation is 'coping behaviour'; the traditional family has to take on much of the responsibilities, which in the North are guaranteed by the welfare state as social rights, and this behaviour has increased lately (see next chapter). Our findings concerning welfare state provision have demonstrated that the total volume of the welfare state expenditure as well as the directed provisions (family policies supporting public support of care of children and elderly and paid parental leave; active labour market policies) tend to support female employment, fertility and parenthood best in the Nordic countries, with France closer the Nordic cluster, and Germany close to the Southern cluster. However, there are sign of retreat from the generous provisions in the North, while some advancement is seen in other member states.

NOTE

[1] The income concept was changed in the 1991 tax reform (broken line = adjusted line). Peaks are effects of the tax reform (1991) and a temporary 50 percent reduction of capital taxation.

SCB Statistics Sweden
Welfare Analysis Program
and
University of Umeå
PO Box 24300
10451 Stockholm
Sweden

JOACHIM VOGEL

THE FAMILY

In the case of the labour market the distribution of resources is based on competition and individual performance. The welfare states' redistribution is focused at solidarity between citizens. In the case of the family the principle is reciprocity and an informal contract between family members concerning responsibilities for the welfare of family members. There is a contract between spouses, between parents and their children, between adults and their elderly parents, and between adults and further relatives. The large variation in Europe in the appearance of families reflects substantial diversity of obligations and informal rights of family members. What can adult children expect from their parents, elderly from their mid-aged children, and where are the limits of responsibility between spouses concerning economic and caring features? This variation of family obligations is also reflected in legislation, delineating responsibilities between the welfare state and the family.

The European union displays a large variation in family structure, family formation, separations, fertility, and caring for the elderly and young. This variation reflects social practise of family traditions, as well as necessities given by the performance of labour market and welfare state in their role as welfare producers. Pooling resources within kinship is the last option when jobs and earnings fail and welfare state provisions are inadequate as well. In this case large and inclusive families are a valuable and necessary resource; we can even speak of family-based welfare regimes. On the other hand, larger families also imply duties and dependencies, which offer less security than general social rights guaranteed by the welfare state. Children's living standards depend on the resources of their parents; care of the elderly is based on the capacity or even existence of grown-up children; support from spouses requires successful partnering.

Social Indicators Research **64:** 393–435, 2003.

Hence, in analogy with its relation to the labour market by *regulation* and *redistribution* ('decommodification') addressed in the previous chapter, the welfare state intervenes with *regulations* (defining responsibilities and rights between family members) as well as *redistribution* (e.g. by providing child allowances, paid maternity/parental leave from work, tax rebates, public child care, and home care for the elderly). These interventions, which could be labelled '*defamiliarization*' (Esping-Andersen, 1999), serve to absorb risks which the family is unable to meet, or to relieve the family from 'extreme risks' that the family (sometimes) is incapable or unwilling to monitor, not to mention situations where there is no family available at all. The logic is to extend social rights based on citizenship to traditionally family tasks such as caring, training, and providing basic living standards to dependents. It should be noted that these policies have a wider impact; they also affect the labour market (supply of labour), gender roles (women's relief from caring duties), deliberating elderly from dependency on their offspring, providing early social training through child care, and stimulate reproduction.

The limits of defamilialization is at the very heart of left-right political cleavage, it is central in catholic/subsidiary thinking, and it is also related to the economic viability of welfare state. Nevertheless, there is a large variation in Europe in the way responsibilities for welfare production is shared between labour market, welfare state and family. No doubt, defamilialization does improve the distributive structure, which is its rationale, but it also weakens the strength and capacity of the family, and contributes to gradual fragmentation of the family. Hence, the increase in equality intended by welfare state intervention also includes negative elements of lost primary group affiliations, sense of belonging, affective relations, and security of partnerships. It is obvious that the European union is (still) a fabric of very divers models of families.

INTER-GENERATIONAL RISK MANAGEMENT

Recent demographic trends in Europe relating to family formation, including marriage and other forms of partnerships, divorces and dissolutions of partnerships, childbearing, parenthood and single parenthood, are changing rapidly. The timing and spacing of these phenomena vary much between EU-member states. There is a common European trend in the direction of fragmentation and diversification of family forms, with the Nordic countries forming a vanguard. On the other hand, in some aspects the three clusters of EU member states seem to develop in opposite directions. In the Southern countries the age of leaving the parental home has increased, partnering tends to be postponed and fertility has declined from the highest to the lowest levels in Europe. Meanwhile, the Nordic countries display a more complex fertility pattern. First, a decline followed by substantial growth, and then again a new decline. Furthermore, there are important comparative differences concerning the cohesion of family bonds, which are related to the distribution of material welfare and opportunities offered by labour market and welfare state. In the South young adults as well as the elderly tend to be incorporated in larger households, in particular when they have lower income (earnings or pensions) or are exposed to unemployment. In the south the supportive function of the family has much kept down and delayed the fragmentation of the family. This supportive function has to a large extent been absorbed by the Nordic welfare state.

The variation between nations, as well as the trends in family formation and reproductive behaviour are complex. The primary causes should not be sought in a general change in post-materialistic values and attitudes related to family formation as such, but in the underlying institutional context defining the individual resources, which determine material living standards. Much of the decisions on family formation and fertility take place in the age of 20–35. The transition to adulthood has been much delayed by the concurrence of prolonged youth education, and stagnation or even contraction of the labour market, with increasing levels of youth unemployment everywhere. Concurrently, we should assume a long-term change in the role expectations of young women related to equal opportunities, in the direction of a full life including a career as well as family life and motherhood, and a democratisation of the gendered power structure within families. This change implies new demands on the welfare delivery institutions. In this period of contracting labour markets and crumbling welfare state provisions we can see an *increasing mismatch* between the welfare mix (i.e. the institutional configuration of the labour market's and welfare state's welfare provisions), and the ambitions of younger women towards equal opportunities and economic independence. This scenario should explain much of the recent change in family formation in Europe, including the move from the parents' home, partnering, fertility and separations.

In the same way we should interpret the opportunities of the elderly. Pension rights available in old age is a matter of having earned pensions by employment in the first place, and pension systems offering liveable pensions levels, be it by private or public pensions. Lower lifetime employment levels, in particular for women, slim survivor pensions and poor public minimum pensions, throw the responsibility for subsistence of the elderly back at the family. The same applies to care for the elderly.

The welfare production of the labour market (through jobs and earnings) and welfare state (by taxes, transfers, and services) defines the complementary obligations required of the extended family. Hence, this variation explains the variation and change of European family forms. In this light we should interpret the family's redistribution of intergenerational risks over the life course, as well as gender roles and the network support of the elderly, within an informal contract between family members. Resources are received during childhood and youth, then returned to the next generation, and then again received in old age. This form of intergenerational risk management is the very essence of the generational contract. We will see that there is a vast variety between EU-member states as to the penetration of this model.

Accordingly, is the gender contract defining gender roles linked to the way caring is monitored. With meagre welfare state provisions women will be entrapped in family duties; with generous public care and family benefits equal opportunities to work and economic independence is promoted.

THE CHANGING OPPORTUNITY STRUCTURE

There is a wealth of demographic data picturing the changing family. These data can be interpreted in two ways; first, as indicators of the *opportunity structure provided by the family as a welfare insti-*

tution, and second, as indicators of *coping behaviour* to adjust to current labour market hazards and welfare state arrangements. The opportunity structure offered by the family is defined by normality: when forms of family behaviour are highly frequent, e.g. staying with parents till the upper 20-ies as in the Southern countries, then this defines 'social practise', including a 'soft' right for young adults as well as an obligation for their parents. Such social practise, rights and obligations, does not exist in Scandinavia, where young adults are in fact moving shortly after age 20; they are expected to do so, and parents sense little obligation to support them after normal schooling.

In the same way are 'gender regimes' defining different role prescriptions for men and women between the two-breadwinner model, and the male breadwinner model. They represent changing models to consider, to accept or abandon in the course of life. In the same vein, the elderly as well as their grownup children have to make decisions on how to monitor caring in old age.

The opportunity structure offered by the family thus defines available options in many realms related to the family's role: we may utilise these options, we may stretch them somewhat further, we may break away towards other, less established family forms, or we may choose to arrange our lives without utilising the "normal" family form, if that is allowed by our overall personal resources. How we will choose between family forms may deviate from 'social practise', usually because of *opportunities and restrictions related to the labour market and welfare state*. The changing opportunity structure offered by the labour market (jobs, earnings) and by the welfare state (transfers and services), will thus influence family formation. For instance: prolonged youth education and increased youth unemployment (increased restrictions related to the labour market) will delay the exit from the parental home; increased female employment (increased opportunity offered by the labour market) will increase separations and singlehood; increased child allowances and public child care provisions (improved opportunity offered by the welfare state) will increase fertility; and viable old age pensions will decrease the proportions of elderly moving to their children's households.

Hence, change in family behaviour can be interpreted as coping behaviour, telling us about the changing welfare efficiency of the labour market and welfare state. This brings us to the essence of this chapter: differences between nations in demographic behaviour reflect not only family traditions (social practise), but also variation in the current opportunity structure offered by the other welfare institutions. In this chapter the same data is utilised for both purposes, to illustrate the opportunity structure of the family, as well as coping behaviour related to opportunities offered by the labour market and welfare state. Decreased opportunity on the labour market or by the welfare state will increase utilisation of family support, against the general basic trend towards fragmentation of family bonds. The model of interacting welfare delivery institutions assumes a balance of responsibility for the welfare outcome at individual level. Efficient labour markets (high employment rates, lower unemployment risk, equality of earnings) relieve the welfare state as well as the family from much of their responsibilities, and likewise do large families and households compensate shortcomings of the labour market and welfare state.

While the existing family structure and family life has a research interest in its own right, the variety of existing family forms offer options for individual coping with external forces influencing living conditions over the course of life. The post-war increase of employment and the expansion of the welfare state relieved the European families from parts of their responsibilities for the extended family and kin. This opened new opportunities for groups usually dependent on the family and patriarchy, in particular for women, young adults, the elderly and handicapped, to choose other family forms, and to adjust their general family behaviour. Hence, the growth in educational subsidies, public jobs, the expansion of pension rights and social transfers have had consequences for the household structure and size, affecting a whole range of family related behaviour.

REACTIVE FAMILY PATHWAYS

The age of leaving the parental home and age of first partnering, the choice between legal forms of partnership (marriage or consensual unions), divorce and de-partnering, singlehood, parenthood, fertility, timing and spacing of childbearing, single parenthood, stepfamilies, and sharing an extended multi-generational household indicate rational decisions based on evaluation of the opportunity structure. The individual is seen as an active agent reacting to external structures (the 'welfare mix'), forming individual pathways through childhood, adolescence, adulthood and old age.

The model of family pathways assumes repeated choice between alternative family forms during the course of life, in response to the existing welfare mix, in order to optimise present and future living conditions. Individual life courses and pathways are meeting the pathways of partners and family members. Couples are joining a common course for life or for a limited period. Children may be born when suitable; they will share the pathways of their parents for some time, later to decide to depart to their own household. Individual pathways are repeatedly negotiated between family members, reacting to the changing options offered by the other welfare institutions. Family life may link its members by moral obligations, affection, sexual attraction, and by pure instrumental considerations related to material conditions; later in life by a common history and by the connection with the next generation.

The existing family structure tends to reflect the welfare mix of the past. In the same vein, it will define the options available in current family formation. Rapidly changing institutional configuration will enforce behavioural adjustment. Looking at the long-term changes in the welfare mix and the overall efficiency of the welfare mix in the European Union, there has been a trend towards relieving the family from much of its welfare delivery responsibilities (defamilialization), supporting individual job careers for women, separations, singlehood, and single parenthood, leading to a general fragmentation of the traditional extended family. Furthermore, there seems to be a long-term trend towards a diversity of family form, as well as increasing mobility between families and family forms. Family pathways are becoming more complex, but the dominant pattern still continues to centre on the nuclear family.

The economic crisis of recent decades, the stagnation of employment and persistent unemployment, and the withering correctives of welfare state arrangements again have changed the welfare mix.

This should produce coping behaviour affecting family formation, including the timing of the separation from the parental family, partnering, and fertility. And accordingly, it should influence the distributive structure with respect to material living standards, and economic and social inclusion.

FACETS OF EUROPEAN FAMILY BEHAVIOUR

Our twofold interpretation of European family forms is focused at *opportunities* offered by the family structure and at family formation as *coping* behaviour. The analysis includes seven aspects:

1. **scale**: the size of families;
2. **exit**: the timing of the move from the parental home;
3. **partnering**: the timing and spacing of partnerships;
4. **childbearing**: the timing and spacing of fertility,
5. **separations**: dissolution of partnerships,
6. **reconciliation**: between family and work;
7. **ageing**: elderly living in extended families.

In each of these aspects we will study the variation between EU member states, as well as the recent trends (if available), in order to explain the impact of the opportunity structure provided in various welfare production models.

In a long-term perspective, much of the traditional family's responsibilities have been absorbed by the labour market and the welfare state. In particular, this applies to the instrumental role of the family as a producer of material welfare in most spheres of life. The basic economic needs of its members are to a larger extent guaranteed by employment and paid work, as well as by social rights guaranteed by the welfare state in the form of income substitutes and public services. This applies in particular to the care-taking role of the family for children (including education), the aged, the handicapped, and in general to the inactive on the labour market. Alongside with this go a gradual change in family-related values, and the demands on the family as a welfare producer.

This general trend also reduces the bonds between household members, opening other options to an independent life outside the realms of the family. The option to leave the nest early, to separate, and to an independent life in old age and when handicapped, could be seen as major democratic advancements. There is a corresponding trend in the direction of secular post materialistic sexual and family values (O'Connor, 1996), in particular towards acceptance of extra-marital sexuality, consensual unions, divorce and de-partnering, and selective mobility. The general picture is one of *fragmentation* of families, where family ties are less reliant by instrumental considerations, but on active choices. The role of the family gradually shifts from its instrumental function towards its *affective function*, towards being a resort of intimacy, affection, and reassurance, meeting emotional and sexual needs. Furthermore, families will exhibit more *instability*, and family forms will develop towards *diversity*, away from the still dominant nuclear family.

In a shorter perspective, say over the last 10–20 years, we are no doubt facing a changing welfare mix in most member states, again towards a shift of responsibility back to the family, which will decrease the options of dependants, increase inequality and female exploitation. This change will have its largest impact on young adults. The labour market continues to withdraw from its responsibilities to with respect to the youth generation. Also in a long-term perspective, the modernisation of working life inflates the education demands, pushing youth education into adulthood. This delays the establishment of youth on the labour market, and thereby their transition into adulthood and towards economic independence. The corresponding contraction of the welfare state will also have its largest impact on the younger generation.

Hence, there are indeed two major trends to be expected in family and reproductive behaviour, one long-term in the direction to fragmentation, instability, diversity, and independence; and one towards a postponement of family formation and reproduction. Since most of the crucial decisions on family formation, partnering, childbearing and departnering are done in the age of 20–35, coinciding with a rapid growth in educational demands, persistent youth unemployment, and welfare state contraction, we should expect to see rapid change in family formation and reproductive behaviour of the youth generation.

In summary, while the age of biological and sexual maturity is decreasing, the age of economic independence is increasing: the labour market absorbs youth labour at later age, and the welfare state seems increasingly unable to accommodate to the closing of options for youth on the labour market. These trends should affect family pathways, in particular in the younger generation. The experience of the last decades indicates that sexual debut, the establishment of new households, partnering, and reproduction appear to be increasingly disconnected in time as well as from economic independence. The timing and spacing of family formation and reproduction should reflect the external institutional conditions. This link will be tested by a series of indicators of reproductive and family behaviour. Family behaviour will be perceived as coping behaviour in relation to the national institutional context. The focus is again on the EU–member states as statistical units, looking for similarities in behaviour related to similarities in institutional configuration.

Family Size

We begin with a general evaluation of the large variation in the family structure of EU member states. The living arrangements and positioning in households is primarily a matter of individual choice; which is influenced much by family tradition and by coping strategies to meet the external environment of options and restrictions experienced on arenas such as the labour market and the housing market, and of personal income resources. A shortage of jobs and of childcare services supports larger families, since women are inclined to adapt to marriage and stay in cohabitation. Low pension levels support multi-generation families taking care of their elderly. Rudimentary social protection also supports larger families. A shortage of dwellings may support larger families: new entrants to the housing market (young adults) will have to wait in the parental home. Finally, there is an economy of scale to exploit: large families make better use of their combined resources since they can share a dwelling and other expenses. For all these reasons, joining and forming larger families are a rational way of coping with available options. Such coping strategies are required in EU member states with inefficient labour markets and poor welfare states, i.e., the Southern cluster.

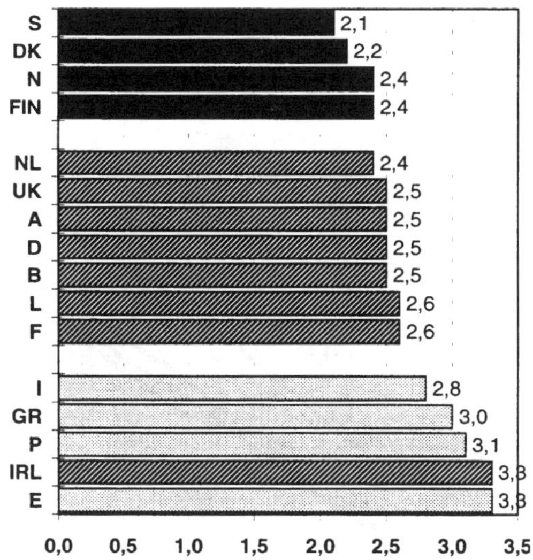

Figure 4.1 Average household size. Source: ECHP/NSS 1994.

Figure 4.1 gives the overall background by displaying the average household size in EU member states. Again we find an almost perfect rank order of countries similar to rankings we have seen in earlier chapters related to labour market and welfare state provisions. There is a Nordic cluster (Sweden, Denmark, Norway and Finland), joined by the Netherlands, with the lowest average household size. The Southern cluster including Spain, Greece, Portugal and Italy, plus Ireland has distinctly higher household size. The remaining central European countries again form the intermediate cluster. The background of these differences are of course complex, including several elements such as the cohabitation rates, age of leaving the parental home, fertility rates and inclusion of elderly in multi-generational households. These elements will be explored separately further on.

The overall trends in Europe go in the direction of smaller households. A recent analysis of the trends since 1960 indicate that the Nordic cluster forms the vanguard and the Southern cluster is the latecomer, with the central cluster in between. Figure 4.2 and 4.3 display the proportion of *single person households*, respectively of large *households with 5+ persons*. It should be noted that the three cluster move in the same direction over the past 30 years on these two indicators, and that the members of each cluster are well united, in level as well as in movement. Such similarity within clusters, and dissimilarity between them, should indicate similar driving forces and modes of adaptation.

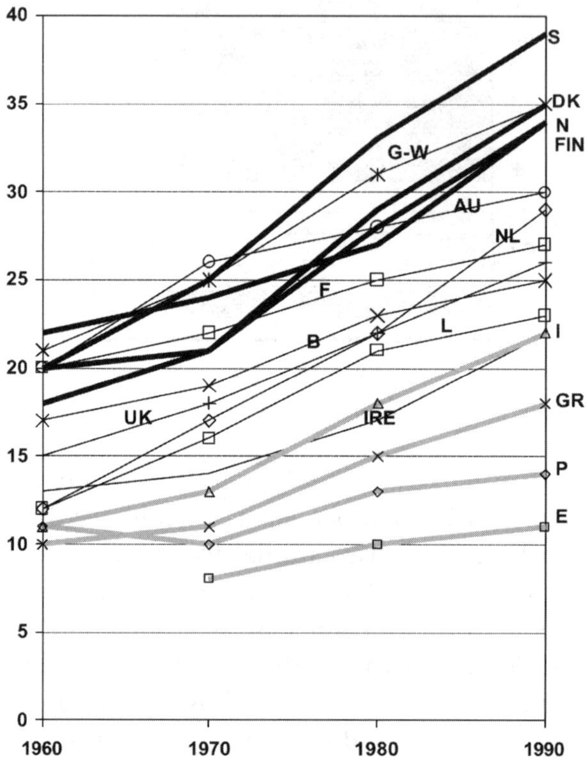

Figure 4.2 Single person households 1960–1990. Percent. Source: Höpflinger 1997.

A closer look at Figure 4.2 reveals that the trend towards single person households is the strongest in the north. In the south some countries are only moderately affected (Spain, Portugal). It took Italy and Greece three decades to reach the Swedish level of single households of 1960. The increase of single households obviously can be decomposed in several subcategories, including earlier exit from the parental home, increase of separations and interruption between partnerships, and dissolution of other types of shared households. Increasing divorce and separation rates producing more cases of transitions between partnerships is the most important category. Earlier exit is not contributing at all. Instead we will see a trend towards delayed exit in many countries (see next section).

The decline of large families displayed in Figure 4.3 follows the same pattern. The representatives of the three clusters are again well united, and there is a common trend with a slight tendency towards convergence between South and North. The major explanation should be an effect from declining fertility in the South, and in particular concerning the third and additional children.

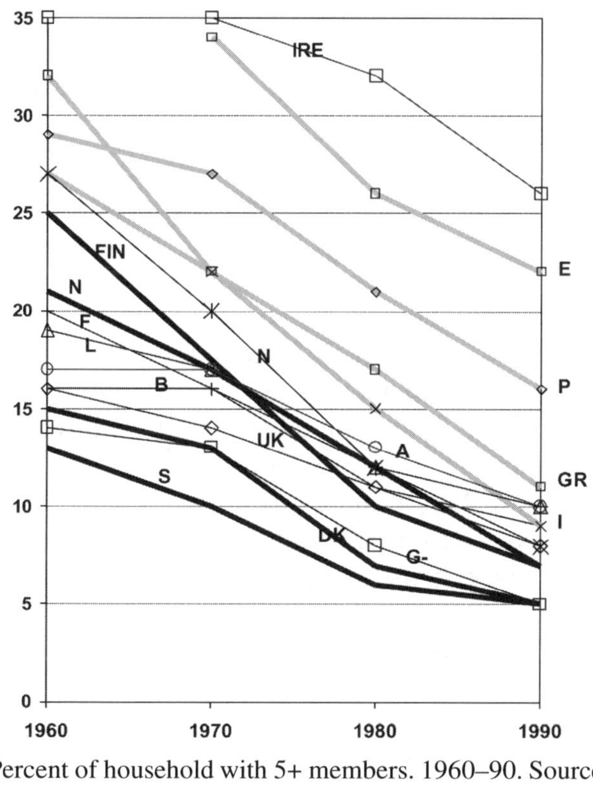

Figure 4.3 Percent of household with 5+ members. 1960–90. Source: Höpflinger (1997).

Leaving the Parental Home

The age at leaving the parental household is usually related to life events such as the end of youth education, the first job and a stable relationship, which will lead to a transition on the individual family pathway, embarking on the first partnership, sometimes after a period of singlehood in a separate household. In addition, there is also a variation in cultural tradition of the normal age for forming a separate household. These choices fall very different in the Nordic countries, the South and in central Europe.

Although there are only minor differences in the length of youth education and the age when the first regular job is taken, young adults move out much later in the South and Ireland, and much earlier in the four Nordic countries, as compared to the intermediate central European cluster. In the North the exit from the parents household follows a straightforward pattern related to the first permanent job or the end of secondary education. In fact, a larger proportion even leaves before youth education ends. Therefore young adults at very low age, frequently still in education, constitute a large fraction of the persons falling below the poverty line in the Nordic countries: they do not stay in the parental home waiting for a partnership and economic independence. In contrast, in the South a large proportion of young adults in their late twenties, stay on with their parents, even after their education is concluded, and even after being established on the labour market.

Recent research on the age of leaving the parental home indicates a sharp increase in Greece, Spain and Italy (Cherlin et al., 1997; Cordon, 1997). This should be seen in the light of prolonged youth education, as well as persistent youth unemployment, being an incentive to further training to be competitive on the labour market. Later exit should be the proper coping strategy, if this is supported by social practise. This interpretation is supported by our data.

The ECHP/NSS database from 1994 gives us a time window to the current age of exit by comparing the rates of young men and women still living with their parents at various age levels. Figure 4.4–4.5 exhibits the vast European differences among the 25–29 year old women and men. Again we find a clear-cut division into three clusters of EU-member states. It should also be noted that young women leave earlier than young men.

Living with parents has important economic advantages, due to the economy of scale in consumption, as well as the parents' financial support, and especially when the young are not fully employed and their economic contribution to the household is low. For many young adults this may be the period in life of their largest consumption capacity, and a period to save money for the new family to come.

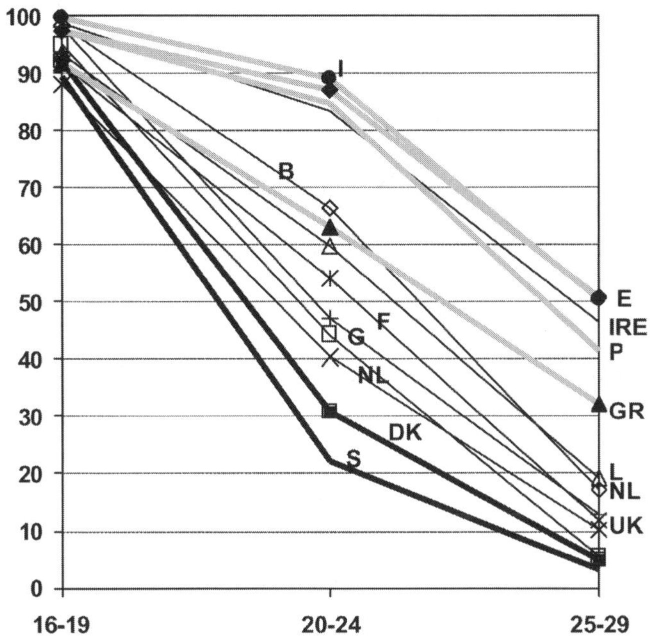

Figure 4.4 Percent of young women living with parents, by age group. Source: ECHP/NSS.

Figure 4.6 underlines the supportive role of the parental household buffering the consequences of inefficient labour markets, by incorporating young adults presently unemployed. The proportion of unemployed young adults included in parental households varies between some 13 percent (Norway) and 78 percent (Italy). Again we can identify the very divers Southern (or Catholic) and Northern clusters, and the intermediate central European cluster. The much larger levels of youth unemployment in the South (Vogel, 1997a) are well buffered by these family arrangements. In fact, even a larger proportion of already *employed* young adults in the South, in ages up to 30, are in fact staying with their parents. This indicates that staying in the parental home is not only a matter of economic necessity, but also a matter of tradition: the parent family seem ready to take on an extended responsibility, as well as their children seem prepared to accept these arrangements.

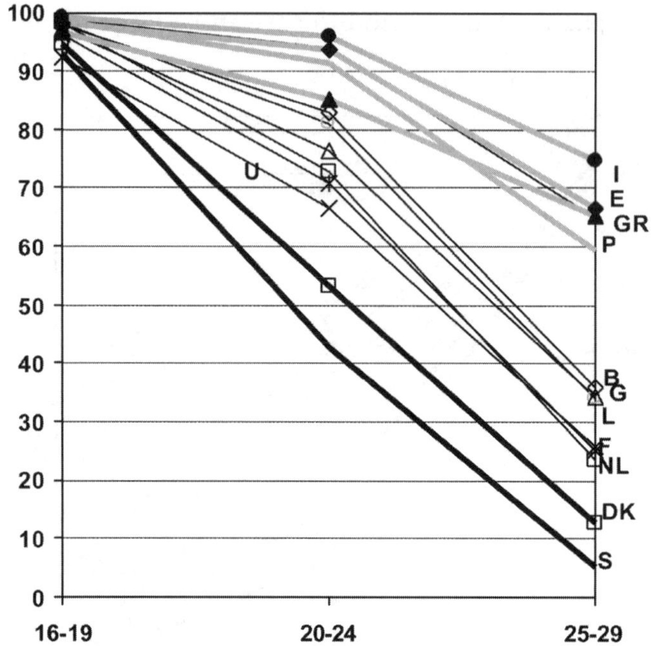

Figure 4.5 Percent of young men living with parents, by age group. Source: ECHP/NSS.

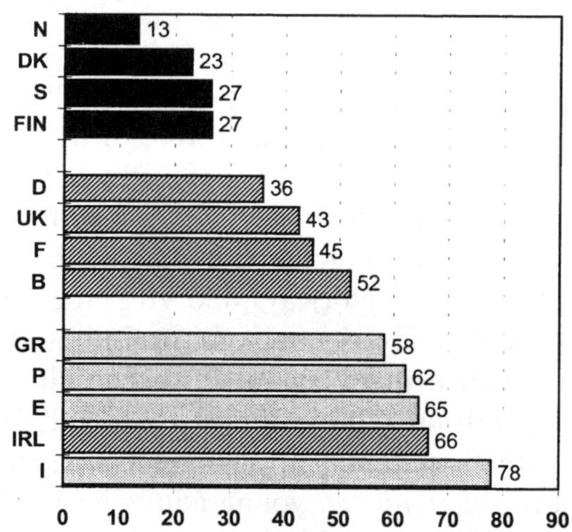

Figure 4.6 Percent of unemployed persons 16–30 years, living with their parents. Source: ECHP/NSS.

Staying with the parents seems to be common social practise, and hence a strong option in the South, but not in the Nordic countries.

In spite of the recent rapid rise in youth unemployment, there is no significant increase in Sweden and Finland in the age of exit, indicating that moving out early is a well-established norm, which is only marginally influenced by a rapid increase in youth unemployment.

The Timing of Partnering

Living within a larger household, with parents or with a partner, has economic advantages (the economy of scale) as well as meets basic emotional needs. At national level high rates of partnership (marriage or cohabitation) will buffer social exclusion on the labour market, and limit the demand on public expenses for social protection.

Late exit from the parental home in the South indicates that drawing on the parental family seems to be a normal coping arrangement to external opportunities. Early partnering seems to be the functional alternative in the North, without a tradition of late exit and several generations sharing households. These two functional alternatives reflect not only the external opportunities (labour market demand and welfare state provisions), but also a variation in basic values relating to role expectations of parents and adult children, as well as sexual norms and the relation between sexuality and partnership.

From late exit certainly follows late partnering, which will be demonstrated next for the Southern cluster. When employment and welfare provisions provide opportunity, partnering as well as fertility will come earlier, as in the Nordic cluster. Recent research (Klijzing and Macura, 1997) based on a comparative study of early partnering (before 25 years of age) surveyed the experiences of two groups of women of different age interviewed in the early 1990s (the age difference was ten years). Figure 4.7 indicates that early partnership is indeed a Nordic tradition, which has not changed, while the opposite coping arrangement (postponing partnering) has in fact occurred in the South. Figure 4.7 shows that the proportion of females who have entered partnership by age 25 is just above 80 percent in the Nordic countries, and there had been no change in this respect over the previous decade (measured by comparing data for women aged 25–29 and 35–39, respectively). In the South, Italy and Spain display much lower levels of early partnering (before age 25). Furthermore, there was a clear decline over the last decade (data for Greece and Portugal are not available). West Germany and the Netherlands have a similar decline, however at higher level. Again, the interpretation points at (increased) coping behaviour in the South, in reaction to less favourable opportunities offered by labour market and welfare state.

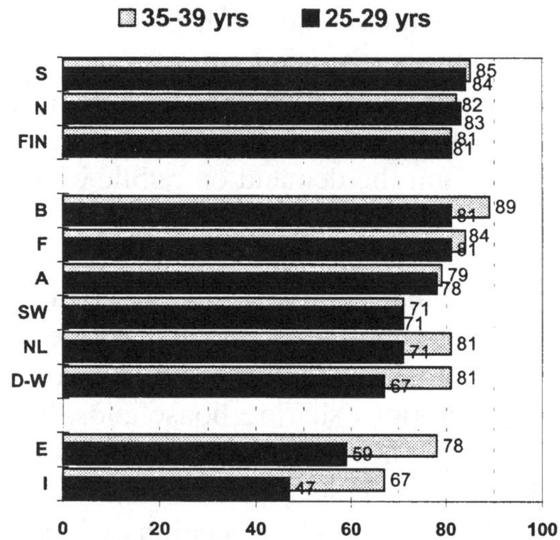

Figure 4.7 Percentage of females who had entered partnership by age 25. Source: Klijzing and Macura 1997.

A closer look at Swedish data from the mid 90-ies (with a dramatic increase in youth unemployment) shows a similar trend as in the ten year perspective for Italy and Spain. The Swedish case supports the conclusion that delayed partnering and fertility is related to decreasing options on the labour market (Statistics Sweden/Hoem, 1998).

Figure 4.8–9 give further details of delayed partnering, by distinguishing between various forms of partnerships. By comparing the behaviour of the 25–29 and 35–29 year old women (interviewed in the early1990s) with respect to their partnering *by the age of 25*, we can display the *change* over the last decade in the *forms* of partnership. Starting with the Nordic countries, we find that more than 80 percent had their first partnership before age 25. There is a decrease in Italy and Spain, as well as in Germany, Netherlands and Belgium.

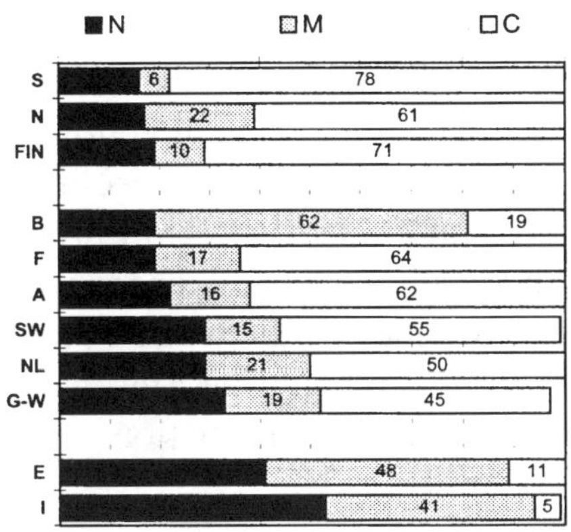

Figure 4.8 Cumulative percentage of women 25–29 years who had never entered partnership (N) by age 25, entered *first* partnerships that were marriages not preceded by cohabitation (M), or consensual unions (C). Source: Klijzing and Macura, 1997.

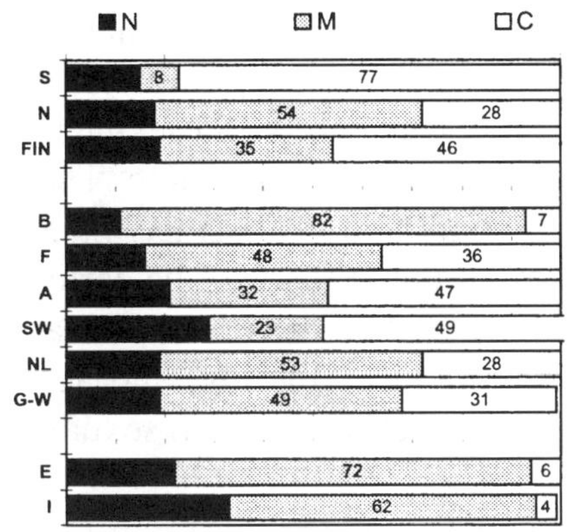

Figure 4.9 Cumulative percentage of women 35–39 years who had never entered partnership (N) by age 25, entered *first* partnerships that were marriages not preceded by cohabitation (M), or consensual unions (C). Source: Klijzing and Macura, 1997.

By comparing between figures 4.8–9 we can also evaluate the various trend, going from marriages (grey) towards starting off with consensual unions (white), which is common to all countries. Figures 4.8–9 also demonstrate the extraordinary North–South divide in starting out with consensual unions. Sweden was an early starter. There is a strong trend in the Norwegian, Finish and French group to choose consensual unions as the first relationship; but this trend towards a Swedish pattern is in place everywhere. The maximum level was reached in Sweden already a decade earlier (as demonstrated in Figure 4.8–9). The development in the South in this direction has been rather limited. Instead we have a strong trend towards staying in singlehood up till and beyond age 25, usually linked to staying in the parental home. In the central cluster we find these two patterns combined: there is a growth of singlehood (as in the South) as well as a growth in consensual unions (as in the North).

The Disconnection Between Sexuality and Partnership

So far we have seen that there is a North-South divide in the timing of partnerships, as well as concerning the form of partnership (marriage or consensual union). While the Nordic countries seem to display little change in their larger volume of early partnerships,

Figures 4.8–9 indicate that there is a postponement in partnering on the way in the South. On the other hand, recent studies indicate that sexual habits and sexual norms have changed in the direction of liberalisation everywhere. The age of sexual initiation has declined by some two years since the 50-ies (Bozon et al., 1997). In Europe sexual debut tends to be earlier in the Nordic countries. These data indicate that there may be a increased time lag between sexual debut and partnering, and accordingly, there should be a growing disconnection between sexuality, partnering and reproduction.

Singles and Couples in Mid-Life

These findings in the previous sections concern the early stages of partnering, before age 25. We have seen that partnering start later in the south, and that recent trends indicate this process has lately been delayed further in the south, but not in the north. The forms of partnerships change considerable at later years, since large parts of consensual unions change into formal marriages, usually at the arrival of the first child.

However, after age 30 the proportion of persons living in partnerships increases in the South, and the proportion living in singlehood will then stay at much lower levels than in the Nordic countries. Figure 4.10 is focused on at the mid-age generation (30–64 years), which covers the ages when partnering is normally completed, and before mortality influences the outcome. Here the Nordic countries (except Norway) and the Netherlands display much higher rates of singlehood in this age group, and the Southern countries have lower rates.

This variation of singlehood should also be interpreted as in terms of coping behaviour. Larger proportions of singlehood are related to better opportunity structure to choose singlehood, which applies to women in the north. The larger Nordic female employment rates provide the necessary economic resources to choose a live without a husband, to stay single or to separate when to the marriage or consensual union does not work. Furthermore, the larger rates of separations and turnover between partnerships (presented further on) in the north produce larger levels of 'frictional' singlehood between consecutive partnerships.

Figure 4.11 displays the various forms of partnership for the entire adult population. Living in a formal marriage is still the dominating pattern in all countries, and the differences between member states are in fact rather limited. However, change is slowly going in the direction of lower marriage/cohabitation rates, alongside with higher female employment rates.

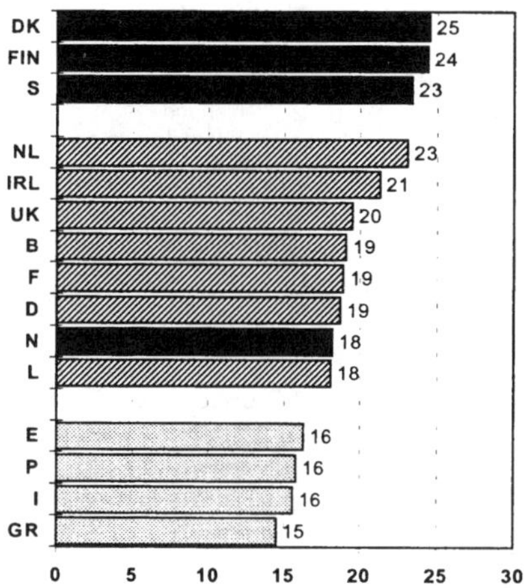

Figure 4.10 Persons 30–64 years living as singles. Percent Source: ECHP/NSS.

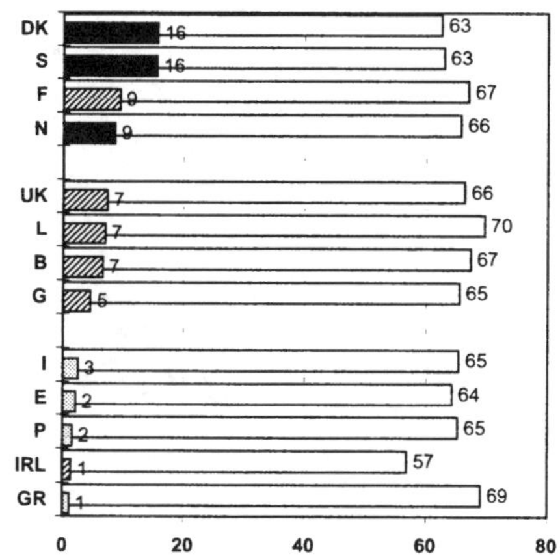

Figure 4.11 Marriages (background) and consensual unions (foreground) in the adult population 16–84 years. Percent Source: ECHP/NSS.

Marriage and Divorce

Long-term time series on partnering and departnering are only available for formal *marriages* and for *divorces*, excluding consensual unions. With this restriction in mind, trend data are certainly distorted by the increase of consensual unions, with variant degree in different countries. Nevertheless, this information is still interesting, if we see it as a crude indicator of the timing of 'seriously established' partnerships, which usually occurs when children arrive.

Women's average age of first marriages has been increasing everywhere, with the Nordic countries being ahead of central and Southern Europe. This trend is exaggerated, since the route to marriages increasingly goes via consensual unions. The direction is the same everywhere, with Denmark and Sweden arriving at the highest marriage age in the 90-ies (preceded by an extremely large volume of consensual unions), and Greece and Portugal at the lowest (see Figure 4.12).

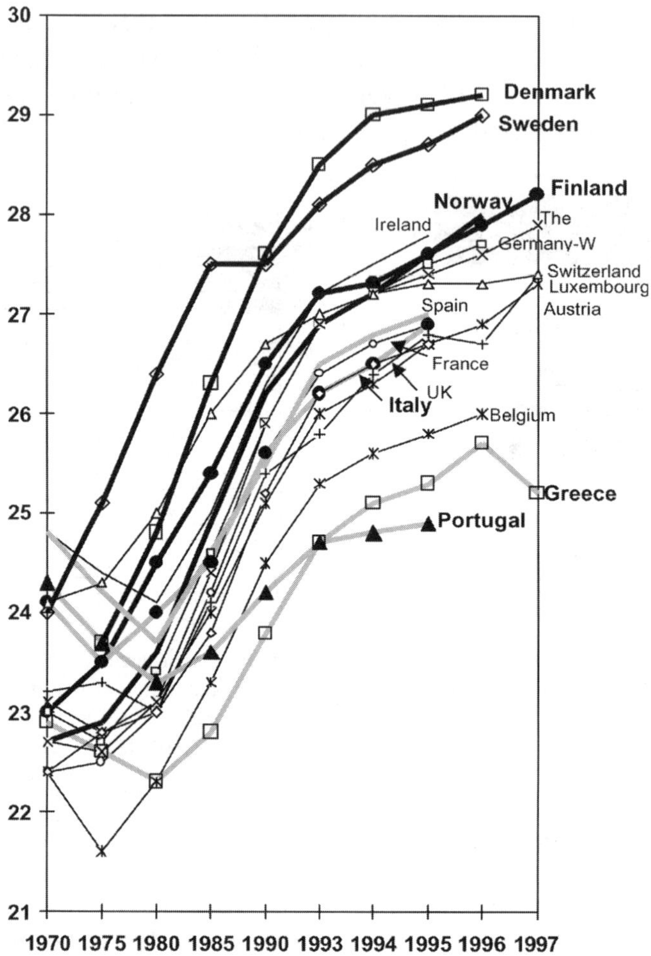

Figure 4.12 Average age of women at first marriage. Source: Newchronos.

We have already seen that this includes different patterns at different age. The Nordic countries have higher total partnership rates (usually consensual unions) in the early 20-ies, but lower total partnership rates (marriage and consensual unions collapsed) later in mid-age (displayed in Figure 4.10 indicating larger rates of singlehood). Again, we can summarise that the Nordic and the southern clusters are well separated. These trends can well be interpreted as variations in coping behaviour. In the north, with extremely high female employment, marriage and partnership is usually not required for purely economic reason. Hence, is marriage to a larger degree a matter of sexual and emotional needs, and thrust in a potential partner and father, and will accordingly occur when these requirements are met. This moment will usually come later in life. In other words: the opportunity structure in the north supports later partnering and higher rates of singlehood, and decisions less dependent on economic considerations, by a more favourable welfare mix (employment; social policy).

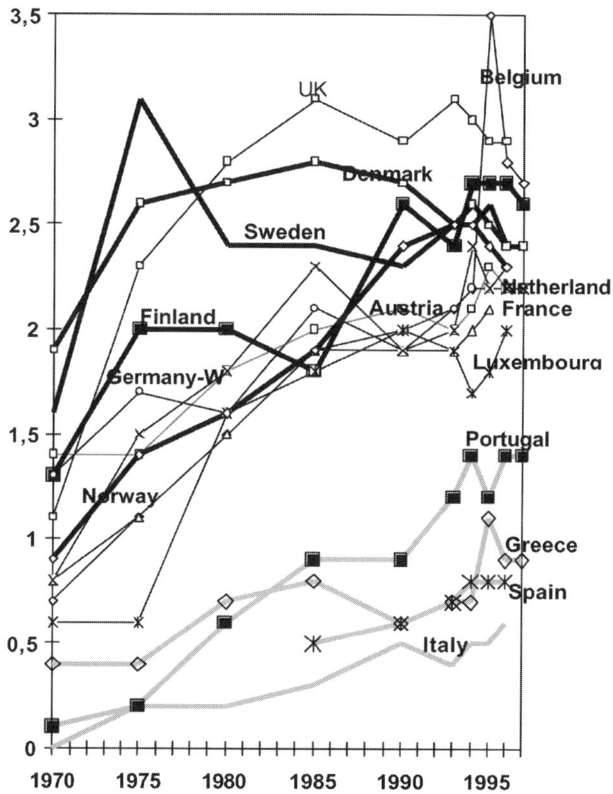

Figure 4.13 Crude divorce rate 1980–95. Divorces per 1000 population.

Figure 4.13 displays the crude divorce rate (per 1000 population). Here we also notice an increase everywhere. The three clusters are still separated, where the Nordic countries have the highest levels and the Southern countries the lowest divorce rate. The levelling off of the Nordic countries could be explained by the parallel increase of consensual unions, with lower stability than formal marriages.

In the South we also observe a gradual growth in the divorce rates, similar to the Nordic countries, but at much lower level.

Divorce trends can also be interpreted as indicating coping behaviour to the current welfare mix. Divorce levels are related to opportunity, in this case female employment rates and available welfare state provisions for single parents (child allowances, public care, housing subsidies etc), which are lower in the south.

Fertility

We have seen some distinct uniformity within clusters of countries concerning the age of leaving the parental home, partnering and forms of partnership, and separations. The variation between clusters in these respects corresponds to a variation of institutional configuration between the performance of the labour market and the welfare state. We continue in the search for coping behaviour by interpreting variation in reproductive behaviour. The indicators concern the timing and spacing of fertility.

Two common elements influencing the welfare mix in Western European countries is the rapid growth in youth education, and the simultaneous increase and persistence of youth unemployment, leading to serious rates of long-term unemployment, postponement of economic independence, economic insecurity and declining thrust in the future, among young adults in Europe. This was the fate of Southern and central Europe from the mid 70-ies, and in the Nordic countries (Sweden and Finland) from the early 90-ies. In the North the expansion of the welfare state continued up to about 1990 towards a gradual improvement of the institutional base of reconciliation between work and family life (including child care facilities, family transfers, maternal/parental paid leave), then interrupted by rapid increase in unemployment and decrease in welfare state provisions. These changes in the institutional conditions or 'welfare mix' and its variation between member states should be reflected in reproductive behaviour.

There is a common trend towards increasing age of childbearing. The average age of mothers at the first child is increasing everywhere since the en 70-ies. This trend corresponds to the common increase in youth education, later labour market entry and secure income. Delayed fertility should be interpreted as coping behaviour. In the South with its much higher levels of youth unemployment, this is a stronger incentive to continued education and delayed childbearing. Furthermore, with the extremely high levels of female education everywhere, we should expect equally high ambitions for a career everywhere. The abandonment of the male breadwinner model is proceeding where there is opportunity, and certainly with younger women in childbearing age (see next section) throughout the European union. With this in mind we should expect an increasing mismatch between opportunity (available jobs) and ambitions for a career, and in particular in the South.

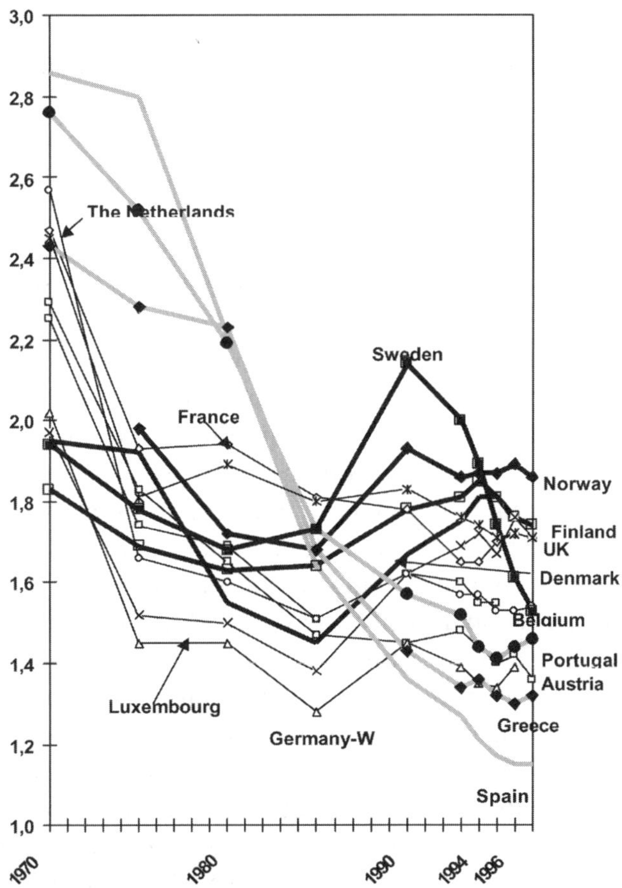

Figure 4.14 Total period fertility rate 1970–95. Estimated average number of children a woman will bear in her lifetime. Source: Newchronos.

Data concerning trends in the spacing of fertility (Figure 4.14) exhibit dramatic and variant change; and furthermore, these trends were similar within the three clusters, and much dissimilar between clusters. In the 1970-ies the Southern countries had much higher fertility rates than the Nordic and central cluster. A rapid decline brought Italy, Portugal and Spain to extremely low rates far below the level of population replacement. Meanwhile, the fertility rates in the Nordic countries increased, topping around 1990–1993 in all Nordic countries. However, since then Nordic fertility again declined or levelled off. Sweden had the largest fluctuation. After topping European fertility at 2,1 came a sharp drop to 1,6 within a few years.

This complex international variation can be explained with reference to the changing welfare mix, and changing opportunity structure. Detailed analysis of the Swedish case (with changing welfare mix in different direction) offers a key to the understanding of fertility fluctuation (Statistics Sweden/Hoem 1998). Nordic data reveal that the end 1980-ies represent a period of extremely favourable labour market conditions, in general and in particular for women, coupled with matured welfare state arrangements (child care facilities and paid maternity/parental leave, see also chapter 3). The employment rates of women and mothers then reached the highest level ever in Western economies. The improved public arrangements supported the double career model of maternity and career, with extremely high labour market participation. There were also additional effects from a longer period of delayed fertility in older female cohorts adding to the period fertility. Hence, for a few years Swedish fertility increased sharply. In the beginning of the 1990-ies a new chapter was written in the history of the Swedish economy. A sudden impact of an international recession and changing domestic economic policies created a sharp decline in employment (by 10 percent points), a fourfold increase in unemployment, a rapidly growing budget deficit, soon to be followed by recovery policies and cut-backs in public sector employment and transfers. This was a much of a shock in the labour market prospects of young women, which triggered a new decrease in fertility corresponding to the sharp downward movement of the Southern countries, as indicated in Figure 4.14. Hence, with respect to the 1990s, Swedish women had similar experiences as women in the south, with similar downward fertility trend.

In Sweden this reversal of fertility levels was most pronounced. A similar but less pronounced tendency is found in Finland and Denmark, which should reflect a similar effect of economic prospects and coping behaviour. It should be noted that all of the Nordic countries had a common increase in fertility in the second half of the 80-ies, with good labour market conditions, and/or in our perspective with an increasingly favourable welfare mix.

Statistical analysis of the recent Swedish decrease in fertility pinpoint the reproductive behaviour of *younger* women as the crucial factor, including a new *postponement of the first child* (Statistics Sweden/Hoem 1998). The mechanisms are increased unemployment and non-employment, decrease of earnings, and a continued increase of education, as well as influence by perceived *local* labour market prospects. This aspect will also be further elaborated later on in a discussion of fertility as coping behaviour with respect to the reconciliation between career and family life.

Finally, Figure 4.15 completes this picture by displaying the trends in extra-marital births. The levels again separate the three European clusters. And there is an increase everywhere, again with the Nordic countries forming the vanguard.

Reconciliation between Work and Family

Labour market activity can be seen as a macro indicator of the labour market's efficiency in absorbing the potential labour force, and of its ability to contribute to economic independence for the largest possible fraction of the population, based on gainful work. However, gainful employment is also a matter of existing gender roles imbedded in traditional value systems, which may change gradually but still have strong impact on individual decisions related to family pathways. There is no doubt a common trend in Europe in the direction changing values towards two-breadwinner model, and towards full employment for men as well as women. However, the pace and level may vary much between member states, in relation to the opportunity structure, i.e. the supply of jobs and the public arrangements supporting of female employment (services, transfers).

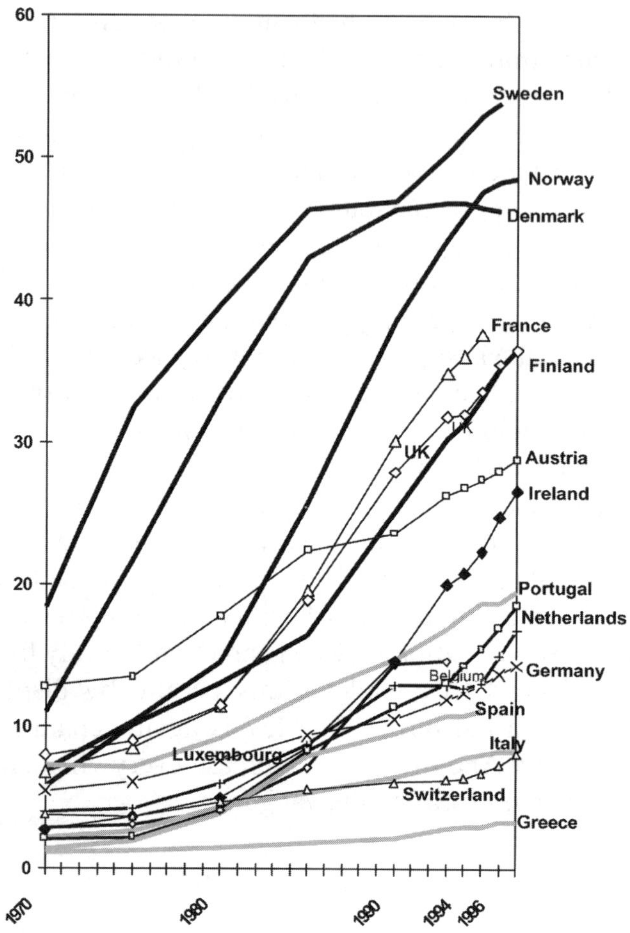

Figure 4.15 Extra-marital birth per 1000 birth. Source: Newchronos.

House Workers

How far has then the reconciliation between career and family proceeded in the European union. Figure 4.16 displays the employment rates of mothers and fathers of pre-school children in Europe. The traditional gender roles still dominate everywhere. However, Denmark and Sweden come closest to a gender neutral sharing of the responsibilities of work and child rearing. The gender gap is much larger in most of the Southern countries. Portugal comes out rather similar to the Nordic countries, due to its higher female employment levels.

Next, Figure 4.17 expands the perspective to the entire population of women (with and without children), by comparing the proportion of full-time housewives in two generations (25–44 and 45–64 years of age, respectively). Again the distinct North-South divide prevails. However, there is obviously a strong trend towards a decline in the volume of housewives everywhere, including the Southern cluster, in the Nordic direction. These findings thus indicate a clear progress towards the two-breadwinner model.

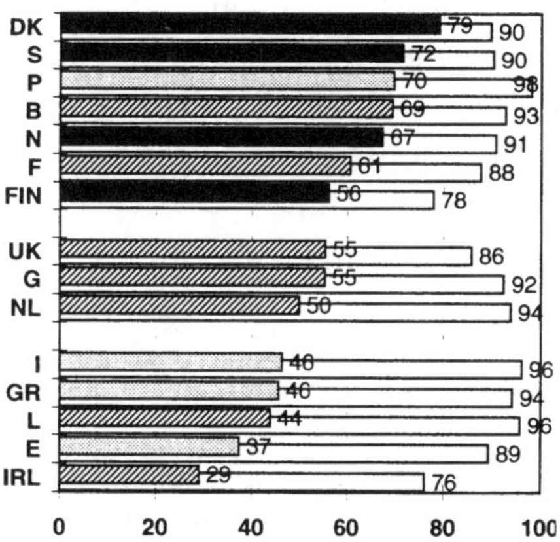

Figure 4.16 Employment rates of mothers (foreground) and fathers (background) of children 0–6 yrs. Percent. Source: ECHP/NSS.

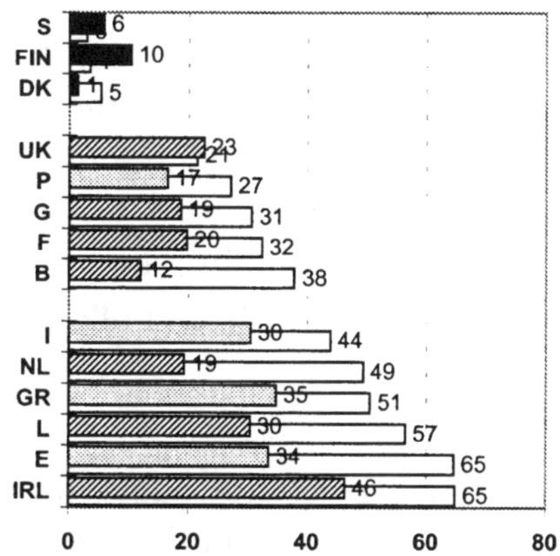

Figure 4.17 Housewifes by age. Percent. Source: ECHP/NSS. Legend: women 25–44 yrs (foreground) women 45–64 yrs (background)

Part-Time Work

Part-time work is in most cases chosen as a way of coping with the demands of family life and a professional role. Evidence (from ECHP/NSS) indicates that a considerable part of reduced working hours actually originate in the lack of full-time opportunities, or lack of childcare facilities. Part-time work patterns reflect family tradition and gender roles as well as welfare state arrangements, such as access to publicly financed childcare facilities. There are five country groups identifiable by similar arrangements:

1. In Greece, Italy and Spain employment rates for women are *generally* low, and this also applies to part-time work. If there are children the first options will not be part-time work but leaving or staying out of the labour market.

2. Finland and Portugal form a second group of higher female employment, and the part-time rate of mothers stays very low.
3. The Nordic countries Denmark and Sweden have the highest overall female employment rates, and a rather low proportion of part-time work among mothers. This Nordic arrangement is supported by generous family transfers and childcare facilities.
4. The highest part-time rates of mothers are found in the Netherlands, UK and Germany, with less supportive public arrangements for mothers, joined be the outsider Norway with better public arrangements. In the case of the Netherlands we can in fact identify a 'part-time work culture', with high part-time rates of free choice (70 percent mention housework or satisfaction with part-time work as a reason for part-time).
5. For the remaining countries we find intermediate employment as well as part-time rates for mothers.

Fertility Patterns

Childbearing is nowadays normally a matter of considerate planning. Increasing youth education leading to wider expectations of work and career, changing values in the direction of gender equality, and access to and knowledge of contraceptives will affect young women's view on the timing and spacing of their fertility. They will plan their fertility to fit their other interests and find strategies to reconcile various conflicting roles in life. They may choose to give priority to motherhood or refrain from motherhood, or they may temporarily delay motherhood. They will evaluate their partner in that respect, and they may choose to wait for the right partner and father for their children. Deciding on the timing of partnering as well as childbearing will be conscious process.

Fertility is increasingly influenced by ambitions related to the work role and is therefore influenced by labour market opportunities. When youth unemployment is high and job security is declining, will the age of establishment on the labour market increase. There are two possible ways of reacting to the delay of economic independency. One way is to prioritise early motherhood and wait with employment. The opposite way is to postpone childbearing. The overwhelming experience speaks for the latter type of coping behaviour.

Young women will also plan childbearing according to the consequences for their general living conditions. For very obvious reasons will the general level of child allowances, taxes and contributions for households with children influence fertility. In the previous chapter we have also demonstrated the large variation within the European union of publicly financed childcare facilities and levels of maternal/parental paid leave. These two conditions are powerful factors to fertility, and in particular for early motherhood. We should be reminded that many countries have wage-related maternal leave payments, which in itself is an incentive to wait with childbearing until such eligibility and reasonable transfers have been earned on the labour market.

In summary, there are good arguments in the European union for a *postponement of fertility*, as well as a *general decline in fertility* (as already displayed in the previous section), for a whole set of reasons. Figure 4.18–20 provides a comparative picture of fertility levels in the most crucial age group, i.e. women aged 25–29. This is the period in life when youth education is completed, but the establishment on the labour market is still ongoing. In these three figures the relation between female employment and fertility is displayed for 1970, 1990 and 1995.[1]

From a Nordic perspective, 1990 was a turning point in fertility, as well as for the provisions of the Nordic comprehensive welfare state model. This was before the deep recession in some of the Nordic states, with optimum female employment as well as welfare state arrangements to support fertility. When looking around in the European union, we note that Figure 4.18 displays a clearly *positive* correlation between female employment and fertility around 1990. And furthermore, there is again a distinct difference in employment levels as well as fertility rates between the three European clusters: countries with the highest female employment also had the *highest* fertility levels. With lower employment, as in the Southern cluster, we also find much lower fertility levels.

It should be noted that all three cluster are dispersed along the Southwest to Northeast axis in Figure 4.18. Except for Portugal (with rather high female employment closer to the Nordic countries) we again find the same three clusters, and they are well separated. Furthermore, the three clusters are well separated. The explanation of these extraordinary clear differences is complex; it relates to a whole bundle of family and gender friendly policies successfully carried out in the Nordic countries, as well efficient labour markets, which by and large are poor or missing in the central and southern clusters. By 1990 the Nordic cluster, in particular Sweden, peaked concerning the opportunities offered by the labour market (providing job opportunity; minimising youth unemployment, and job insecurity) as well as the welfare state (with high levels of public care for children, and subsidised paid maternal and parental leave). This coincidence of all three factors provided good opportunity and incentives for high as well as early fertility, as compared to the central and southern cluster. Hence, the consolidation of work and family was successfully supported by the Nordic welfare state arrangements and labour market in this period.

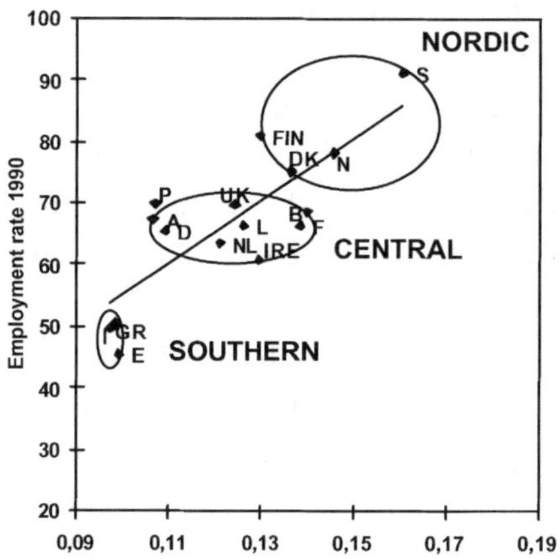

Figure 4.18 Employment and fertility rates for women 25–29 years. 1990.

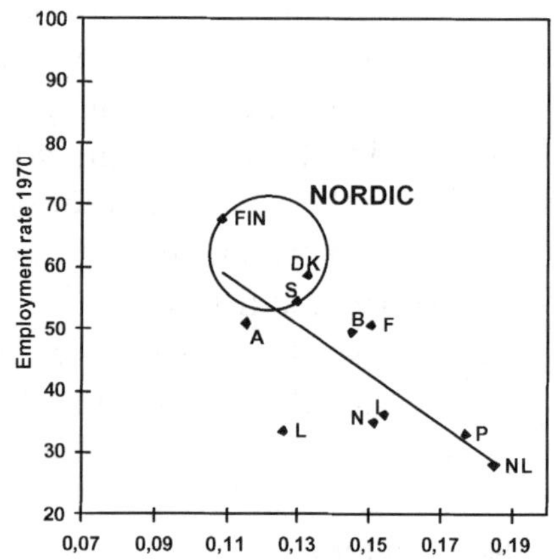

Figure 4.19 Employment and fertility rates among women 25–29 years. 1970.

In Figure 4.19 we move 20 years back in time, and look at the situation about one generation ago, providing the corresponding relationship for employment and fertility levels of European women 25–29 years of age (these figures are drawn in the same scale to facilitate comparison). 1970 was well before the large expansion of the public sector in the North, with large increase of new female jobs, family policies and support for the two-breadwinner model. Accordingly, in 1970 there was a completely different correlation between employment and fertility. There was a *negative* correlation between employment and fertility, which indicates different underlying pattern of factors supporting (early) fertility as well as different behavioural reactions of potential mothers.

If we compare the two figures we will find that female employment was much lower in 1970. Fertility levels were generally higher in 1970, which should not be surprising, since this was the traditional and normal role expectation within the male breadwinner model.

Already in 1970, in the early phase of Nordic family policies, we can observe that the Nordic countries formed a separate cluster well separated from the rest of Western Europe, with the highest female employment levels. However, in 1970 the Nordic cluster had the *lowest* fertility rates in Europe; family policies were less developed and the opportunities to combine work and family were poor. 20 years later, with the new family policies and excellent job opportunities meeting the ambitions of an increasing group of well-educated young women, the Southern and Nordic cluster had changed places. The Nordic cluster had now arrived at the *highest* fertility levels in the European union. Sweden, Finland, Denmark and Norway moved towards Northeast. Unfortunately there is no complete information available for all Southern countries for 1970. For Italy and Portugal, we record increased employment combined with *decreased* fertility. This is also the dominant tend for the central cluster over these 20 years.

However, the deep recession in the 1990s, in particular in Sweden and Finland, again changed the relation between employment and fertility. Figure 4.20 shows that in 1995 the Nordic countries had again regressed towards South-East, with decreased employment as well as fertility, in this age group. Youth unemployment had again increased, with delay of job entry and secure income between 1990 and 1995. Furthermore, job security decreased, and recovery policies reduced the efficiency of the welfare state in supporting high fertility. It should not be surprising that Sweden and Finland, with the largest decline in employment, also suffered the largest decline in fertility. For the Southern member states we find continued low female employment, coupled with decreased fertility as well. In addition, there is of cause the common international environment to consider. The common denominator for all EU-member states in this period is a general decrease and delay in job and economic security, objectively as well as subjectively, following enhanced international competition and recovery policies.

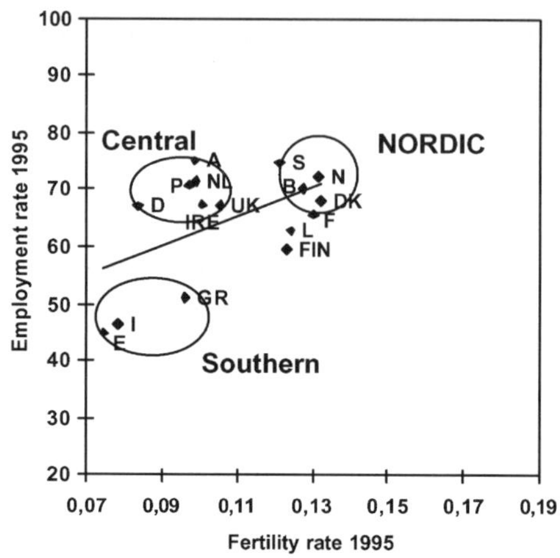

Figure 4.20 Employment and fertility rates among women 25–29 years. 1995.

The following three figures will further clarify the divers fertility patterns in the three clusters during the period 1970–1995. First, Figure 4.21 shows the positive relationship between employment and fertility within the *Nordic* cluster over the period 1970–1995. We plot each of the four countries for the years 1970, 1990 and 1995, with respect to employment and fertility levels. For the Nordic countries high employment goes along with high fertility level. When employment increases, fertility also goes up. This is illustrated in Figure 4.21 as movement of the member states from Southwest to Northeast. The interpretation should be that female employment as well as fertility is increasingly supported by welfare state arrangements (child care, paid parental leave). Hence, career and maternity can be combined, and fertility comes as a consequence of realised job opportunities. However, in the recent deep recession (in particular Sweden and Finland of the early 1990s), lost job opportunities decreased and delayed fertility.

Figure 4.22 displays the corresponding trend for the *Southern* cluster.[2] Here we find that the countries are moving from Southeast to Northwest: increased employment is accompanied by lower fertility (Italy and Portugal). This is a logical consequence of lower childcare and maternal leave provisions.

Finally, Figure 4.23 gives the corresponding trend for the central cluster. The general picture is the same: with increased female employment, we get decreased fertility.

In summary, these findings underline the importance of the unified support of job opportunities and welfare arrangements (subsidised child care facilities and paid maternal leave). All three have to be in place to produce high fertility levels. This combination is also productive in limiting poverty and set free resources for generous welfare provisions in other areas.

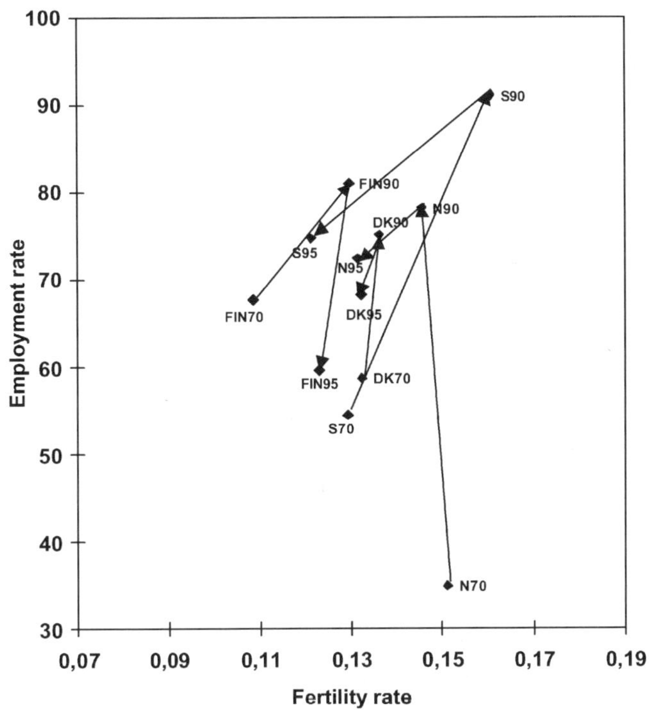

Figure 4.21 Trajectories of employment/fertility rates from 1970 to 1995. Women 25–29 years. Northern cluster.

The Household Situation of the Elderly

The household situation of the elderly reflects the traditions in family formation as well as the economic resources of the elderly. With meagre pensions moving in with adult children will be a necessity, if not normality experienced over generations. Furthermore, grandparents are welcome to care for grandchildren, when public childcare is non-existent, scarce or expensive. Hence, the elderly may be a valuable resource to younger generations, for caring duties as well for pooling economic resources.

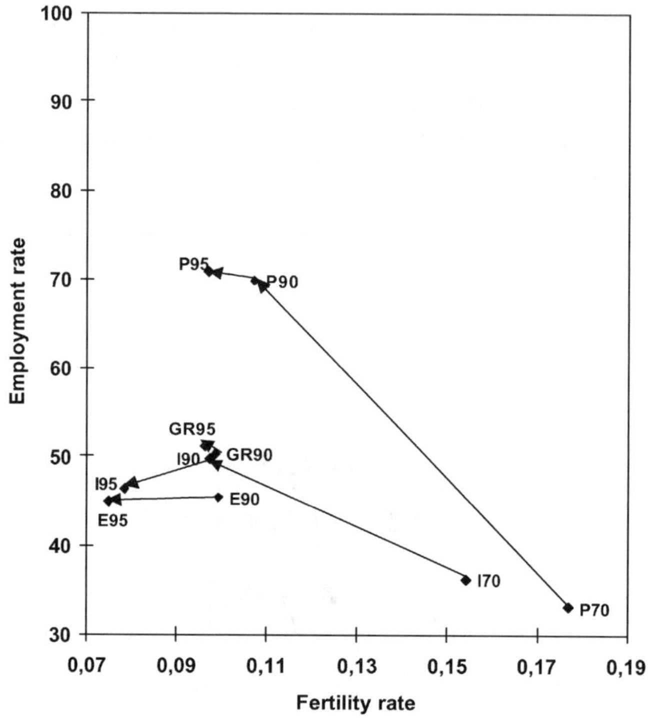

Figure 4.22 Trajectories of employment/fertility rates from 1970 to 1995. Women 25–29 years. Sorthern cluster.

Concurrently, there will emerge a responsibility for their children to care for them towards the end of life. In countries with poor caring services for the elderly as well as for children, as well when there is a tradition supporting large multi-generation families, elderly will experience less of isolation in their old days. This should be expected in the southern cluster.

The following series of data displays just that. Again we find clear-cut as well as unusually strong differences between the Nordic and southern cluster. Elderly living with their children are practically non-existent in the North, very frequent in the South and intermediate in the central cluster. Again, Ireland joins the southern cluster.

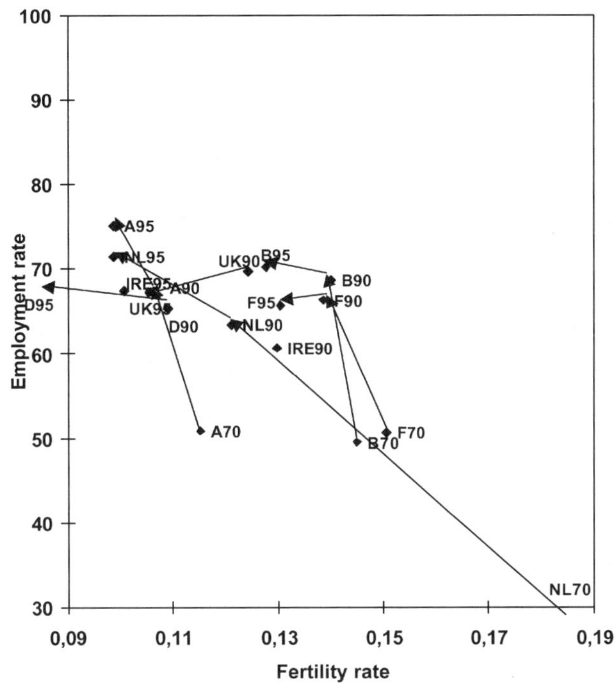

Figure 4.23 Trajectories of employment/fertility rates from 1970 to 1995. Women 25–29 years. Central cluster.

Figure 4.24 counts the proportion of elderly persons 70–84 years living with children in the age where these normally should be perceived as the household head with the largest income (30+). There is indeed a very clear clustering, with perfect separation of member states into the three major clusters. About 30–40 percent of elderly women in the southern countries live in their children's household. Figure 4.24 distinguishes between men and women (men's values are displayed in the foreground in white colour). The gender variation is explained by differential life expectancy and age differences between wives and husbands, leaving women in widowhood for about average 7–8 years. We can see that men tend to complete their life in a pair relation, while women tend to move to their children when they loose their husband.

The next Figure 4.25 is a corresponding calculation of elderly living in households with *grandchildren* included. Again, we find a perfect separation between the three clusters, however with Ireland again falling in the Southern cluster.

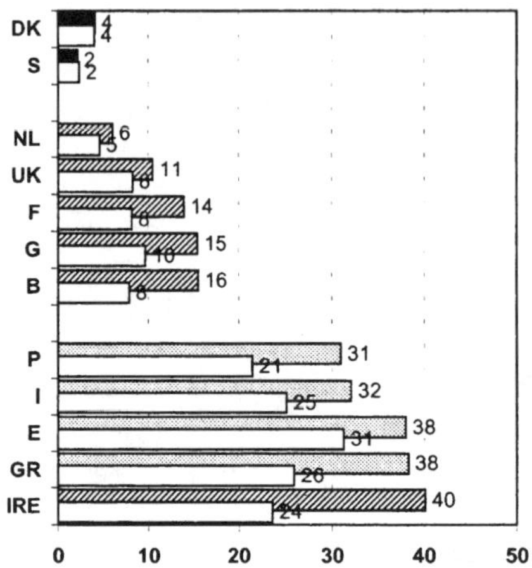

Figure 4.24 Elderly men and women (70–84 yrs) living in their children's households. Percent.
Source: ECHP/NSS. (foreground=men)

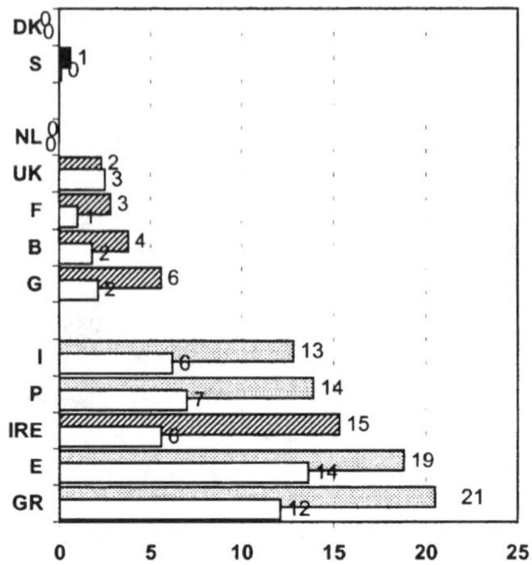

Figure 4.25 Elderly men and women (70–84 yrs) living in households including grandchildren. Percent.
Source: ECHP/NSS. (foreground=men)

Finally, the last three figures are focused on the single elderly women *without a surviving partner*. They are usually concentrated at the upper age levels. Almost half of these women in the Southern/Irish cluster live with their children (Figure 4.26). This is about ten times as much as in the Nordic cluster, where care is usually given in institutions or by public home care. This figure increases further when we add other types of households, with other relatives of the elderly (Figure 4.27).

The last Figure 4.28 demonstrates well the important role of the family network in old age in the southern countries and Ireland. Only one third in this group of elderly women without a surviving spouse lives alone in Ireland, while this applies to about 95 percent in the North.

In summary, the family network obviously provides a valuable support to the elderly in these countries, offering nearness to the closest relatives as well as physical and economic security and potential help in every day activities. From an economic point of view the sharing of households is a rational mode of coping when income and pensions are insufficient. This appears to be widespread social practise in the catholic countries, but almost non-existent in the North.

However, what appears as a positive solution could also be seen as an indication of constraint and lack of command over personal matters, if pensions and other forms of elderly care are poor. And, in addition, this practise is not always available for all elderly who really would need it. Also, not living in larger households is normally a consequence of choice, when personal resources (pensions, savings) are sufficient. This is mostly the case in the Nordic countries.

DISCUSSION

In general, as already demonstrated in chapters 2 and 3 for labour market and welfare state performance, we have found a corresponding clustering of EU member states with respect to family characteristics and coping behaviour. The major findings in this chapter are summarised in Figure 4.29, which collapses the ranking of member states on six major indicators onto a Traditional Family Index.[3] Again, the data produces three distinct clusters of European nations. There is a coherent Nordic cluster (Sweden, Denmark, Finland) with lower household size, early exit, early partnering, higher fertility, larger divorce rates and singlehood rates, and elderly seldom cohabit with their mid-aged children. The Southern countries, including Ireland, depart concerning all these aspects. The remaining central EU member states take an intermediate position in most aspects. Netherlands is rather close to the Nordic cluster, while Norway falls closer to the central cluster. There are very few exceptions from the clustering found for labour market and welfare state characteristics in chapters 2 and 3. They concern first of all Ireland, which in all classifications is located in the southern (catholic) cluster. Portugal as well as France and Belgium display a rather Scandinavian pattern of consolidation between maternity and employment.

Where trend data is available, the data indicates that the central as well as southern cluster clearly move towards the Nordic family type. But there are exceptions from this rule, related to a mismatch between opportunity and ambitions: the Southern countries seem to move towards later exit of children, later partnering and declining fertility.

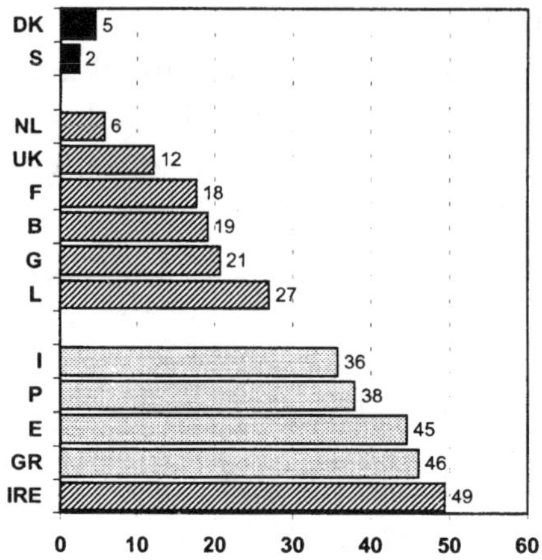

Figure 4.26 Elderly non-married or cohab. women (70–84yrs) living in households including *children*. Percent. Source: ECHP/NSS 1994.

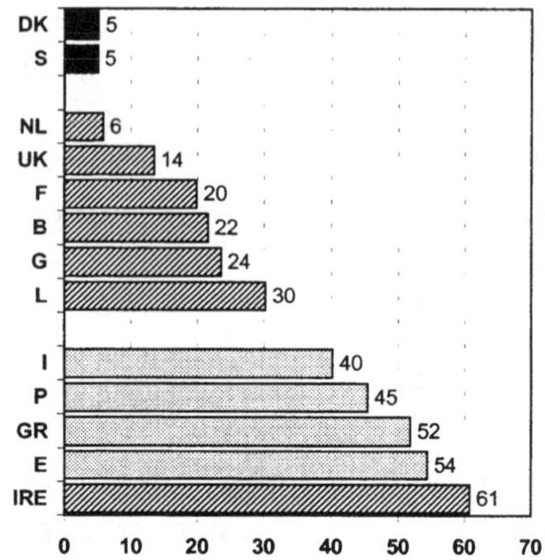

Figure 4.27 Elderly non-married/cohab women (70–84 yrs) living in households including *relatives*. Percent. Source: ECHP/NSS.

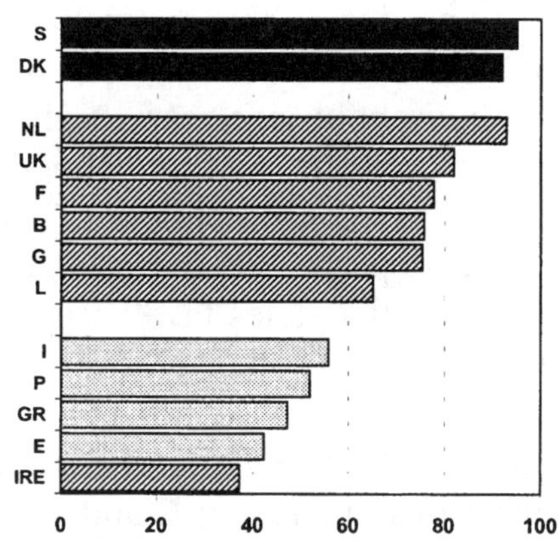

Figure 4.28 Elderly non-married or cohab. women (70–84 yrs) living in one-person households. Percent. Source: ECHP/NSS 1994.

The common denominator behind these findings concerning the variation and trends in European family and reproductive behaviour is the efficiency of the labour market and the welfare state in providing welfare resources. Fragmentation of the family prevails in all member state. Data also point at an*increasing mismatch* between the welfare mix (i.e. the configuration of the labour market's and welfare state's provisions), and ambitions of women in the direction of equal opportunities and economic independence. This implies in particular the two-breadwinner model, with full employment for men and women, including work as well as parenthood for women as well as men; it also precludes required provisions such as public care for children and elderly and paid leave for family matters.

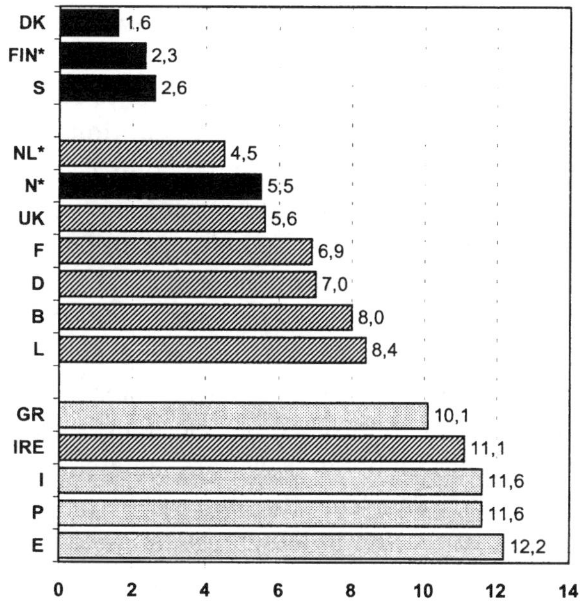

Figure 4.29 The traditional family index (average rank on 6 indicators). Source: ECHP/NSS.

We assume that the EU-member states share a common and a gradual change in the gender role expectations of women, supported by attitudinal effects of the growth and equalisation of education. The most crucial elements are the problems relating to the establishment of young adults on the labour market, and the reconciliation between work and family during the first 10 years of adulthood, when childbearing begins and when children are small and require care facilities. These changing welfare demands meet a reality of external conditions, which by and large are unchanged or even deteriorating in large parts of Europe. The labour market is not producing the *additional* jobs required. Instead the entry to the labour market is delayed by increasing demands of youth education and qualification. Youth unemployment and involuntary inactivity is increasing, as well as income insecurity. The welfare state cutbacks in public transfers and services are pushing responsibilities back to the household sector.

This is the environment where we should place the recent European variation and trends in family formation and reproductive behaviour. The model of family pathways assumes active individual decisions between varieties of available options of family formation. Transitions to other family status, such as leaving the parental home, to embark on the first partnership or to stay in singlehood, to marry, to divorce and to leave a partnership, to enter parenthood, are decisions that are influenced by the institutional context. They can be interpreted as *coping strategies* to control living standards. We have seen in this chapter that the timing and spacing of these transitions are linked to variation and change in labour market and welfare state performance in EU member states.

In summary, we have recorded a postponement of the move from the parental household, of delayed partnering and a strong trend towards declining fertility, in the Southern cluster as well as in some of the central European countries (e.g., Germany). However, in the Nordic countries, with elaborated welfare state support, we find a different pattern. The move from the parents and partnering was not postponed, in spite of recent rapid increase of youth unemployment. On a general level, youth unemployment has been less severe in the North, and the welfare state support given by family policies, paid leave and childcare facilities expanded throughout the 1980-ies. The Nordic fertility decline was then stabilised, and fertility again increased in all four Nordic countries throughout the 1980-ies, towards much higher levels than in the Southern countries. Sweden is the most interesting case because of its large variation in fertility that moved in different direction over a rather short time span. The recent peak in Swedish fertility around 1990 can well be interpreted as a rather unique combination of full employment for women as well as men, and of generous public provisions for child care and paid maternity/parental leave; in other words, an efficient labour market/welfare state mix. A new recession in the 90-ies again decreased fertility. Accordingly, the Swedish trends can also be interpreted with reference to coping behaviour. Microanalyses clearly indicate that this new Swedish decline was directly related to the reactions of young women to local labour market prospects, affecting the timing of the first child.

Postponement of the move from the parental household, of partnering and childbearing also seem to disconnect sexuality and family formation. The time span between sexual debut and the establishment of stable partnerships and first childbearing is increasing, and the traditional 'legal marriage' pattern is gradually changing towards later partnering, informal partnerships, and 'trial and error' relations with large levels of de-partnering. This decrease in the objective security of partnerships adds a *subjective* component working in the direction of further postponement of the time when women feel secure to embark on childbearing. The combined consequences of *postponed* partnerships and increasing *insecurity* of partnerships will shorten the childbearing period, which in itself will contribute to decreased fertility.

NOTES

[1] Employment rates are given in percent and fertility rates as average children born per annum for each age year in the interval 25–29 years. Source: New Chronos.
[2] Data for 1970 is incomplete.
[3] The index gives the average ranking of the 15 nations according to the following indicators:

1. the national average household size,
2. the percentage of single adults in the age of 30–64 years, i.e. after the family formation period, and before mortality affects the outcome (we are here primarily concerned with the propensity to stay single),
3. the percentage of adults living in a consensual union,
4. the percentage of young adults under the age of 30 still living with their parents,
5. the percentage women aged 70–84 living with their mid-age children (30+).

SCB Statistics Sweden
Welfare Analysis Program
and
University of Umeå
PO Box 24300
10451 Stockholm
Sweden

JOACHIM VOGEL

INCOME AND MATERIAL LIVING STANDARDS

This chapter explores the distributive structure of *income* as well as *material living standards* (household assets, housing standards). These two aspects are used as two parallel sets of indicators of the consequences of the institutional mix, with different theoretical as well as technical features.

Income is a resource of a special character. Income and financial assets are "generalised resources"; they are useful on most arenas, and they are consequences of other types of resources that have been transformed into money (such as education, paid work, health, and social networks). When looking at income from a welfare perspective, our prime interest is the total *equivalent disposable income*, calculated in relation to the household members who have to share this income. The idea of the disposable income is to construct a measure of economic resources that is comparable between individuals living in very different household situation. The disposable income is composed of several sources related to the three welfare delivery systems. The bulk of income comes usually from earnings (paid work), and related income substitutions such as pensions, sickness payments and paid parental leave, which are provided by the labour market or welfare state. Additional market-related income comes from property and capital, and direct taxes are deducted. Finally, the family is the third source affecting the disposable income, adding the effects of support within the household, which is accomplished by pooling of all household member's income, effects of the economy of scale boosting the value of income in larger households, and cash transfers and benefits in kind between households, usually from parents to children.

The relative levels of these two components as well as their compensatory role vary much between individuals and households, as well as between nations, along with the households total labour market participation, the level and distribution of earnings, the

Social Indicators Research **64:** 437–469, 2003.

volume and distribution of capital and property, the volume and distribution of welfare state intervention (social transfers, taxes, services) and finally the family structure and inter-household transfers. In other words, the disposable income may have different origin with respect to the impact of the labour market, welfare state and family. The level as well as the distribution of disposable income is shaped by the configuration of these three welfare institutions. In search of European models of welfare production we will in this chapter add the distribution of income and material living conditions to characterise the typology.

Indicators of *material living standards* give a complementary picture of the effect of the distribution of current and recent income. Accordingly, material living standards should confirm the general picture of the institutional configuration. Further, material living standards are more robust indicators from a technical point of view. Household equipment is easily defined as compared to the composite nature, many sources of measurement errors, and sensitivity of income. Better validity level of material standards thus strengthens the findings for the income distribution.

Chapters 2–4 confirmed there is sharp division and clustering of EU member states by their institutional configuration, and that there are a rather limited number of such combinations. Each of these models should produce a characteristic distributive pattern. With respect to disposable income the Nordic model, with higher employment and extensive social protection and taxation, should produce a comparatively egalitarian income structure, and accordingly, a more egalitarian distribution of material living standards. The Southern model, with lower employment rates and rudimentary social protection, should produce larger inequality. Stronger family support in the south should be a functional alternative to welfare state and labour market, with limited and specific impact. The central EU member states should perform in intermediary position between the Nordic and Southern models.

COMPARATIVE INCOME STATISTICS: DATA SOURCES

Social indicators are normally designed for immediate understanding, by using popular common-sense concepts easily understood by most readers. This is not possible with respect to indicators of income and poverty. There are several complex theoretical and conceptual considerations, as well as serious technical limitations to be well understood. Arriving at robust conclusions on the European income distribution is extremely difficult, and more so in a short and selective chapter. The magic of tables and numbers should not overshadow that the income data presented here are much less reliable than other type of simple data utilised in this report.

In contrast to simple statistics, measurement of disposable income combines large numbers of information, including each household member's annual income from various sources, taxes and tax deductions, and data on the current and previous household composition. Misclassifications may occur on each of these variables. Furthermore, much of the required information is difficult to remember and recall in personal interviews, for the entire household, and for the entire previous year. In addition, much information will be missing (underreported, not registered or unknown to the respondent), or irrelevant. Since income is usually calculated per annum, and dynamic households are changing composition and size over the observed year, the pooled annual income/transfers/taxes for the current household members interviewed much later may be misleading. Good corrections are practically impossible to manage.

However, in spite of these problems is the European household panel a milestone towards improved comparative income statistics. The ECHP is the first ex-ante co-ordinated income survey designed for comparative income analysis in Europe. Parallel studies (the Luxembourg Income Survey; OECD/Förster, 1999) applied ex-post harmonisation of already existing national surveys. Further, the ECHP/NSS is the only complete data set with coverage of all EU-member states (except Austria).

In addition to the technical problems already mentioned further obstacles emerge in comparatives analysis. First of all, the European Panel uses personal interviews to collect income data. Recall of monthly income from all sources is difficult and may lead to distortion and probably to underreporting. The Nordic databases using register data will be more complete, which on the other hand will affect comparability with survey based income assessments in other countries. Comparability is also affected by the large variation in response rates, ranging from some 30 to 90 percent for the ECHP/NSS database. This relates in particular to the poverty estimates. Poor as well as affluent households are likely to be over-represented in the non-response stratum.

Finally, the harmonisation of income data also extends to factual definitions of income applied in the fieldwork, of economic activity and household structure, which are also involved in the calculation of monetary income. Furthermore, earnings are related to paid work only. Unpaid household production is not included in the measurement, but certainly contributes differentially to material living standards in different countries. This component is probably larger in the Southern member states, with lower employment rates, thereby underestimating the material standard in these countries. On the other hand, in the Northern welfare states the higher value of free or subsidised public services is not fully covered. The last two factors imply that the PPP-adjustment applied does not provide full comparability.

All these technical obstacles affect the comparability of income data. Methodological research is poor, and in summary, there is little evidence of comparative data quality. On the other hand, fortunately our analysis produce distinctive and coherent enough findings concerning the ranking of member states on income issues.

Indicators of Income Distribution

The following four indicators of income distribution have been selected:

1. **Inequality of (net) earnings, measured by Gini-coefficients**. Earnings are defined as post-tax personal income from employment and self-employment. *Net* earnings serve as a substitute for *gross* personal earnings, which would be the preferred social indicator of "market income". Unfortunately, this information was not available in the ECHP. This indicator is specially compared between men and women.
2. **Inequality of disposable income, measured by Gini-coefficients**. Disposable income includes all income sources (work, capital, property, social transfers, minus taxes) summated for all household members, and adjusted for the number of consumer units (adult equivalents), according to the OECD

modified scale (1 for the first adult, 0.5 for further members over age 14, and 0.3 for younger children). All household members are attributed this equivalent disposable income, and are thus assumed to share the household income alike. This procedure accounts for the economy of scale in larger households, and allows income comparisons between families of different size. Note that all indicators are calculated for persons, not households.

3. Based on the disposable income, two poverty rates are defined. **Poverty rate I** measures the percentage falling below 50 percent of the *national* average disposable income. **Poverty rate II** measures the percentage falling below 50 percent of the pooled average disposable income for all participating countries.
4. Accordingly, the **affluence rate** is defined as the percentage falling above 150 percent of the *national* average disposable income

All estimates are expressed in annual averages in ECU at the price level of 1993, adjusted for purchasing power parities (PPP). They are thus designed to give comparable purchasing power estimates for all member states.

The indicators of material living standards will be presented later on in direct connection with the presentation of findings.

EARNINGS

The concept of earnings, short for income from work, covers wage and self-employed income as well as income related income substitutes, minus direct personal taxes. Earnings are calculated for all persons aged 20–84 years. They indicate the *personal* dependency on income from work for all adults, in contrast to the normal way of presenting statistics of earnings (for all persons *with* earnings, i.e., the active labour force). In the tradition of social indicators, however, we are here interested in the total adult population. The relevant Gini-coefficients for earnings (for persons 20–84 years) have already been presented in chapter 2 as indicator of labour market performance. Here we will add some strategic findings on the distribution of earnings between men and women, and between mothers and fathers, respectively. These findings directly address the relation between the role of the labour market and the family, including the issue of gender roles, household production, and economic dependency between spouses. They explain the divers strategies in the north and south with respect to women's reliance on the labour market versus the family.

The Comparative Perspective

Figure 5.1 shows the share of *net earnings of women* in each of the member states, expressed as a percentage of men's earnings. Female employment rates, women's volume of part-time work, and their relative wage levels as compared to men's wages shape the international variation. Again, we identify the familiar clustering, with the Southern countries having lower relative earnings for women (Greece, Italy, Spain) joined by Ireland, the Netherlands, Germany and Luxembourg. These countries can be identified as cases of Gender Regimes *in transition from patriarchy* or *Housewife Contracts* (see chapter 1). In the lead are all of the four Nordic countries, representing the two-breadwinner regime, all with high employment rates among women as well as lower gender-related wage differences. Finland is in the lead, which is explained by an additional factor, namely a very high rate of full-time employment among women. Portugal deviates from the other Southern countries, as a consequence of high female employment rate.

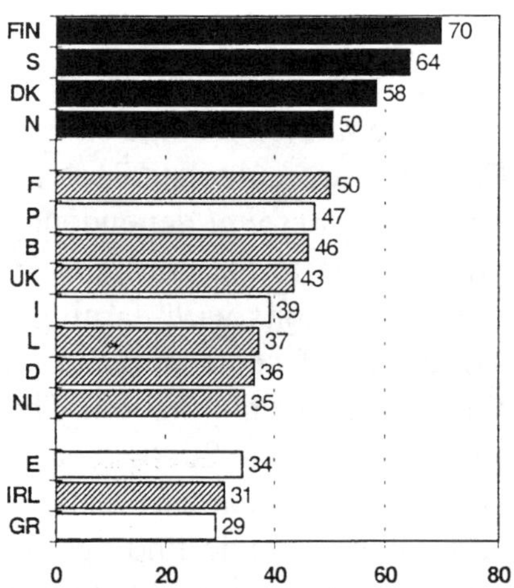

Figure 5.1 Net earnings of women as a percentage of men's earnings. 20–84 years. Source: ECHP/NSS.

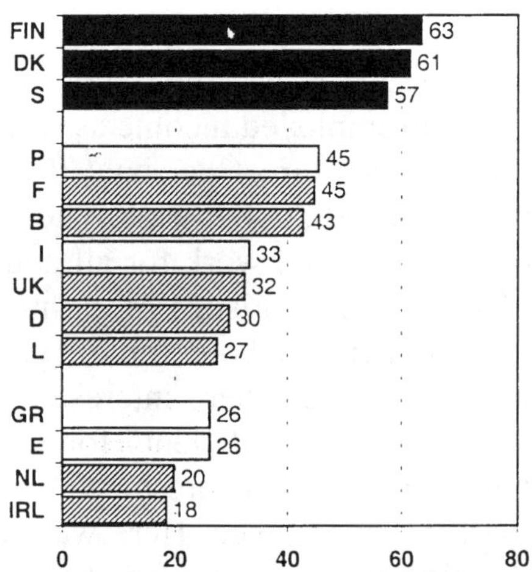

Figure 5.2 Net earnings of mothers as a percentage of net earnings of fathers. Source: ECHP/NSS.

Figure 5.2 extends this structure to parents. Again we find the Nordic cluster unmistakably separated from the remaining EU member states. The gender gap in earnings is much lower in the north. The Nordic countries exhibit a different pattern of combining a career and motherhood. In the Southern countries, as well as Ireland, the Netherlands, Luxembourg and UK, we find a much stronger division between gainful work and parenthood, with a much larger share of housewives.

The Swedish Case

The corresponding trend data for the Swedish case demonstrates how the initiation of the two-breadwinner model and the increase of public jobs usually provided for women proceeded over the past 25 years (Figure 5.3). This transformation went ahead at rapid pace in the 1970s and 80s, but came to an end in the mid 1990s dramatic employment crisis. The remaining gender difference reflects employment levels as well as wage differentials between men and women. The former factor was the most influential. In summary, this change greatly increased the self-subsistence and economic independence of Swedish women. This Swedish development started in 1975 from a level most EU-member states had not even or barely reached by the mid-1990s; for most of them little progress was made in the past 20 years.

OVERALL INEQUALITY OF EQUIVALENT DISPOSABLE INCOME

The adjusted disposable income is computed per household and then attributed to its members. This implies that all member make use of the monetary resources alike, which of course is an oversimplification and sometimes unrealistic. This applies in particular to young adults living with their parents, as well as to (single) elderly who have moved in with their middle-aged children. There are large differences in family formation between the South and North of Europe, as already demonstrated in chapter 4. Furthermore, in the North, are young adults over 18 staying with their parents usually considered as separate households.

Figure 5.4 begins with a global outlook on the distribution of disposable income. The Gini-coefficient measures the expected average difference in incomes, relative to the average, between any two pair of persons randomly chosen from the population. This index ranges between 0 and 1, where higher values are associated with higher inequality of income. The Gini-coefficient for adjusted disposable income sums indicates in one number the combined effect of inequality created on the market, and after the corrective effects of welfare state intervention and family arrangements.

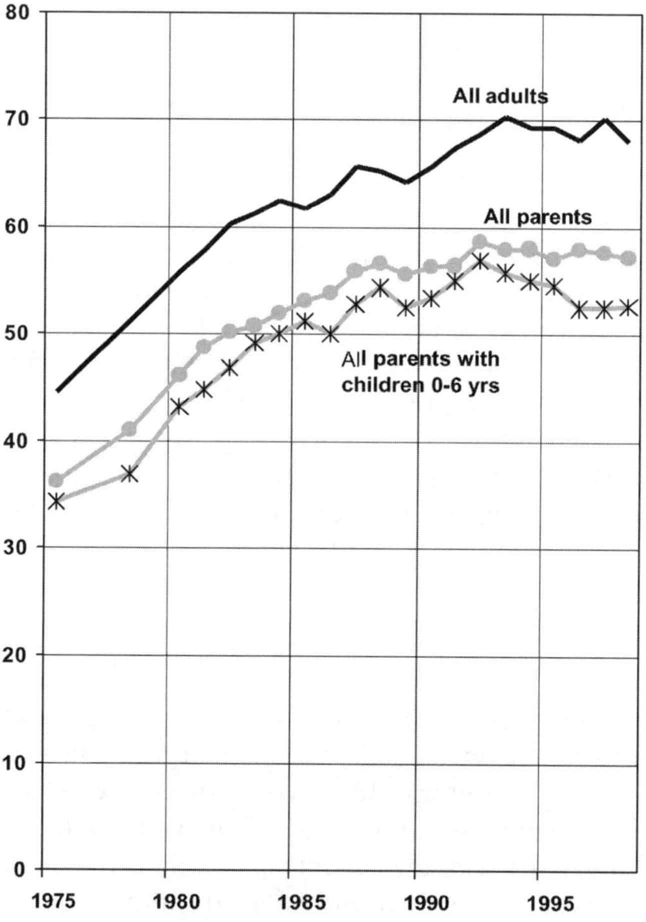

Figure 5.3 Female earnings as a percentage of male earnings. By family type. Sweden 1975–98. Source: HINK.

The Comparative Perspective

The pattern of material inequality in each of the member states is related to the unique configuration of the three welfare delivery systems, i.e., the labour market, the welfare state and the family. Similar institutional arrangements and performance should produce similar welfare outcomes at individual level. This is clearly demonstrated in Figure 5.4, where lower Gini-values indicate lower levels of inequality. The European Union is again divided into the already familiar three clusters. Inequality estimates are highest in the Southern cluster, joined by UK. All of the four Nordic countries fall at the lowest level of inequality, as measured by the Gini-coefficient, while all of the Southern countries fall into the highest cluster.

UK leaves the central cluster and joins the Southern cluster. This should be expected from UK's social expenditure share of GDP, which is lower than all other central and Northern member states (except Luxembourg), as well as from recent economic policies. This result also corresponds to earlier income statistics based on the Luxembourg income survey (Atkinson et. al. 1993), which indicate a general pattern of growing inequality in most countries, where UK displays the largest growth in Gini-estimates.

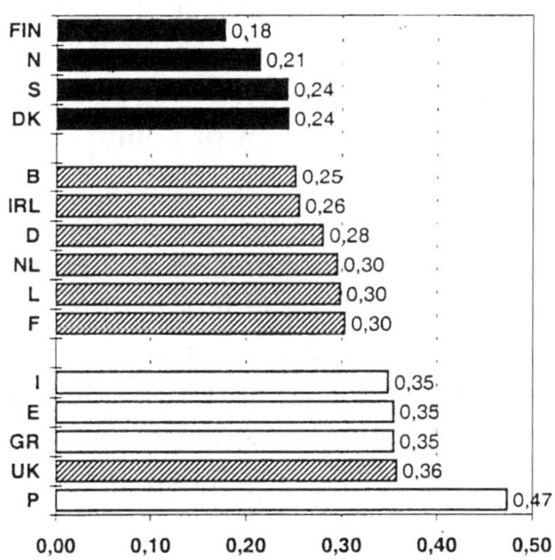

Figure 5.4 Inequality of equivalent disposable income (Gini-coefficients). Persons 20–84 yrs. Source: ECHP/NSS.

Trends in Income Inequality

ECHP is the first ex ante coordinated data source covering all EU member states. However, this survey started in 1994, and does not provide trends for earlier periods. Unfortunately, alternative sources for trend analysis of the full set of EU member states are not available. However, coordinated trend data based on ex post coordination of national income surveys for an incomplete set of OECD countries are available (Gottschalk and Smeeding 1999 using the Luxembourg Income Survey; OECD/Förster, 2000). These studies seem to indicate that Gini- coefficients increased from the late 1970s in most countries, and that the rank order between nations has not changed much. UK, Sweden, Denmark and the Netherlands seem to exhibit major growths in Gini-coefficients (Gottschalk and Smeeding 1999). Atkinson (1999) gives a similar picture using national sources as well as the Luxembourg income survey (Figure 5.5).

The dominant economist interpretation of these trends identifies globalisation, increased competition, flexibilization of working contracts, and technical change as the driving forces behind the trend towards higher levels of income inequality, hence a stronger market impact (wage differentiation), as well as reduced welfare state influences (tax, transfer and service cuts). However, in analysing detailed data for some OECD countries Atkinson (1999) found that annual statistics for a set of countries (Canada, France, Finland) deviated from this pattern (see Figure 5.5), with rather stable Gini-levels over longer periods. This indicates that there is still space for *social norms* operating in the direction of equality, within the labour market (differentiation of wages) and through politics (continued expansion of taxes, transfers and services). This is also underlined by Gustafsson and Johansson (1999), who report that large public sectors as well as high levels of union enrolment are related to lower levels of income inequality.

The Swedish Case

Turning to the Swedish case, annual trend data will give us opportunity to follow income inequality over three decades, in relation to the changing institutional configuration in Sweden (Figure 5.6). Over the 60s and 70s Swedish Gini-levels decreased, as a consequence of a changing welfare mix, characterised by increased employment levels as well as substantial expansion of the welfare state's taxes and transfers. However, from the early 1980s and throughout the 1990s, increasing income inequality has again been measured for Sweden as well. During the 1980s employment rates and welfare expenditure were still expanding. The shift in income inequality level during the 1980s was primarily due to expansion of higher income levels. In addition, the lowest incomes declined during the 1990-ies, and the proportion living in poverty increased as well. The increase of inequality (and poverty) in the 1990s corresponds to a substantial decline in employment rates as well as subsequent reduction of public welfare provisions, moving Sweden towards the central cluster.

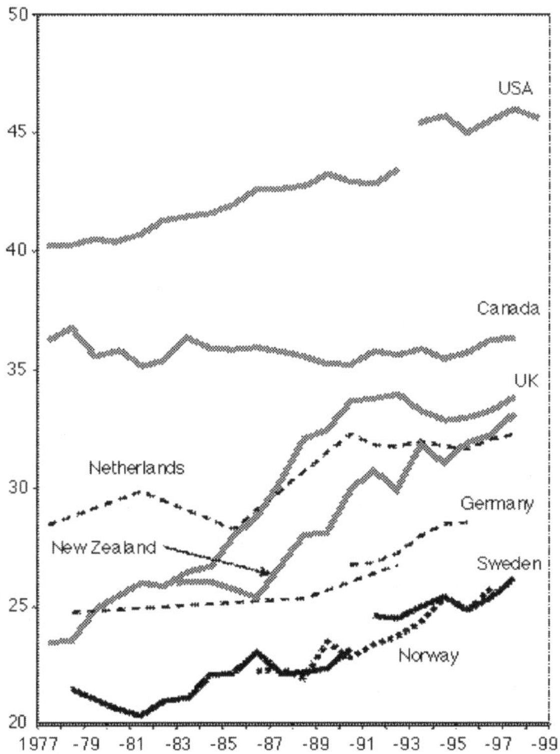

Figure 5.5 Inequality of disposable income in selected EU-countries. Gini-coefficients (expressed as percentages). Source: Atkinson 1999.

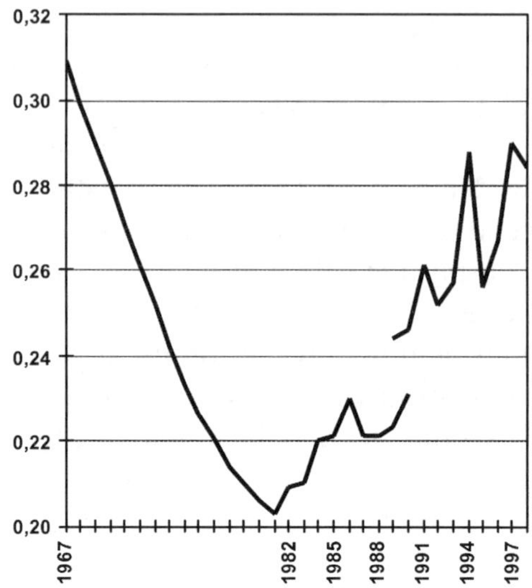

Figure 5.6 Inequality of equivalent disposable income. Sweden 1967–1998. Gini-coefficients. Source: ECHP/NSS.

Poverty

Concepts and Measurement

The theoretical and technical problems involved in income analysis are enhanced when we move on from average income to the margins of the income distribution, whether they are poverty levels or levels of high income. The presentation of poverty rates as well as affluence rates has to follow common conceptions and usage of these terms to be accepted by the users and ordinary readers. This requires further discussion and delineation of these categories.

It has to be understood that monetary income has to be related to a period, usually the last year. When we are computing the disposable adjusted household income we sum up the income during *the previous year* of all household members we can identify at a later point in time, namely *the time of the interview*, which is usually sometimes during the following year. However, neither income nor households are stable over a year. Some household members may have started their working-life late during the previous year, which affects their total annual earnings. Cases of low annual income may in fact be associated with a very high monthly income during less than 12 months. Furthermore, households may have recently changed in size and composition. There may have been a divorce or marriage, new children may have arrived or left the parental home. Annual disposable income does not catch and correct for these transitions, since income data relate to the last year, and household size to the time of the interview.

These problems are usually acceptable when we are dealing with statistics on average income. However, when we look at poverty there is a risk of contamination of the "truly poor" by such transitory cases (or mismatch of income and household classification), blowing up the poverty rates, and adding cases that normally would not be considered as poor. This will affect the level of poverty, and to some extent also the variation between nations. The same argument applies to high-income groups, which may be unstable because of contamination by temporary income peaks or recent change in household size.

However, what we are looking for is enduring poverty, in the sense of exclusion from normal standards of living:

- *'The poor shall be taken to mean persons, families and groups whose resources (material, cultural and social) are so limited as to exclude them from the minimum acceptable way of life in the member state in which they live' (European Counci's decision of 19 December 1984)*

This definition suggests that transitory cases, normally not associated with the image of poverty should be excluded as far as this is technically possible. However, the available data does not permit longitudinal identification of such cases.

Two types of poverty rates are presented in this report. They are both using *objective* criteria for inclusion (a monetary poverty line), and they apply a *relative* perspective linking poverty to the normal income standard in society. The first poverty line is defined by taking 50 percent of the *national* average adjusted disposable income (as defined earlier). The other uses 50 percent of the *Union* average as a poverty line. This poverty rate corresponds to the general idea of the levelling of level of living disparities between the member states. Here we are presenting data indicating the distance from that goal.

The Comparative Perspective

Figure 5.7 gives the poverty measures for EU member states, for 1993. The poverty line is here defined as 50 percent of the *national* average equivalent disposable household income. Again the 15 member states fall into the same three clusters identified earlier, and they also display three rather distinct levels of poverty rates. The lowest poverty rates are found in the Nordic welfare states (Denmark, Finland, Sweden and Norway), all of which have about 5 percent of their adult population in relative poverty according to the chosen criteria. These four countries form the Encompassing Welfare State Regime Cluster characterised by a large public sector, high levels of social protection expenditure, high tax rates, comprehensive social security schemes, high employment rates, and higher labour union enrolment.

The intermediate poverty cluster has about twice as high poverty rates, well above 10 percent. This central European cluster includes Germany, France, Belgium, the Netherlands and Luxembourg. Again, UK joins the Southern cluster including Greece, Spain, Portugal and Italy with higher poverty rates, ranging between 18 and 27 percent.

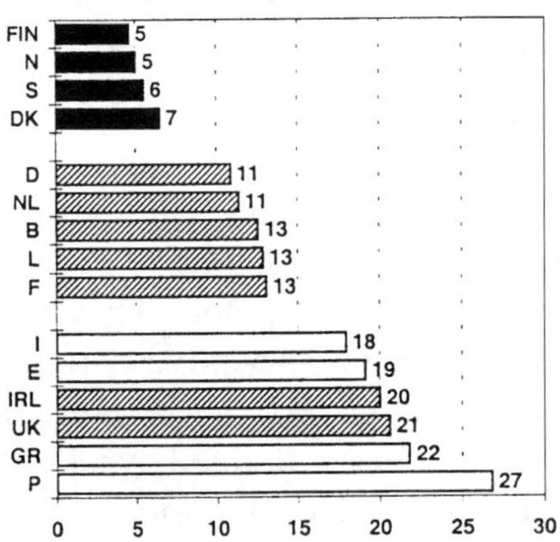

Figure 5.7 Poverty rates in the European Union. The poverty limit is 50% of the *national* average equivalent disposable household income. Percent.
Source: ECHP 1994 and Nordic surveys.

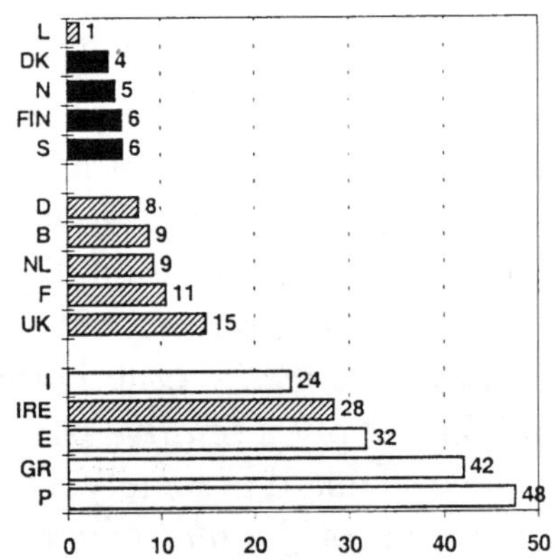

Figure 5.8 Poverty rates. Persons falling below 50% of the *union* average adj. disposable income. Percentage.
Source: ECHP 1994 and Nordic surveys.

Figure 5.8 gives the corresponding poverty estimates, applying a common European poverty line for all countries (50 percent of the *EU* average adjusted disposable income), defined at equal purchasing power. This estimate is much higher in some of the member states, in particular in the South. This is of course a consequence of the lower general income level in the South. This outcome underlines the vast variation in the material standards within the European Union. There is a variation in these poverty rates ranging from 1 to 47 percent points (Luxembourg and Portugal). Note that these differences reflect the joint effects of many different factors, including employment rates as well as wage levels, the structure of occupations, social protection expenditure and tax rates, family patterns, in other words the full variation in 'welfare mix'. It should also be noted that the most extreme poverty rates are found in the Southern family welfare states.

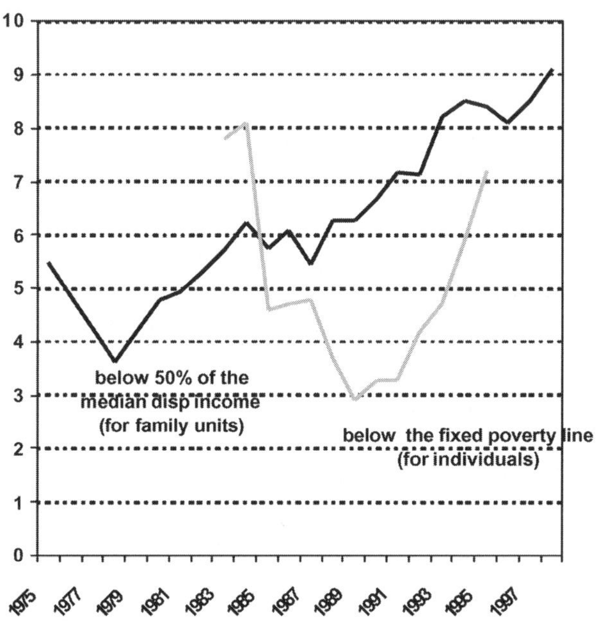

Figure 5.9 Poverty rates for Swedish family units and individuals 1975–1998. Percent. Source: HINK and ULF.

Poverty Trends in Sweden

Turning to the Swedish case, we can again trace the changing Swedish welfare mix (see also chapter 8) in the poverty trends. Figure 5.9 shows two poverty indices for Sweden, one for *all family units* reaching back to 1975, and one index for a 'cleaned' population of *individuals* (16–84 yrs, excluding youth living with their parents, students, and self-employed). After decades of declining poverty rates, there was a distinct shift toward increasing poverty around 1991[1]. From 1983 to 1990, the proportion of the population living in poverty declined from 8 to 3 percent, which is in line with increased employment and welfare state provisions. During the 1990s, the proportion again increased to 7 percent, as a consequence of a sudden decrease of employment rates (by 12 percent), and increase in unemployment (from 2 to 8 percent), followed by subsequent cuts in transfers and services. Hence, also in the Swedish case we can connect the changing welfare mix and the poverty trends.

The Structure of Poverty

Next, we will look into the structure of poverty by identifying population segments with higher and lower poverty levels, within EU-member states and in Sweden over the past 15 years, respectively. Among many problems of subsistence, poverty should be clearly related to three major problem areas related to the institutional conditions, ***lack of market income*** (unemployed persons), ***dependents*** (e.g., having at least 3 children, being a single mother) and ***poor pension rights*** (retired persons). In the following we will look at the relative poverty levels of these four groups, within clusters of EU-countries and for Sweden over later years. In each case we confront the poverty rates of these categories with the overall poverty rate (Figure 5.10–13).

All of the four figures indicate that all the Nordic countries not only have the lowest overall poverty rates, but also low levels of *excess* poverty among these four groups (these countries are plotted near the diagonal). Again, the Nordic countries form a cluster distinctly separated from the other EU-member states, in the direction of lower levels of social exclusion for unemployed, families with many children, single mothers and retired persons.

The central cluster is also well united, but located at higher poverty levels, with a larger tendency towards social exclusion in the case of unemployment and dependents (location towards the right of the diagonal), but not in the case of the retired. Again, UK moves out of the central cluster into the Southern cluster with much higher overall poverty level, as well as greater levels of social exclusion indicated by excess poverty among the unemployed, persons with many dependents, single mothers and the retired.

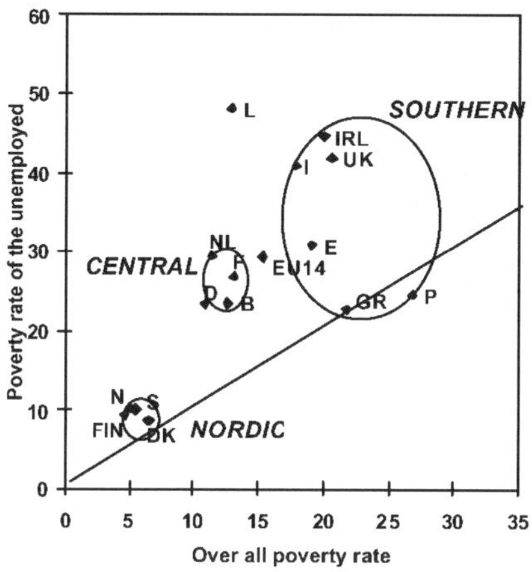

Figure 5.10 Poverty rates among the unemployed vs the overall national poverty rate. Source: ECHP/NSS.

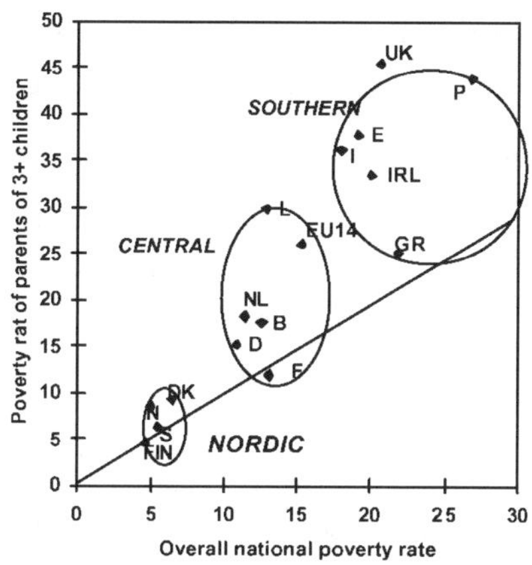

Figure 5.11 The poverty rate of persons with 3+ children vs the overall poverty rate. Source: ECHP/NSS.

The Southern cluster, on the other hand, falls apart. The overall poverty is high, but there is no *excess* poverty in some cases. Italy and Spain have no excess poverty among the retired, which could be explained by inclusion of elderly with lower pensions in larger household. This should indicate that retirement (with lower pension rights) tends to be monitored by the family to a larger extent in Italy and Spain. The same applies to the unemployed (primarily youth) in Greece and Portugal (Figure 5.10).

Table 5.2 (see appendix) also gives further details of the poverty levels in other population segments.

The structure of poverty in Sweden is given in conjunction with poverty trends in Figure 5.14. Poverty levels vary greatly between different segments of the population, and the structure of poverty changed little with the overall level of poverty over this period. Poverty levels increased sharply during the 1990s in relation to the new unemployment shock, followed by reductions in most transfer systems. Swedish data demonstrates that the changing levels of poverty left the well-situated population in full employment and without maintenance burden largely untouched. Sweden as well as other developed nations is facing a pattern of marginalisation related to labour market problems (youth, immigrants, households with less than full employment, social class), and households with responsibility for dependants (single mothers, many children). Fully employed households were not affected at all. The same applies to old age pensioners, where we can observe the gradual effect of the fully installed public pension scheme.

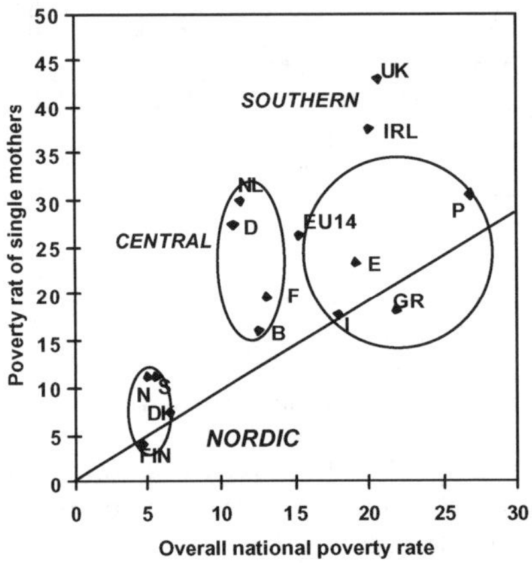

Figure 5.12 The poverty rate of single mothers vs the overall poverty rate. Source: ECHP/NSS.

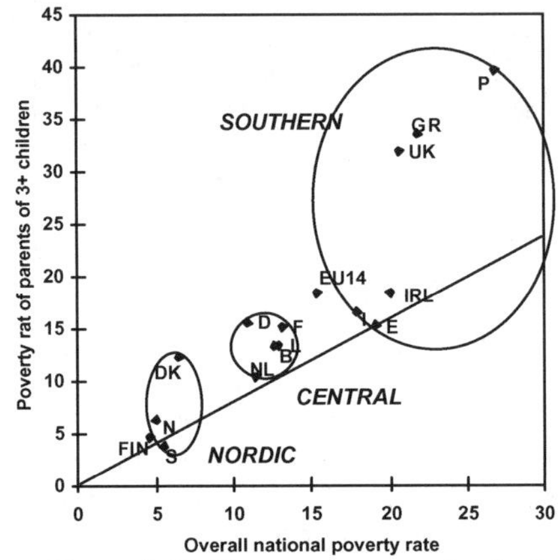

Figure 5.13 The poverty rate of retired persons compared with the overall poverty rate. Source: ECHP/NSS.

AFFLUENCE RATES

The Comparative Perspective

The third aspect of income distribution covered in this chapter is the volume of rich people, here defined as the proportions of adults living in households with an equivalent disposable annual income above 150 percent of the national average. Affluence defined in this way is a consequence of a complex composite of earnings of all household members (contribution of the labour market), taxes and public transfers (welfare state) and the economy of scale and support of the family structure. Furthermore, this indicator is a *relative* construct, and therefore affected by the entire income structure, including the volume of the lower tail. We should expect the following:

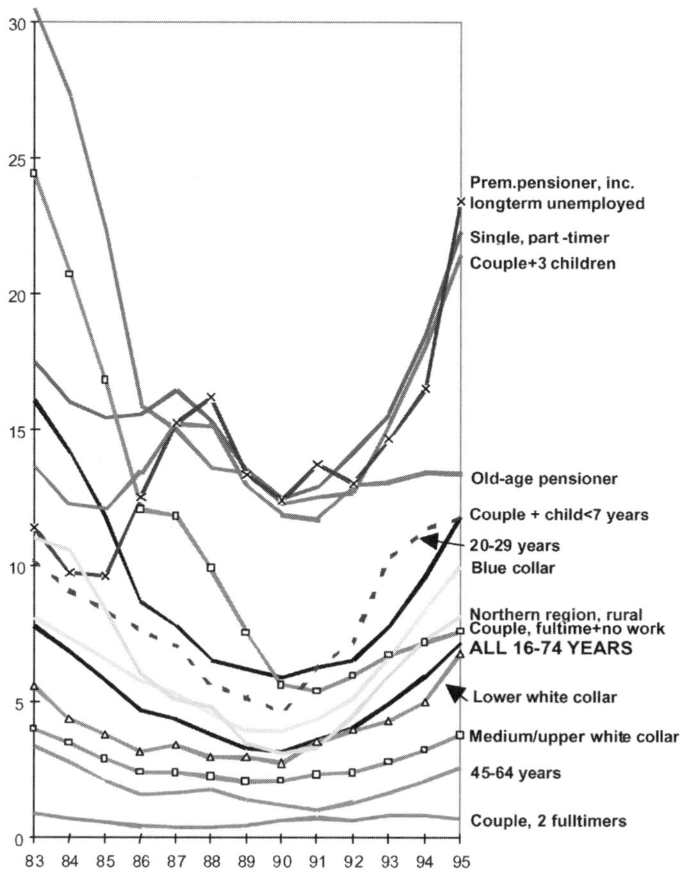

Figure 5.14 Persons living in poverty. Sweden 1983–1995. Percent.

- Higher tax levels in the Nordic welfare states should limit affluence rates;
- Larger households should support higher affluence rates due to the economy of scale in the Southern cluster;
- Fully employed household should more often pass the *relative* affluence line in the Southern cluster (as a consequence of higher poverty levels);
- The central cluster should fall in intermediate position.

Figure 5.15.a shows the affluence rates simultaneously with the poverty rates. Again we record three clear-cut clusters. We can see that affluence rates as well as poverty rates are the lowest in the

Nordic cluster. However, affluence rates do not differentiate between the Central and Southern clusters.

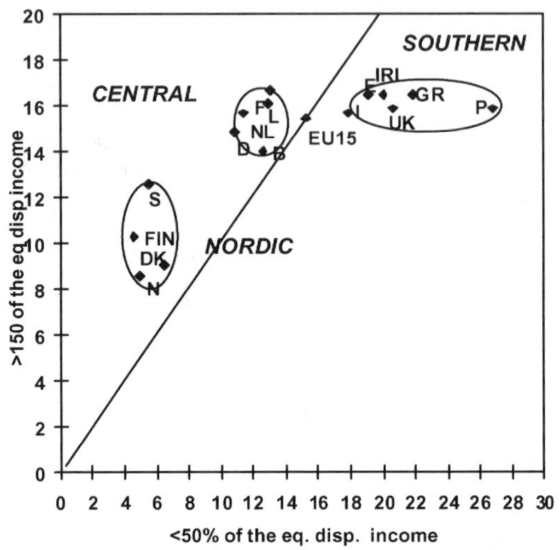

Figure 5.15.a Affluence vs poverty rates (>150 and <50% of the national equivalent disposable income). Percent. Source: ECHP/NSS.

The Swedish Case

Trend data for Sweden (Figure 5.15.b) display a long-term change towards higher wealth rates over the past 20 years, which in the early 1980s introduced a change in the Gini-coefficients. The wealth rate is here calculated as the ratio between the disposable incomes at upper percentiles (P90, P95 and P99) divided by the P25 income. In *relative* terms the income gap between the top and bottom of the income structure has decreased up to the early 1980s (increasing marginal tax rates, increased public transfers, centralised wage negotiations). Then followed a period of increased relative affluence rates. In 1991 a tax reform reduced the marginal tax rate for upper income levels as well as for capital income. The peak for 1994 is explained by a further temporary reduction of capital taxation by 50 percent.

Additional information on wealth in given in Figure 5.16 concerning the development of net capital assets (as registered in tax returns). The total net assets of the upper percentile and top deciles are calculated as their share of the macro estimate of (registered) and taxed assets of the total population. We can summarise that from the mid 1980s the trend towards equality was also broken and reversed, with respect to assets.

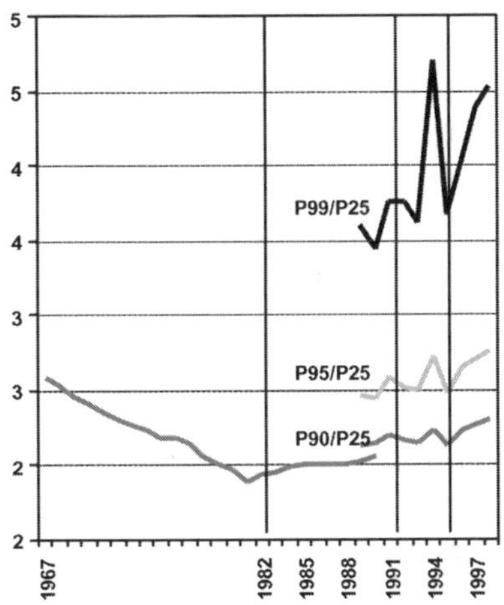

Figure 5.15.b Affluence rates, expressed at the ratio between the disposable income of upper percentiles and P25. Sweden 1967–98. Source: HINK.

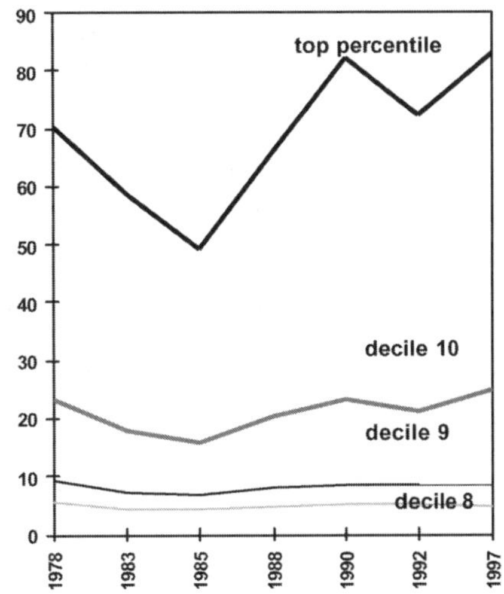

Figure 5.16 Net capital assets of decile groups. Percent of the total net assets. Sweden 1978–1997. Source: HINK.

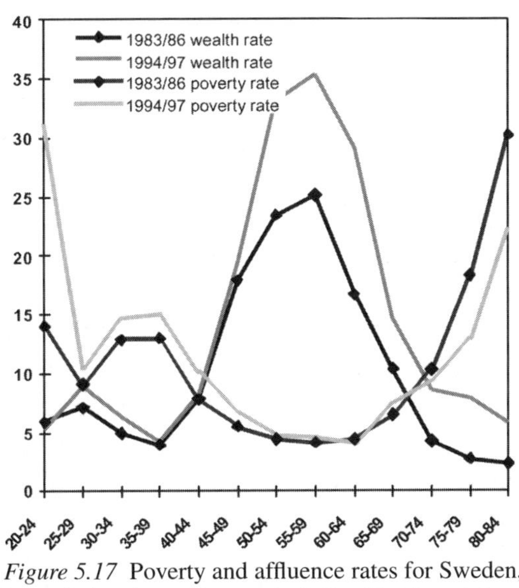

Figure 5.17 Poverty and affluence rates for Sweden, by period and age. Poverty is defined by the minimum subsistance level, and wealth by 150% of the average adj. Disposable household income. Percent. Source: ULF.

Finally, Figure 5.17 presents one of the major findings in trend analyses on the levels of wealth and poverty in Sweden. This analysis targets the changing age differentials, using multivariate method to control for social class, family type, gender and region. There is a general movement towards *higher* affluence rates, as well as *lower* poverty rates, in higher age groups, and the opposite in lower ages. The interpretation relating Swedish income trends to the welfare mix follows in the final chapter. In summary, in the Swedish case we have seen a clear reversal of the dominant trends towards declined inequality of income and poverty, followed by increased income disparities, in particular during the 1990s.

DETERMINANTS OF INEQUALITY

Income Determinants in EU Member States

The variation of disposable income can be interpreted from two perspectives: First, from an analytical perspective to trace the determinants of inequality of income, which is next on our agenda, and second from a descriptive perspective. The comparative decomposition of income and material living standards by gender, generation, family type, education, labour market status, and nationality will unfold to what extent such categories are privileged or underprivileged in the various member states, and the relative impact of these characteristics within member states. Table 5.1 (see appendix 1) presents relative descriptive estimates for each subgroup, calculated as a percentage of the national average, in order to exhibit such structural differences in the distribution of disposable income. Table 5.2 then presents the corresponding multivariate analysis of the distribution of disposable income for the 14 member states, with respect to some of the major social cleavages of our interest. The applied model controls for gender, generation, social class, employment and household type. Norway is excluded, since the socio-economic classification is not available. These findings are presented in graphical form in Figure 5.18–23, focusing on three of these dimensions, i.e., social class, generation and family type. The estimates present *relative* disposable annual income, i.e., the *difference* in average income between the first mentioned group and the second group (reference).

First, class inequality is illustrated by comparing the income levels of upper and lower non-manual workers respectively, with the income of manual workers. The first analysis on *lower non-manuals* (Figure 5.18) follows the expected structure to the letter, with the exception of Luxembourg, with larger wage differentials related to the special industrial structure and large volume of well-paid non-manual employees. The Nordic cluster again displays the lowest level of inequality, the Southern cluster displays the highest levels and the central cluster is in intermediate position.

The next Figure 5.19 concerns the upper end tail of the social structure (upper non-manual), which should be relative more affected by misclassification and lower comparability. The data reveal that the variation of disposable income by social class in this case is the largest in Luxembourg, France, Germany and UK. Finland, Sweden and Belgium seem to have the lowest level of inequality in this respect, along with the Southern cluster.[2]

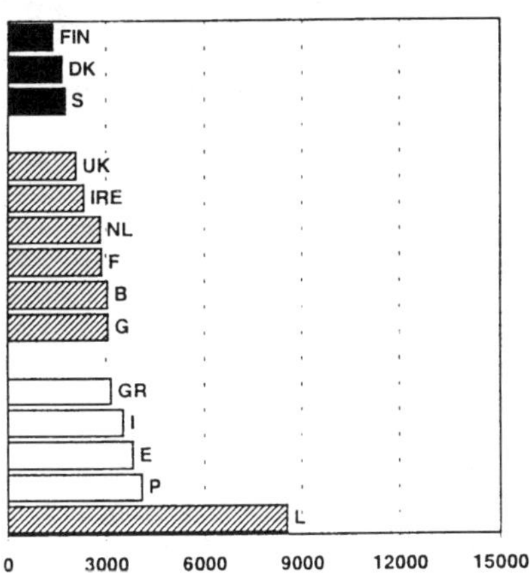

Figure 5.18 Relative disposable income of lower nonmanual employees, as compared with manual workers (reference). Ecu in PPP. Source: ECHP/NSS.

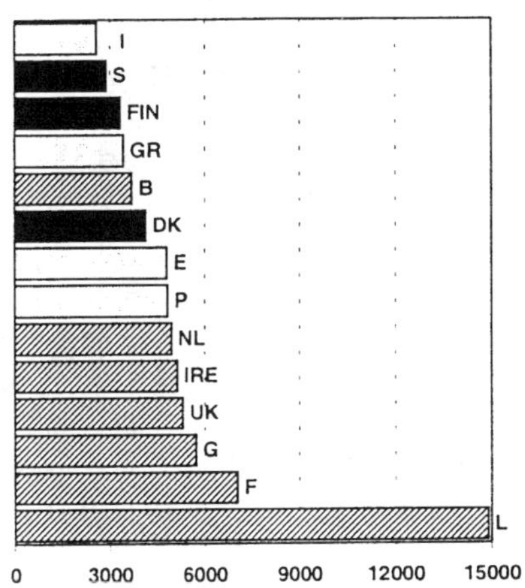

Figure 5.19 Relative disposable income of upper nonmanual employees, as compared with manual workers (reference). Ecu in PPP. Source: ECHP/NSS.

Next, we proceed to the generation gap. Compared to the most affluent generation (45–64 years; reference) young adults (20–29 years) have the weakest position in the Northern and central welfare states (Figure 5.20). In the South, Greece, Spain, Portugal, and Italy have considerably small differences between these two generations. This should be a consequence of the large variation in the age of leaving the parents already addressed in chapter 4 (the scale effect), as well as selection in the categories staying on in the parental home. In the North young adults are likely to leave early, and definitely when they start to earn money. In the South a large proportion stays on even after their labour market entry. The contribution of their earnings to the (parental) household is valued twice as much as compared to a single person's household (a consequence of the economy of scale adjustment in the calculation of the disposable income). It can well be argued that this way of looking at household income is not entirely realistic. Nevertheless, here we see that the Nordic and central early exit pattern imply larger income gaps between generations, going in unexpected direction.

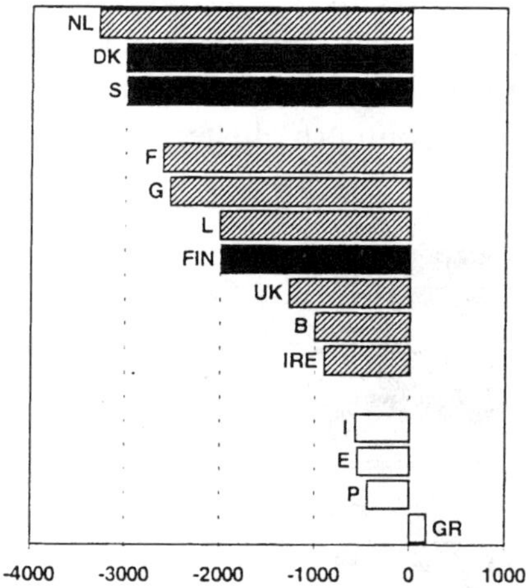

Figure 5.20 Relative disposable income of young adults (20–29 yrs), as compared with persons 45–64 yrs (reference). Ecu in PPP. Source: ECHP/NSS.

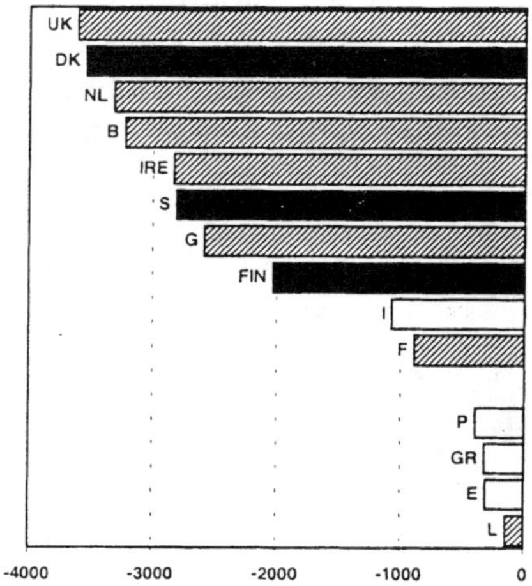

Figure 5.21 Relative disposable income of elderly (65–84 yrs), as compared with persons 45–64 yrs (reference). Ecu in PPP. Source: ECHP/NSS.

Among the elderly (Figure 5.21) we have a similar family effect. The income gap between the elderly and the mid-age generation is much smaller in the South, as compared to the central and Nordic member states. Again, the interpretation draws on the family tradition in the Southern countries. In the South the income level of the elderly (65–84 years) is much closer to the affluent generation of the 45–64 year old. This should be explained by a more frequent inclusion of elderly with poor pensions in the families of their middle-aged children, especially in the case of elderly women (widows). In the Northern and central countries the nuclear family model dominates, and such practise of intergenerational family support is therefore less frequent. It should be noted that the exit age as well as the inclusion of the elderly does not vary much between the Nordic and central cluster. Hence these countries differ little on these issues; the major divide goes between the Southern cluster and the remaining EU-member states.

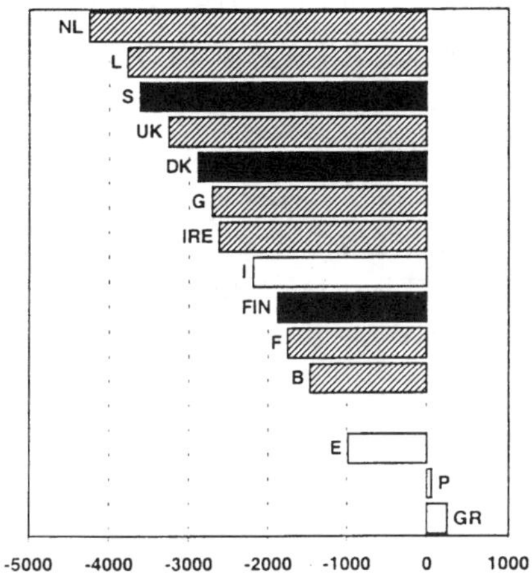

Figure 5.22 Relative disposable income of couples with children, as compared to couples without children (reference). Ecu in PPP. Source: ECHP/NSS.

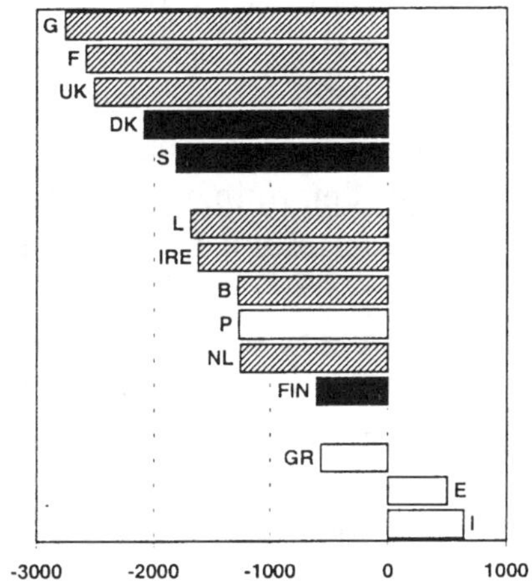

Figure 5.23 Relative disposable income of single parents, as compared to couples with children (reference). Ecu in PPP. Source: ECHP/NSS.

Multivariate analysis also confirms the earlier findings concerning the economic consequences of having children. Figures 5.22–23 indicates that the Southern cluster performs best, with lower impact on income of having children. This comes as no surprise, with respect to recent family formation patterns with postponed partnering, delayed exit, and delayed and decreasing fertility (see chapter 4). Furthermore, the traditional family in the South will incorporate young families and grandchildren. Belgium and France also seem to have a lower effect of having children, as compared to the Nordic countries. It should also be noted that the same applies to the relative income situation of single mothers. Here we have an indication of larger problems in Germany, France and UK.

The Nordic countries are, generally speaking, in intermediate position, in this case not separated from the central cluster. In the Swedish case are these findings not surprising. Sweden's recent recession and recovery policies have had strong impact on young families, as recorded in recent Swedish social reporting. The deep recession, massive decline in (youth) employment and public welfare cutbacks are recognised as the major welfare issues to monitor in the new century.

Determinants of Material Living Standards in EU Member States

Income inequality, poverty and affluence are indicators concerned with inequality in a *general* sense, irrespective of social cleavages such as gender, generation, social class, region or family. In the previous section we have applied multivariate technique to isolate the major determinants of disposable income. Next, we will corroborate these findings by repeating the analyses using indicators of consumption in the form of consumer durables. In order to compare such inequality patterns between nations we need to decompose the consumption structure by social cleavages, as well as construct an index, which measures the overall level of material inequality in such a way as to allow comparisons between nations as well as between dimensions. Such an inequality index was constructed and included in Swedish Social Reporting (Vogel, 1988; Vogel, 1997; Ribe, 1987). In this section we use this technique to compare the determinants of inequality between nations.

The inequality index is an extension of logistic regression analysis, adding several model specifications. The index has the following characteristics:

- Pairs of contrasting subgroups are selected from each dimension to represent the variation by gender, generation, social class, family etc.;
- By LOGIT-analysis we control the structural differences deriving from the other dimensions;
- We consider an imaginary population where the two contrasting groups have equal structure in all other included dimensions;
- The inequality index equals the difference in the percentage in each of the two groups having a certain good (e.g., a car);
- Indexes are calculated separately for a set of material indicators, as well as an average for these indicators;
- The index varies between +100 and –100, where +100 signifies total inequality (all in the first group have the good, and none in the other group); –100 means that the situation is reversed;

and 0 indicates perfect equality (equal percentages of the two groups have the good).

- The numerical index scores for each pair of groups (and dimension) are thus directly comparable. Hence, with this method we can compare the relative impact of the dimensions in different countries, and in the case of Sweden we can measure the corresponding trends for 1975–1995.

For technical details and separate indexes for each indicator see Vogel (1997).

Class Inequality
The following three figures give the corresponding inequality indexes for the European member states of 199.4[3]

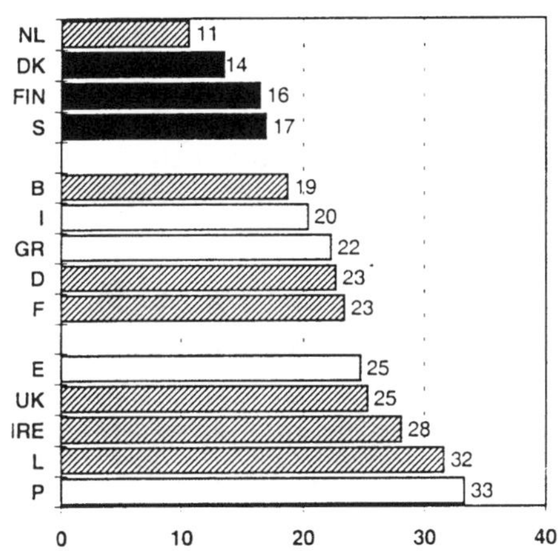

Figure 5.24 Inequality between manual and upper non-manual workers. Average index score. Source: ECHP/NSS.

The class dimension is analysed by comparing manual workers to upper non-manual employees, including larger managers and employers (with at least 10 employees). The numeric size of the index tells about the relative impact of social class, or in other words, the contribution of market effects (employment, earnings) on the distribution of material living standards at national level. Class inequality appears to be the lowest in the Nordic encompassing welfare states, characterised by inclusive labour markets and extensive social intervention, and the Netherlands (Figure 5.24). Class inequality is the largest in Portugal, again joined by UK, also

Luxembourg and Ireland. Luxembourg is extreme in its income distribution with a large volume of households with very high income. The location of UK in the high-level inequality cluster has already been demonstrated with other indicators, and is again confirmed here. Greece and Italy display rather moderate class inequality by this measure, which has to be further analysed. The remaining central European countries are again in an intermediate position. This figure exhibits a ranking rather similar to the earlier findings concerning income inequality and poverty.

Inequality Between Generations

Inequality between generation concerning material living conditions is measured in the same vein by comparing the three generations pair wise. First we take a look at the 20–29 year old versus the parental generation of the 45–64 year old (Figure 5.25). Then we continue with a comparison of the elderly (65–84 years) and the 45–64 year old (Figure 5.26).

The ranking of member states according to inequality between generations (20–29 vs. 45–64 years) produces an entirely different ranking, in fact *a completely reversed ranking* of the three major clusters, in the same direction as found in the previous section for disposable income. Figure 5.25 again indicates that young adults are best off in the Southern countries, and worst off in the North, relatively speaking, and again with the central European member states in intermediate position. It should be noted that the three clusters are perfectly separated.

This outcome is (again) explained by the very different role of the family in the South as compared to the North. Young adults in Italy, Greece, Spain and Portugal are staying much longer with their parents, especially when they are in education and before they are permanently established on the labour market, or in a stable partner relationship. This means that they share the economic resources of the larger parental home, including durables, housing conditions and the pooled disposable household income. The incorporation of young adults in the parental households is an advantage due to the economy of scale: resources as well as costs and goods can be shared. A special feature is the selective nature of young adults leaving their parents early; they are usually well established in the labour market and/or a new family context.

In the Nordic countries young adults tend to leave their parents much earlier, and even before they are established on the labour market, have sufficient income, and before they form a new family. Leaving at a certain age (around 20) and often continuing youth education is a common Nordic pattern. Therefore, as compared with the South of Europe, there is a much larger volume of young adults under the age of 30, with marginal income, still in education and living in single person households. A closer look at Swedish poverty statistics reveals that the larger share of Sweden's relatively low poverty rate is explained by such cases, while other age groups, including the elderly, have very low poverty rates, due to high employment levels and public income maintenance schemes, including the public pension program.

Hence, the separation of generations in households explains why the generation gap is much more pronounced in the Nordic cluster than in the Southern cluster, characterised by closer family ties. In other words, the Southern family tradition seems to be more efficient in limiting the generation gap created by differential access to work and market income (late entry to the labour market, youth unemployment, lower youth wages). Welfare state arrangements in the North do not sufficiently relieve these consequences of the younger generation's family formation pattern. On the other hand, young adults in the North gain independence earlier. The price is lower living standards during the period of establishment. Currently, as youth education is gradually prolonged a growing proportion of young adults is living in poor conditions, and there is a corresponding growth of the generation gap.

When it comes to the relative material conditions of the elderly the same clustering of EU-countries has been recorded (Figure 5.26). Here we compare the elderly (65–84 years) with the 45–64 age group. Again the Southern countries have the lowest level of inequality, and the Nordic countries have the highest index scores. Again, there is an almost perfect separation of the three clusters.

The interpretation corresponds to that for young adults. In the South there is (still) a large proportion of the elderly living with their mid-aged children, often in three-generation extended households.

These elderly usually have lower pension rights and income. This also means that single elderly persons in one-person households tend to be positively selected with respect to income. Consequently, the difference in material living conditions, related to income, is reduced by the sharing of resources in extended households.

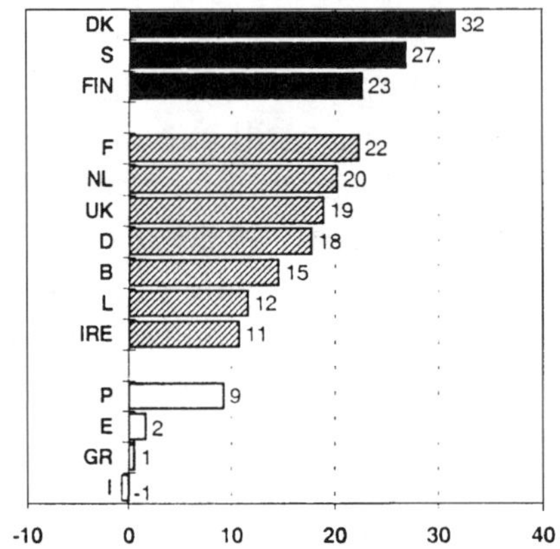

Figure 5.25 Inequality between persons 20–29 and 45–64 years. Average index score. Source: ECHP/NSS.

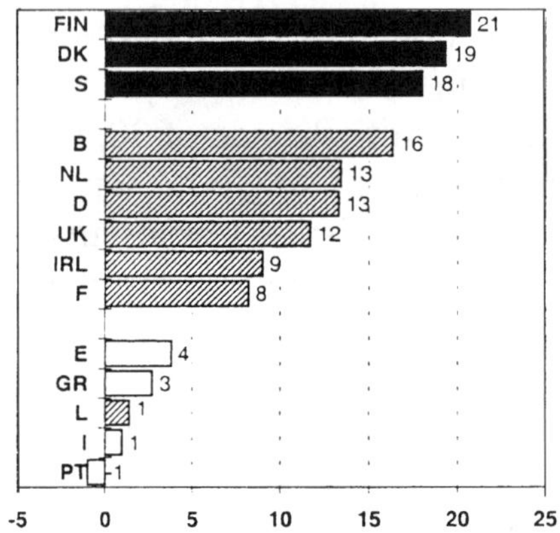

Figure 5.26 Inequality between persons 65–84 and 44–64 years. Average score. Source: ECHP/NSS.

In the Nordic countries elderly persons living in with their children's household are extremely rare. On the other hand, higher employment rates during the active years also provide better pension rights. The resulting country ranking implies that the extended family in Southern Europe has an important impact, in fact surmounting the effect of the Nordic full employment tradition and public pension rights.

Determinants of Inequality in Material Living Standards: Sweden 1975–1995

The corresponding multivariate analysis for Sweden over the period 1975–1995 is presented in Figure 5.27.[4] This analysis indicates that up until the early 1980s, there was a narrowing of *class differences* in Sweden; after that followed stagnation. The institutional background is increasing differentials in earnings, and, in the 1990s, increased unemployment and public recovery measures.

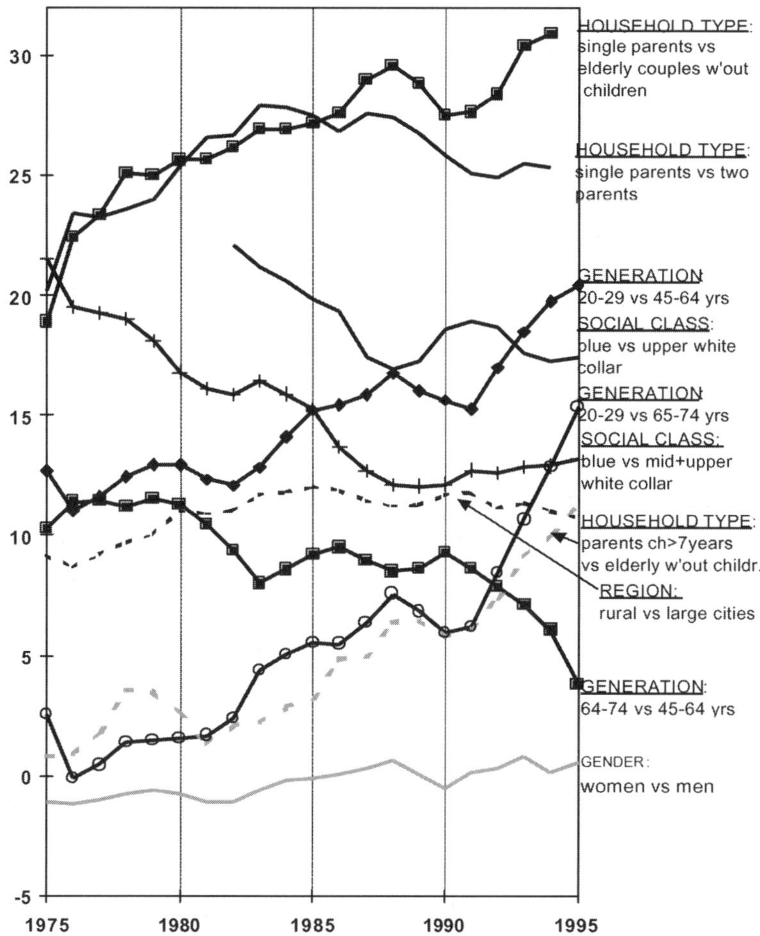

Figure 5.27 Material inequality by social class, gender, generation, household type and region. 1975–95. Inequality index (based on 11 indicators, see text). Pairwise comparisons between categories. N=130 000. Source: ULF.

Generational differences have been increasing for a long time, but there was an especially sharp increase during the 1990s along with the deep recession. The main institutional factors are decreasing employment (by prolonged youth education, and increasing youth unemployment). The material living conditions of young adults aged 20–29 years deteriorated in relation to the two older generations in the study (45–64 and 65–74). In addition, the material standard of the elderly improved in relation to both young and middle-aged adults, as a consequence of increased pension rights and public pension levels. From the mid-1980s, the generation gap between young adults and the middle-aged increased to become as large as the corresponding class differences.

The situation of single parents and families with young children became worse in consequence with the impact of labour market hazards during the 1990s on young families, along with reductions in the transfer systems. Regional differences in material living conditions remained largely unchanged during the entire period from 1975–1995.

CONCLUDING REMARKS

Our data indicate that the welfare outcome with respect to material aspects, including disposable income as well as material living standards, in each of the member states is related to the unique configuration of the three major welfare delivery institutions, i.e., the labour market, the welfare state and the family. Similar institutional arrangements and performance produce similar distributive structure at individual level. The comparative analysis of this report, which is conducted at the macro level, suggests there are three clusters of EU member states (the Nordic, the Southern, and the intermediate central cluster), each of which with distinct distributive features related to market forces, welfare state arrangements and family patterns. The countries included in each of these three clusters exhibit considerable uniformity in all three institutions. Furthermore, the longitudinal study of the Swedish welfare mix during the past three decades demonstrates the same co-variation between institutional configuration and distributive outcome.

This similarity within clusters, and dissimilarity between clusters, also extends beyond the income distribution and material living standards addressed in this chapter. Additional studies focusing on coping behaviour related to family formation (see chapter 4) and public health (chapter 6), also demonstrate the link to the welfare mix.

These findings indicate there are *three different national strategies of welfare production*, the general nature of which only can only become visible with a larger set of national cases, in this case 15 EU member states. The findings have been demonstrated in spite of the technical deficiencies for comparative analysis of the ECHP/NSS database. Distinct findings under poor technical conditions speak for the assumptions presented in the first chapter. In addition, we have examined the case of Sweden over the past 30 years, tracking the evolvement of the Swedish model of welfare production, with its parallel change in institutional conditions and distributive outcome. It should be noted that the findings and clustering of member states, as well as Swedish trends, are generally distinct with rather few unexpected deviations, producing consistent rankings on most indicators.

The link between institutions and distributive outcome will be elaborated further in the concluding chapter.

NOTES

[1] Poverty trends for *individuals* are calculated according to the traditional *absolute poverty line* used in Swedish statistics. This line is defined by the National Board for Health and Social Affairs based on a fixed sum defined by budget studies. Individuals living in households with disposable incomes below that standard after taxes and transfers are regarded as poor.
[2] The socio-economic as well as income measurement is dubious for this category. In addition, larger and differential non-response should contribute to less reliable findings. The findings for Luxembourg correspond to the current labour market structure and wage levels.
[3] Small scale farmers, which in the Southern countries form a larger part of the labour force, are here collapsed with manual workers.
[4] Inequality indexes are in this section based on the following sample of eleven indicators: Absence of overcrowded housing; High standard of housing space; Ownership of a dishwasher; car; a second home; a caravan; a boat; a video; dishwasher; a freezer; access to a daily newspaper.

SCB Statistics Sweden
Welfare Analysis Program
and
University of Umeå
PO Box 24300
10451 Stockholm
Sweden

TÖRES THEORELL and JOACHIM VOGEL

HEALTH

The previous chapter has documented that there is considerable variation in material living conditions between clusters of EU member states. There are differences in material living standards as well as differences between member states with respect to income distribution, education and socio-economic conditions. These conditions are being currently discussed as factors of relevance to the level and distribution of health in populations. In addition all of the European states have experienced pronounced structural changes in labour market and living conditions in general during the two recent decades.

This chapter will extend this analysis of European welfare regimes and distributive outcome by exploring health variations. In addition this chapter will extend the field of observation to recent comparative studies including Eastern Europe. The inclusion of Eastern Europe expands the variation of socio-economic living conditions and welfare provisions, which further illustrates the link between the social context, economic outcome and health outcome.

According to the general hypothesis these differences in welfare should also be reflected in health outcomes. In Northern Europe during the recent decades there have been small socio-economic income differences as well as high material standard for low-income citizens. This should be reflected in low morbidity and low mortality as well as lower socio-economic differences in morbidity and mortality. In Southern Europe the family has been a major provider of health care. According to the hypothesis this may increase health inequity since differences in family income are not buffered. In addition the health care system has been less extensive and the programs for disease prevention have been less advanced than in the northern European countries. The Western part of the middle European countries occupies an intermediate position. Thus, with some exceptions for specific illnesses, higher morbidity and mortality as well as higher levels of health inequity are expected

Social Indicators Research **64:** 471–493, 2003.

in the Southern European countries. In the eastern European countries, finally, the past decade has been a period of transition, going from a situation with the state as the main provider of welfare to a mixed situation. High mortality and morbidity as well as increasing socio-economic health gaps are hypothesised.

HEALTH MEASUREMENT AND COMPARATIVE HEALTH REPORTING

The primary target of health reporting is the public health, the measurement of which raises fundamental technical problems. Any attempt to develop a set of social indicators for *international* comparison of public health add further obstacles. In order to clarify some of these problems this chapter starts with a general discussion of health measurement in the context of surveys and comprehensive social reporting.

Illness is a personal event as well as social phenomenon. The personal experience of illness is a complex product of bodily feelings, individual resources to cope with health problems and its social consequences, such as disability, financial problems and social exclusion. The personal experience of health and illness is also influenced by environmental and social demands for health, defined by the individuals' roles in various arenas. Hence, illness is not only related to biomedical malfunctioning, but also to the social context. Malfunctioning, in this extended sense, has of course a basic causal background in biological ageing, and environmental influences from work, leisure and health-related life style, but in addition there are also influences from the social context.

Accordingly, health researchers offer three different models of morbidity, relating to the biological, subjective and social levels of experience. The related concepts are disease, illness and sickness. ***Disease*** refers to biological or physiological reactions, to injuries or changes in the internal bodily environment. This individual-oriented and biological model usually utilises clinical and objective symptoms to locate a biological malfunctioning, usually in relation to environmental risk factors.

Illness refers to the subjective dimension (individual feelings of pain and discomfort). Illness is related to the consequences of disease, and has to be understood in its social context. Issues such as individual expectations and aspirations are of relevance.

Finally, ***sickness*** is understood as a social identity, i.e., an inability to meet obligations in real life. Sickness is identified by others as individual malfunctioning in relation to the special roles a person is expected to perform. Hence, sickness is the social consequence of disease and illness.

These three models have different implications for any measurement of public health, as well as for the understanding of comparative morbidity statistics. An integrated system of social indicators preferably uses interview data, where morbidity is measured simultaneously with other social indicators, in particular risk factors (age, work environment, life style, natural environment, material resources, social networks). This approach typically leads to personal interviews with random samples, asked about their general health status. This approach was used in the ECHP and the Nordic Level of Living Surveys. It is important to understand the validity of such information collected from respondents in standardised interviews, since they affect the comparability of national estimates. This information gives the layman's self-rated status, primarily according to the illness model. These interviews measure subjective awareness of bodily disorder (pain, discomfort), including diagnosed disease of which the respondents are been made aware by their doctor. However, this awareness depends of the volume and efficiency of the National Health Service, as well as the cultural tradition of consulting the health service. Several diseases are not always accompanied by discomfort, in particular in their early stages, and hence not uncovered and made aware by the patients. When we compare morbidity statistics based on surveys from different countries, we have to consider these circumstantial effects affecting the international variation of self-rated heath levels. In spite of identical measurement (identical questions in a questionnaire) there is a cultural factor involved.

Another comparative problem is the individual demand structure. Self-ratings of health are influenced by the current demands from employment, family obligations, and the general cross-pressure of daily life. Higher demands produce higher stress levels and hence higher levels of discomfort (illness) at constant health (disease). In other words, the environment not only affects disease, but also the subjective health (illness) reported in health surveys.

This complicates any understanding of the links between risk factors and health, based on a few simple survey questions in a general social survey. The mechanisms through which health is affected by material deprivation (poverty) and social exclusion (unemployment and long-term unemployment, exclusion from social networks) are complicated and difficult to disentangle with the limited information of a general survey. There is little doubt that the international variation of disposable income levels, income inequality, income security, poverty, long-term unemployment, family support, etc. contributes to the variation in public health (disease as well as illness) between member states. At best the data presented in this chapter on morbidity, which essentially is the first comparative presentation for the European Union, will initiate hypotheses and serve as an appetiser for more detailed comparative health surveys.

Possibilities for comparing socio-economic conditions in European states have improved during recent years. This is partly due to a growing number of survey studies for characterising living conditions but also to the decision to facilitate direct comparisons by means of standardisation and emphasis on comparability within the framework of the ECHP.

Our understanding of differences between European states in socio-economic conditions and their association with inequity in health heavily depend on the comparability of health outcome variables between the states. There are three different options for making comparisons – none of them representing an ideal method. A short description of the three possibilities as well as a discussion follows:

MEASUREMENT OF MORBIDITY: METHODOLOGICAL ISSUES

Self-reported Health According to National Surveys

Self-reported health has been shown to be a valuable indicator of health. According to several reports, poor self-reported health correlates with elevated mortality and objective measures of morbidity (Nilsson and Orth-Gomér, 2000). Therefore questions about self-rated health have substantial potential value in efforts to compare health levels between European countries. There are obvious comparability problems, however. First of all there are language problems. The translation of questions about self-rated health is problematic in itself. Secondly, even when translation problems have been solved, the health concept may have different cultural meanings in different countries. Thirdly, the data collection procedures themselves differ between different European countries. For instance, there are markedly different survey response rates in different countries. Fourthly, a comparison in self-rated health may be problematic even when the response rate is identical in two countries, since the reasons for non-participation may be markedly different. These reasons may be related to the determinants of health as well as to the health outcome itself. For instance, there may be a much lower response rates at the lower educational level than at higher educational levels. This leads to an underestimation of the prevalence of poor self-rated health in that country. A fifth problem is that the level of self-rated health is related to the amounts of contacts that the citizens have with the health care system. In a country with good access to health care there will be more contacts and these contacts will make the citizens aware of objective health problems. A person with a diagnosis which is associated with no symptoms (for instance elevated blood glucose indicative of an early stage diabetes) will be more likely to report a poor self-rated health than a person who has the elevation but is unaware of it – several chronic diseases have a long asymptomatic period preceding symptoms. Hence, countries with poor access to health care will have relative underestimation of self-rated health.

Despite all these methodological difficulties comparative research in self-rated health should still provide valuable insight in the determinants of health inequities. The ECHP/NSS database is at present the best coordinated comparative source for such analyses. However, these data have to be interpreted with due precaution, and they should also be evaluated in conjunction with objective health outcome measures.

Use of National Registers for Morbidity and Mortality Comparisons

Most countries have well functioning mortality registers. This facilitates reliable national comparisons. The limitations and possibilities for European mortality comparisons have been discussed by (Kunst, 1997). The speed at which annual register data become complete differs between countries in Europe. In some countries there is a delay of several years before mortality statistics are completed. Furthermore there are differences in quality of diagnostic procedures as well as procedures for calculating specific measures. While overall mortality estimates are generally reliable, variations in the calculation of specific death causes may impede comparisons of specific diagnoses. For instance, the diagnostic procedures in cases of suspected myocardial infarction differ not only between but also within countries. In areas with a high forensic autopsy rate, diagnoses of myocardial infarction occurring outside a hospital are more precise. When the procedures are less advanced diagnostic mistakes are more likely to occur and prejudice regarding excess risk in certain population groups may affect the classifications. For instance, if there is a common belief that the myocardial infarction risk is higher among highly educated men (which is opposite to scientific consensus) the risk among highly educated men may be overestimated in areas with a low autopsy rate and prejudiced ideas about myocardial infarction risk. In some countries death non-medical persons establish death causes. In other countries physicians always establish the diagnosis. This may also affect the risk of erroneous assessments of incidence.

Hospital registers and primary care registers are accessible for studies of morbidity in some countries. For cross-national comparisons, however, such registers are difficult to use for studies of differences in social inequity of morbidity. First of all, there are differences in accessibility of care and patterns of consultation of caregivers when illness occurs, and these cross-national differences may affect socio-economic groups differently. Secondly, there are differences between countries with regard to diagnostic procedures in health care, and again such differences may affect the observed prevalence or incidence of specific illnesses differently in different social groups.

Direct Comparisons with Individual Examinations between Randomly Selected Subjects in Contrasting Countries

A number of such studies have been performed which address specific scientific questions. Such detailed studies are usually not performed in several countries, and more general conclusions are therefore difficult to draw although they may highlight important differences.

SOCIAL INDICATORS

The morbidity indicators used in this report are collected by two standard questions in health surveys, both related to the illness model. The first question concerns "Your health in general" (sex response categories between very good and very bad). The other is linked to the daily activities ("Are you hampered in Your daily activities by any chronic physical or mental health problem, illness or disability?"). It is quite obvious that both indicators carry subjective elements, and that there is room for underestimation of disease as well as socially defined health problems, likely to have impact on the comparability between nations. The second indicator is probably more robust, since it tries to relate to daily activities. Unfortunately the information on morbidity in the ECHP is restricted to a few simple indicators, which did not give altogether consistent results.

The third indicator concerns dental status, and identifies satisfaction with own teeth, dentures or false teeth; based on interview data collected 1996 by the EUROBAROMETER.

The fourth indicator utilised is the traditional life expectancy indicator.

Finally, a set of life style indicators will be presented, relevant as indicators of health-endangering behaviour. This set of life style indicators to be applied to the set of EU member states includes smoking, alcohol consumption, obesity and road accidents.

The agenda of this chapter is to explore to what degree these indicators also divide the European Union in the already familiar clusters of member states found in earlier chapters.

MORBIDITY

The interview data on morbidity indicators give a confusing and contradictory picture of the variation of public health in member states. This variation reflects not only differences in health-related determinants, but also cultural factors and methodological problems related to the measurement process.

The first indicator concerns the rate of persons rating their "general health" as "good or very good" (Figure 6.1 and Table 6.1; see Appendix). The dominant geographical ranking of member states in the earlier chapters is not fully reproduced. The Southern, central and Nordic countries are blended, but there is still a tendency that the Nordic countries as a group perform better than the central and southern cluster. The Nordic countries (Denmark and Sweden), but not Finland, are located at the upper end, while the Southern countries concentrate towards the end. However, we have to remember the subjective element involved in these ratings, already addressed in the introduction. Furthermore, there may exist a certain national cultural propensity of taking a more or less positive (or pessimistic) attitude in general subjective ratings in surveys of this character. For instance, it has been noticed that the Danish sample is overly positive on most issues measured in the ECHP (including self-rated health), which does not always correspond to the objective conditions registered for the same sample.

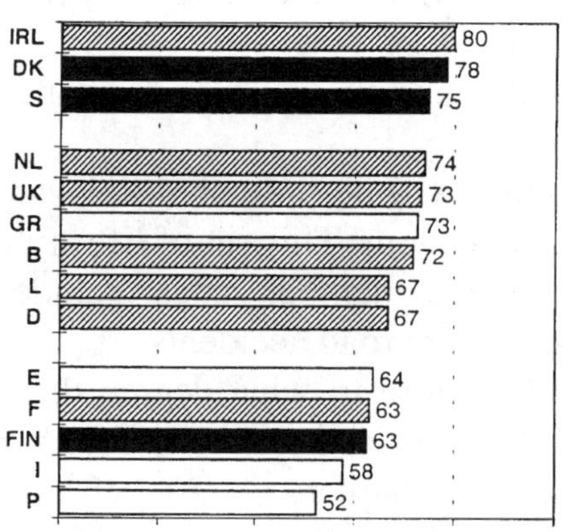

Figure 6.1 Self-rated health is "good". Percent. Source: ECHP/NSS.

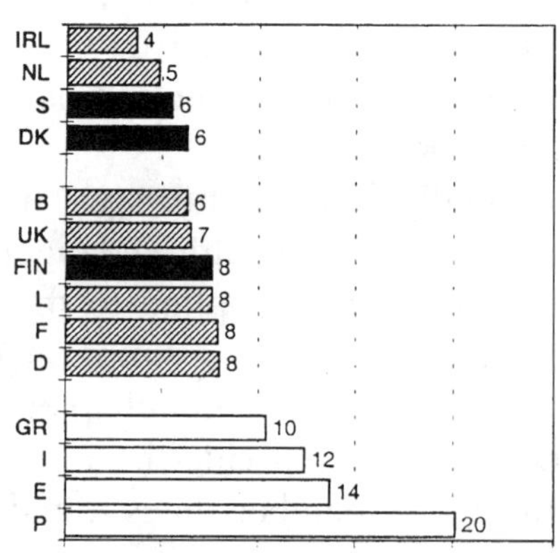

Figure 6.2 Self-rated general health is "bad". Percent. Source: ECHP/NSS 1994.

The next indicator uses the same interview question, but presents the lower end of the distribution, i.e., the proportion reporting that their general health is "bad or very bad" (Figure 6.2 and Table 6.2). This ranking of member states is of course very similar to the last indicator. However, here we get a ranking much closer to the clustering of member states found for other social and indicators presented in this report and by Vogel (1997), in particular employment, welfare state provisions, income, poverty and family structure. Again, all of the four members of the Southern cluster (Portugal, Spain, Italy and Greece) have distinctly higher levels reporting their health is "bad", as compared to the central and Northern member states. Two of the Nordic representatives in this table are in the favoured group. The variation between nations on this indicator is rather large. The proportion with "bad" general health is four times as high in Portugal, as compared to the leading countries (20 versus 4–6 percent).

It appears that the notion of "bad health" used in the interviews could be more robust in relation to subjective influences in the measurement process (as compared to "good health"). Hence, the distribution of health is best evaluated by using the proportion rating their general health as "bad". The major discriminator is of course age. The proportion of disease and illness inclines with biological ageing, but at various pace in the member states. From Table 6.2 we can conclude that South versus Central/North divide is concentrated to the ages over 45. In particular, after 65 years of age these differences between the three clusters are very large. In the leading countries (Ireland, the Netherlands, Sweden) just over 10 percent report "bad health", as compared some 50 percent in Portugal and over 30 percent in Greece and Spain.

For all morbidity indicators there are slightly higher levels of illness reported among women in all member countries. This probably reflects a gender variation in every day demands (higher cross pressure from work and family), as well as attitudes towards bodily concern and following up health problems by contacting the health services.

Table 6.2 also reveals that higher educational level is related to better health status in all member states. This is a mixed outcome of two major factors. Higher education is generally related to better working environment and other life conditions. Furthermore, higher education is related to lower age.

Table 6.2 also indicates that disposable income is related to health. Here we can see the joint negative effects of a range of factors related to income, such as unemployment, low wages, poverty, lack of family network support, and the environmental effects of low-paid jobs.

Finally, the disaggregation by socio-economic group again brings out the subjective character of self-rated health measurement. The general picture is straight forward: manual worker report illness more often, and small scale farmers have the highest rates, reflecting physical job demands. However, this pattern is far from consistent for all of the member states.

In summary, there is partial support for the hypothesis that the Nordic countries have better health than the Southern countries since Portugal, Italy, Spain and Greece all belong to the countries with a higher percentage of subjects reporting bad health, whereas Denmark, Sweden and Holland all belong to the "good" group of countries. Finland is a notable exception from the rule. We have no explanation for this finding.

LIMITED CAPACITY

The second morbidity indicator concerns persons being *severely hampered in their daily activities*. Here we measure illness in relation to the normal activities of the respondent. Figure 6.3 and Table 6.3 give a different picture as compared to the rating self-perceived health in the previous section. This can be attributed to the different ways of measurement. This time the two Nordic countries (Sweden, Finland) as well as France move in the foreground with higher levels of illness, and all of the Southern countries move downward in this ranking.

Figure 6.3 illustrates that this morbidity indicator is highly sensitive to circumstantial factors. The explanation to these discrepancies is probably, as already mentioned in the introduction, the social context. In the Southern countries, characterised by much lower employment rates in upper ages, as well as better family network support in larger traditional families, the demand structure is more favourable. In particular, the strong family tradition buffers the stressors of daily life originating from unemployment, poverty, and old age isolation from practical and emotional support (see also chapter 4). Accordingly, when it comes to health in relation to the *daily obligations* the southern countries (and in particular the elderly) come out better than expected from the earlier subjective ratings.

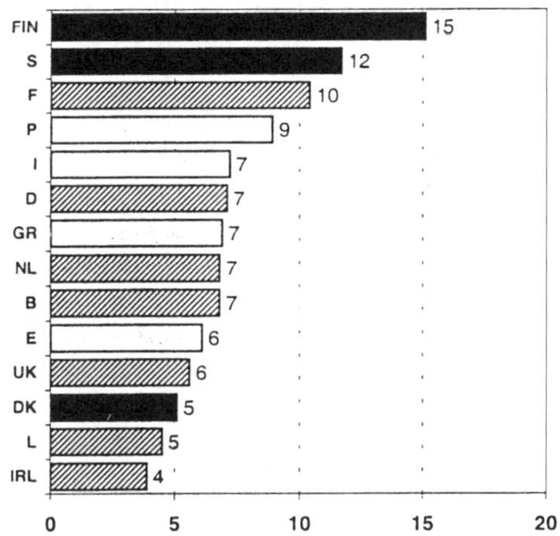

Figure 6.3 Persons severely hampered daily activities. Percent. Source: ECHP/NSS.

A closer look at Table 6.3 supports this interpretation. Here we can verify that the elderly are less exposed in Greece, Spain, Italy and Portugal, as compared to the Finland, Sweden, Norway, France, and UK, with lower levels of health limitations reported in the South. This difference points in the direction of lower overall daily demands in the South.

Poverty and Health

Which then are the segments of the population most exposed to health problems? There is a descriptive and an analytical answer to this question. The following data give a descriptive account of the relation between economic stress and health. We use the classification of monetary poverty (see chapter 5) identifying persons living in a household with less than half of the average national disposable equivalent income. This defines a poverty line, which is relative to the national context, and hence varies between nations. In the relative sense, persons living in these households represent the lowest part of the income structure. The health indicator is the self rated health question earlier presented, with the categories bad or very bad. Similar analyses can be performed with other classifications of exclusion from normal living standards, such as unemployment, poor social networks, poor education or lower social class affiliation. We chose poor households for this analysis, since this indicator overarches several sources of exclusion.

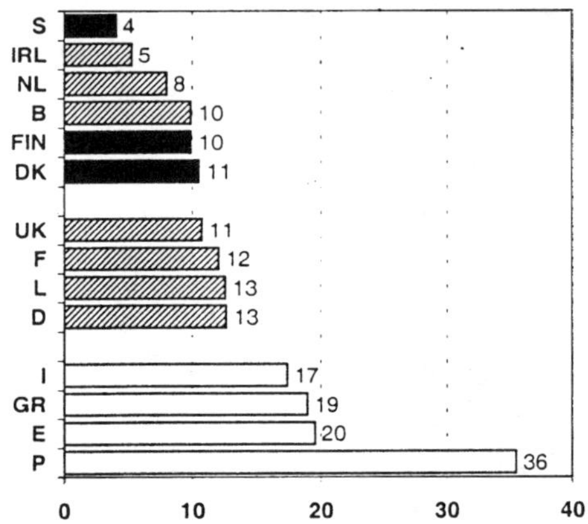

Figure 6.4 Self-rated health (bad) of persons living in poor households. Percent. Source: ECHP/NSS.

Figure 6.4 demonstrates again a clear North-South divide. In particular in the Southern cluster we find high levels of health problems, while the Nordic countries concentrate at the better end.

The next two figures elaborate this picture further. Figure 6.5 shows the *deviation* (from the average) in the percentage of persons with bad health among those living in poor households. We find rather limited variation between the Nordic and central member states. The Southern countries, on the other hand, form a cluster with extremely high levels of bad health in poor households. This is further elaborated in Figure 6.6, where we add the health level in rich household, which here are defined as households with more than 150 percent of the average equivalent disposable income (or three times the poverty line). Figure 6.6 again demonstrates that the Southern cluster is extreme, in the European context. It should be noted that the health variation is rather limited among the rich, but the health variation between member states among. the poor is rather large.

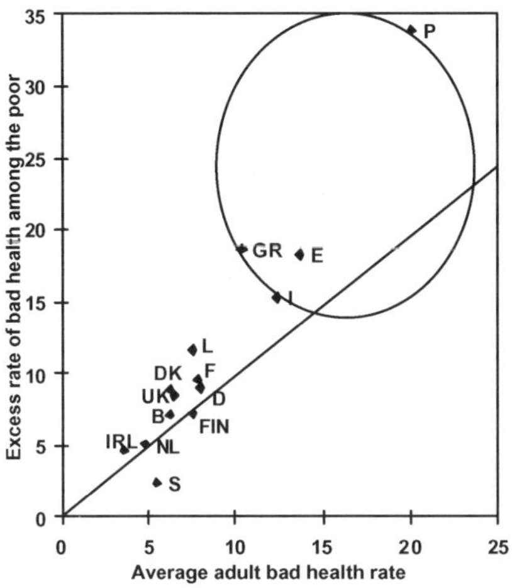

Figure 6.5 Excess bad health rate among the poor vs the average rate of bad health. Percent. Source: ECHP/NSS.

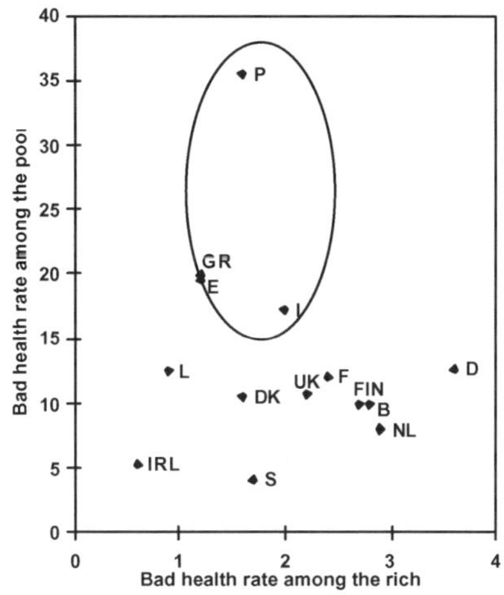

Figure 6.6 Persons living in rich and poor households, reporting bad health. Percent. Source: ECHP/NSS.

So far for a descriptive account of the health variation between poor and rich households, and between member states. The analysis of this variation, however, is extremely complex. Social and economic exclusion and health are interrelated, with causal links in both directions. Furthermore, the previous chapters indicate that the set of relevant processes and health determinants should vary much between member states. Health status is strongly related to age, which also is involved in processes of exclusion. For instance, poverty in Sweden is primarily a matter of early exit from the parents household, while in the South (Portugal, Greece) it tends to relate to ageing and poor pension rights. To explore the causal background multivariate techniques are required to capture the diverse health determinants in the member states. And finally, health in itself influences social and economic exclusion.

MORTALITY AND DEATH CAUSES

According to the general hypothesis, mortality is expected to be low in the Nordic countries with their emphasis on the state providing welfare. There are no studies of all the European countries except studies of mortality data gathered by the WHO, with standardisation for age but not for other relevant confounders. Illustrative maps of age adjusted mortality rates in European countries have been published (Józan and Prokhorskas, 1997). The mortality pattern reported in these sources does not confirm the hypothesis. The highest life expectancy at birth for men was found in Iceland, Sweden, Holland, Italy and Greece whereas the lowest was found in Turkey and the former Soviet Union countries. The situation was similar for women. Accordingly, the Southern state and the northern EU countries were winners in this competition.

The quantitatively most important cause of death in the European countries is cardiovascular disease that has historically shown a geographical pattern with high incidence in the Northern and Eastern countries. Since cardiovascular disease is the major determinant of longevity in the European populations it is important to know that morbidity and mortality have a complicated relationship to one another. A high morbidity would logically be associated with a high mortality. However, if the health care system is efficient, the mortality may be low despite a high morbidity. This should be born in mind when the longevity pattern is interpreted. It has been shown repeatedly that the incidence of myocardial infarction is high in the Northern and Eastern countries, and this is also confirmed for ischaemic heart disease (the broader cardiovascular concept) (Józan and Prokhorskas, 1997). Genetic, climatic, dietary and social factors have been discussed (Keys et al., 1996; Rosseneu et al., 1994). Despite this, cardiovascular mortality is relatively low in the Northern countries (Józan and Prokhorskas, 1997). There is a low cardiovascular mortality in Iceland, Spain, France, Belgium and Italy and it is relatively low also in Greece, Sweden, Denmark and Holland for men. For women the cardiovascular mortality is low in Norway, Sweden, Holland, Holland, France, Italy and Spain and relatively low for Finland, Belgium and Greece. Accordingly, the pattern is similar to the one for longevity – despite a disadvantage in cardiovascular incidence the Northern European countries have a relatively low mortality.

Furthermore, if the health care system is egalitarian in its treatment of patients with the disease, a low degree of social inequality in the mortality pattern for this disease might be found. Kunst et al. (1997) have pointed out that the health inequity patterns are different for different diagnostic groups. There is evidence that the social inequity in cardiovascular mortality is low in these countries (Hallqvist, 1989). It may be that the health care system in the northern countries is so effective that with regard to mortality it can compensate for the high incidence of cardiovascular disease. The Southern countries on the other hand have a low incidence to start with.

There are also many technical difficulties in the interpretation of differences in the social patterning of mortality in different countries (Kunst, 1997). One of the most important difficulties in comparisons of mortality specific to social groups in different countries, for instance, is that the definitions of social groups differ between countries. Manual workers, for instance, could be identified in several ways and this may lead to marked differences in the proportion of manual workers as well as registered health levels.

If occupation is recorded in different ways for the general population, versus those who have died, systematic errors may arise in the statistics relating occupation to mortality. The educational system is also different as well as ways of recording income. Several indices could be calculated, however, and if all the three indicators of social conditions are used – income, education and social group – the total analysis may indicate consistent differences. For instance, in a study of (occupationally based) social group in relation to mortality in 11 European countries, Kunst (1997) showed that France consistently had a more pronounced social group difference in mortality in the 1980s than Ireland, Denmark, Finland, Italy, England/Wales, Portugal, Norway, Spain, Switzerland and Sweden. This tendency was found both in relative terms (comparing risks in different strata) and absolute terms (taking the sizes of the manual and non-manual classes into account). Alcohol consumption was suspected to account for a substantial part of this pattern since the age specific mortality rate ratio of unskilled workers versus higher-level employees and professionals for alcohol related mortality (liver cirrhosis and cancer of upper digestive tract) was very high in France (4.68 and 5.23, respectively).

One of the drawbacks in using mortality statistics in the study of social patterning of ill health is the delay in the production of statistics. No statistical complex analysis can be performed before all the mortality statistics from several countries have been completed. The study by Kunst et al. was limited to the 1980s whereas no information could be subjected to in-depth analysis during the 1990s. Alcohol consumption has decreased in France during recent years (10), and this may explain why France has improved its position with regard to expected longevity and general mortality during the 1980s so that its position in 1991–1993 was quite favourable compared to the Czech republic, Denmark, the United Kingdom, Italy, the Netherlands and Norway. In particular for French women age standardised mortality was lower than in these other countries (Juel et al., 2000). On the contrary Denmark had worsened its position, particularly for women. In 1991–1993 the age standardized mortality rates in Denmark was the second highest (after the Czech republic) among these countries. The development in Denmark may be due to an adverse development of diet and smoking habits (particularly in women compared to other European countries) as well as of alcohol consumption.

According to WHO statistics (Gorski, 1998) one of the most striking findings is that higher gross national product (GNP) is associated with low infant mortality. Infant mortality could be regarded as a good indicator of availability and effectiveness of health care in a country. However, there are interesting exceptions to this rule. Countries with small income differences have often emphasized public health care, and in this group, for instance China and Cuba who have been relatively poor countries in the 1970s and 1980s, infant mortality has developed favourably compared to other countries. On the contrary, the US, a country with a very high BNP per capita, has had large income differences, relatively small emphasis on public health care and a relatively high infant mortality.

Within Europe, countries in Eastern Europe have higher age standardised mortality as well as more pronounced differences in mortality between manual and non-manual classes than countries in the west. Kunst et al. (1998) found that the social group mortality rate ratio (manual/non-manual classes) was 2.25 and 2.89 in the age group 30–44 and 1.83 and 2.65 in the age group 45–59 in the 1980s in the Czech republic and Hungary respectively. The corresponding numbers in the United States, England and Wales, Finland and France ranged between 1.42 and 1.76 for the age group 30–44 and 1.32 to 1.71 for the age group 45–59. The total age standardised mortality was also much higher during this period in the Eastern countries Estonia, Czech republic and Hungary than in USA, France, Norway and Finland.

With regard to specific causes of death the excess mortality in countries that belonged to the Soviet Union has been particularly pronounced in suicide (Ginter, 1995) and coronary heart disease (Józan and Prokhorskas, 1997). According to a recent publication from the MONICA-WHO study, the health inequity caused by socio-economic differences in the prevalence in overweight has been increasing recently in the world (Molarius et al., 2000). The difference has been particularly observable in men. In Russia, the longevity among men was decreasing during several years in the 1990s, and although the trend has been reversed during the latest years, Russian men have a strikingly low longevity compared to most countries in Western Europe.

REGIONAL STUDIES: LINKÖPING AND VILNIUS

A direct comparison between two samples of 50-year old men in Linköping in Sweden and Vilnius in Lithuania (Kristensson, 1998), 101 in Linköping (82% participation) and 109 in Vilnius (76% participation), may serve as a good example of direct comparisons that address specific scientific questions. The aim of this study was to compare the risk factor pattern in Linköping (where the risk of developing a myocardial infarctions is average by European standards) to that in Vilnius, and to explore socio-economic differences in risk factor patterns in the two countries. A number of factors were examined such as working conditions, coping patterns, life style (exercise, smoking and alcohol consumption) and biological risk factors. Vilnius belongs to the cities with a high myocardial infarction incidence. It was predicted that there would be a more adverse risk factor pattern in general in Vilnius men, and that differences between social classes would be more pronounced in Vilnius than in Linköping.

The biological analyses showed that blood pressure was higher in Vilnius and the serum concentration of LDL cholesterol (which stimulates the progression of artherosclerosis) higher in Linköping, whereas smoking habits were similar in the two cities. On the other hand, men in Vilnius had a lower concentration of vitamins with antioxidant capacity (for instance carotene) and more disturbance in antioxidant activity than those in Linköping. It is generally believed that a high antioxidant activity can slow the artherosclerotic process. Non-invasive studies of arteries showed that the Vilnius men had more advanced artherosclerosis than the Linköping men.

An interesting observation was that the two groups reacted differently with regard to the cortisol concentration in serum and saliva (both indicators of physiological arousal, the saliva concentration is highly correlated with the serum concentration) to a standardized stress test in the laboratory. The Vilnius men started with higher concentration but had much less rise in cortisol levels during the test than the Linköping men. Thus, during the experiment the Linköping men had higher mean levels than the Vilnius men. This reaction pattern in the Vilnius men could be interpreted as an indication that they were more aroused and slightly depressed but that they also were less able to react with rise during mental arousal than the Linköping men. According to stress research theory, a reduced ability to react with cortisol elevation could be an indication of physiological exhaustion. For instance, in the chronic fatigue syndrome lack of cortisol elevation in challenging situations is a common finding.

The psychosocial examination of the two groups (which was done by means of questionnaires) showed more job strain (a combination of high psychological demands and low decision latitude at work), less social support at work as well as less emotional support and less social integration in life in general in the Vilnius men than in the Linköping men. The Vilnius men also described themselves as having more problems with coping, self esteem and sense of coherence as well as having more vital exhaustion and depression than the Linköping men. Quality of life, self-rated health and future health expectations were also less favourable in the Vilnius men.

An important finding in the Linköping-Vilnius study was also that there was a social patterning in the differences. There was a higher proportion of men with blue collar jobs in Vilnius, and for some of the differences (job strain and depression in particular), the blue collar men in Vilnius were worse off than white collar workers in both cities and also worse than blue collar workers in Linköping. Similar tendencies were observed with regard to antioxidant status. Thus, when social class was taken into account it became evident that part of the difference between Vilnius and Linköping was due to the fact that the Vilnius blue collar men had worse conditions than the other studied groups.

The Vilnius-Linköping study shows that the excess cardiovascular illness risk in middle aged men in Vilnius could not be explained by differences in accepted risk factors for cardiovascular disease. Instead social and psychosocial factors seemed to be of considerable importance. The differences in antioxidant capacity could be due both to dietary habits (which differed in different social groups) and to chronic psychosocial stress (which was markedly worse in Vilnius than in Linköping).

The main findings in the Vilnius-Linköping study are confirming observations in similar comparisons. For instance, a comparison between Kaunas (in Lithuania) and Rotterdam (Bosma et al., 1994) showed that Kaunas men had a more favourable cardiovascular risk factor profile than men in Rotterdam – despite a higher mortality. The large WHO examination, the so called MONICA study, of risk factors and changing risk factors patterns in Europe enabled a comparison of data from 15 European communist countries and 25 democratic MONICA populations. This showed that a combination of the classical CHD risk factors could explain only part of the observed CHD mortality differences between the countries. It is obvious that these investigations, both performed in the middle of the 1980s were unable to predict the rise of CHD mortality that followed in Lithuania and the other Baltic countries. It is also obvious that cross-national comparisons, if information from official registers is combined with detailed individual examinations of representative samples, may be very important in efforts to increase basic understanding of illness mechanisms.

SUICIDE IN FORMER SOVIET REPUBLICS AND IN EUROPE

Recently, mortality registers in the former USSR have been made accessible for researchers. This has made it possible not only to study mortality trends but also to make comparisons with other European countries. Suicide is a specific cause of death that has been studied recently by means of these registers. For suicide in men, pronounced fluctuations in the Baltic countries have been observed. In conjunction with perestroika in the former USSR (including a restrictive alcohol policy and the first tentative steps towards democracy) male suicide rates in the years 1986 to 1990 fell considerably below those in the preceding years. Female suicide rates also decreased but the decrease was less pronounced and not consistent across the three Baltic countries (Värnik, 1994). In an expanded analysis, comparisons between 22 European countries (Värnik et al., 1998) and the Slavic and Baltic regions with regard to age-specific suicide rates for the period 1984–1990 were made. Data showed that there was a similar decline in suicide rates in the Slavic regions of the former Soviet Union in 1984 to 1986–1988. For men, the fall amounted to 41% in the Slavic region and to 30% in the Baltic region. For women the corresponding decreases were 18% in the Slavic and 16% in the Baltic regions respectively. During the period 1986–1988 to 1990 there was a slight increase again in men – but not in women – and this change was more pronounced in the Slavic region than in the Baltic. Accordingly, the increase in men was 15% in the Slavic and 5% in the Baltic region, whereas no consistent changes were observed during this period for women.

Despite the favourable suicide development during the 1980s in the former USSR, the suicide rates were still higher in 1990 in the former USSR than in the 22 European countries. The most pronounced difference was found for men in the age group 45–54 among whom a two-fold difference was found in the former USSR compared to the European countries (Austria, Bulgaria, former Czechoslovakia, Denmark, Finland, France, former GFRG, Greece, Hungary, Iceland, Ireland, Italy, Luxembourg, Malta, Netherlands, Norway, Poland, Portugal, Sweden, Switzerland, United Kingdom and former Yugoslavia).

Analyses of possible causes of the relatively marked fluctuations in suicide rates particularly among middle-aged men have pointed at excessive alcohol consumption as a possible cause of increased suicide rates. Alcohol consumption has been calculated in multivariate analyses to account for more than 50% of male and 27% of suicides in the former Soviet Union. Other potentially important factors have to do with religion (the catholic churches and Islam prohibit suicide whereas protestant churches do not), society's role (repressive societies may increase suicide risk) and gender roles (influencing the male to female suicide ratio).

HEALTH RELATED LIFE STYLE VARIABLES

Life style variables related to health such as smoking, alcohol consumption, overweight and injuries have been examined in the EUROBAROMETER 1995. In countries, which emphasize public health through political action, a healthier life style pattern would be expected since prevention is part of the political agenda. In addition, when health care is easily available for most citizens advice regarding smoking, alcohol, physical activity and safety measures in the traffic would be expected. According to our general hypothesis Nordic countries would be expected to have healthy patterns, and those in the south unhealthy.

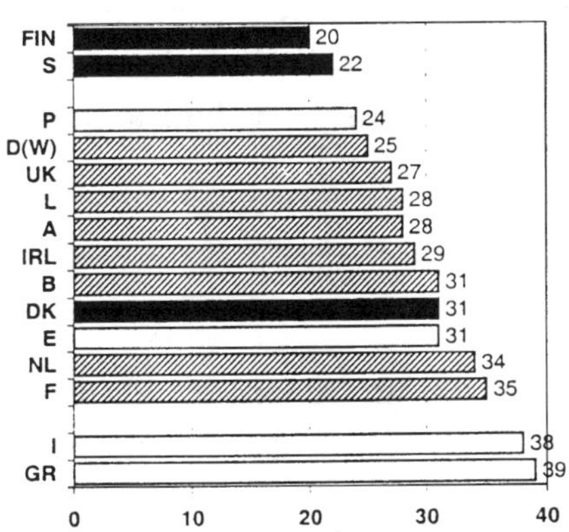

Figure 6.7 Daily smokers. Percent. Source: EUROBAROMETER 1995.

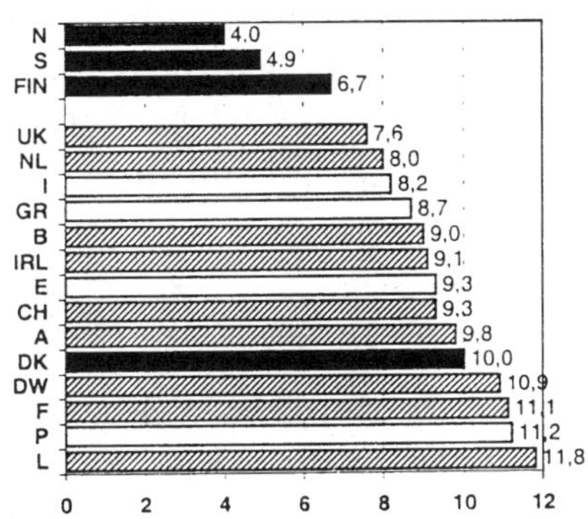

Figure 6.8 Average alcohol consumption: Average litres pure alcohol per person/year available on the market. Source: WHO.

Figure 6.7–10 show the data for smoking, alcohol, body mass index and injuries. Two Nordic countries (Sweden and Finland) report very healthy patterns with regard to smoking, alcohol and traffic accidents. Norway is also in the best group with regard to alcohol and road accidents but information is missing for smoking. Denmark is in the expected good group for traffic accidents but belongs to the worst tertile with regard to smoking and alcohol. Sweden occupies the top position with regard to health body mass index but Denmark and Finland have bad body mass index positions.

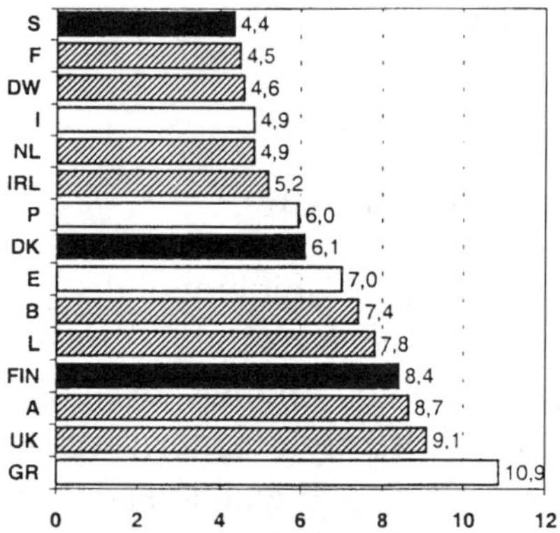

Figure 6.9 Body mass index. Pooled data for men and women. Source: EUROBAROMETER 1996.

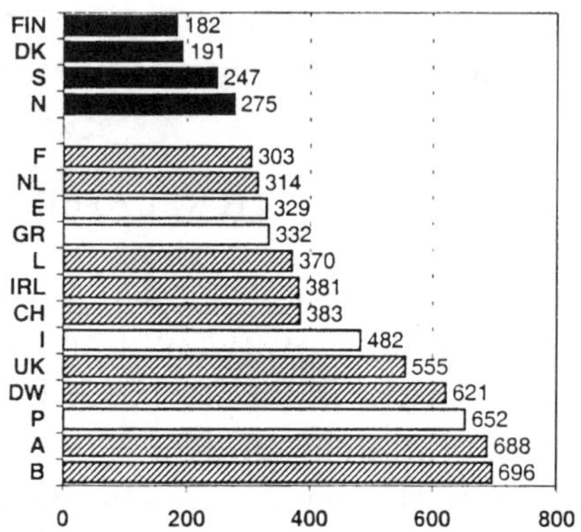

Figure 6.10 Injured persons per in road accidents. Per 100 000. Source: WHO.

Thus with the exception of body mass index the Nordic countries have healthy patterns, which confirms the hypothesis. Denmark is a notable exception with regard to smoking and alcohol. This probably has a historical background – the Danes have had a liberal attitude to alcohol and smoking since a long time.

CONCLUSIONS

Comparisons between European states with regard to different aspects of health could be performed in many ways. There are different problems with different outcomes. The production of mortality statistics is delayed by many factors. Studies of morbidity in representative samples of the populations to be compared are expensive and technically difficult to compare. Questionnaire studies of self rated health are difficult to interpret because of differences in verbal formulations and in culturally determined meaning of words, accessibility of health care – which may influence the participants' awareness of symptomatic medical conditions and of course also increase survival of persons with specific diagnoses – and differences in insurance systems and social security regulation.

Despite all these difficulties direct comparisons between EU countries tend to show that self-rated health is associated with welfare regimes. The Nordic countries, which have emphasised the role of the state in providing welfare, in general belong to the countries with a good self-rated health in the population. Furthermore, these countries also have been more successful in providing employment opportunities for a larger share of their working age populations. When the comparisons are extended to the former Soviet countries the contrasts are striking. Newly published detailed studies on the individual level show that poor self-rated health is associated with stress-related bodily changes, which may partly explain the association between poor self-rated health and poor expected longevity.

These observations are in line with those of an American team of researchers who showed that self-rated health in the USA is related to social capital (Kawachi et al., 1999). Those who lived in areas with a low level of social trust had trust had worse self-rated health than others, even after adjustment for a number of individual factors such as income, education and smoking.

SCB Statistics Sweden
Welfare Analysis Program
and
University of Umeå
P.O. Box 24300
1451 Sweden

STEFAN SVALLFORS

WELFARE REGIMES AND WELFARE OPINIONS: A COMPARISON OF EIGHT WESTERN COUNTRIES

In this last chapter, it will be asked to what extent the different institutional configurations which have been explored in previous chapters correspond to patterns of public support for welfare state intervention. In order to do so, a broader set of countries, chosen to represent different welfare state regimes both within and outside Western Europe are compared.

The chapter is thus placed at the intersection of comparative welfare state research and comparative attitude research. In the former field, as witnessed by the other chapters of this volume and several other recent studies, a thorough mapping of welfare state regimes and institutions and their distributional consequences have been conducted. Patterns of public and political support for the welfare state have, however, been a less prominent theme.

In the latter field, a rapidly growing number of studies have been conducted of how citizens of different countries perceive and value their societal arrangements. These studies have rarely been based on an institutional understanding of the countries in question and thus lacked in interpretative and explanatory depth. As recently lamented by Jowell, "analysts of cross-national data frequently abandon offering explanations and interpretations in favour of league tables of distributions showing merely 'gee whiz' national differences" (Jowell, 1998: p. 168).

Comparisons of patterns of social attitudes are linked to wider sociological issues. From a comparative political economy framework, it may be asked to what extent political institutions, most often found at the national level, correspond to attitudes among populations of different industrialised countries? Does a global market economy and capitalism create the same kind of social attitudes worldwide? Or do national institutions and political traditions play the decisive role in forming attitudes?

Social Indicators Research **64:** 495–520, 2003.

In this respect, the impact of institutions is therefore a central topic. Institutions should here be understood as "the rules of the game", or using a more strict definition "the formal rules, compliance procedures, and standard operating practices that structure the relationship between individuals in various units of the polity and economy" (Hall, 1992: p. 96; cf. Levi, 1990). Institutions are hence something more than the constitution and the law, in that they also include more informal rules ("standard operating practices"). Still it seems necessary not to widen the definition of institutions too far as to include any set of structured interaction, because the possibility will then be lost to distinguish between the importance of formal political institutions and other social facts (Levi, 1990: pp. 404–405; Rothstein, 1996: p. 145). The definition of institutions should therefore include only objects of human design and intention, such as social security systems, political party systems, collective bargaining systems, and so on, while leaving social facts such as family interactions, class structures or norms outside the definition. Even with such a fairly narrow definition, it is clear that the presence and impact of institutions are immense in modern societies.

Institutions affect human action in a number of ways. First, institutions modify the structure of rewards and costs. Through welfare state intervention, for example, or through labour market legislation, the structures of rewards and costs are modified. Second, institutions structure possibilities and incentives. Competition, recruitment and social mobility are structured by political institutions, which therefore affect the incentives of social actors.

While most institutional theories would agree that institutions affect rewards, costs, possibilities and incentives, a third way in which institutions are effectual are often disregarded in purely "rational choice"-approaches to institutions.[1] This is that institutions affect perceptions and norms (Rothstein, 1996, 1998). This is because institutions (a) affect the *visibility* of social phenomena, (b) affect what is considered politically *possible* to achieve in a given setting, and (c) embody, and hence create, *norms* about what is fair and just (Rothstein, 1998). Institutions provide "normalcy", that is, they suggest to people what is "the normal state of affairs", and what is deviant or even impermissible.

To give a few examples, welfare policy institutions may affect the visibility of benefit claimants; in this way citizens' perceptions of the number and characteristics of such claimants are affected. Institutions also show whether a certain policy is possible to implement: is the state able to distribute child allowances to all parents or is it not? Welfare institutions also embody normative principles and practices, for example (in most cases) that the public health care which is provided should not be affected by ability to pay.

To assume that there is some relation between national institutions and social attitudes does not imply that institutions determine attitudes. The relationship is instead a probabilistic one and one of mutual dependency and development. Certain institutions tend to make some attitudes more likely than others, and given a certain set of preferences some institutions are more easily implemented or changed than others.

The concept of "regimes" is denoting institutional configurations, that is, constellations of institutions with some internal coherence (Esping-Andersen, 1990; Pierson, 2000). Different nation-states display qualitatively different modes of connecting labour markets, welfare policies and families. As shown in the previous chapters of this volume, as well as by considerable amounts of previous research, this has important effects for the stratification system in different dimensions and thus also for the kind of distributional and political conflicts that arise. The question I seek to tackle in this chapter is to what extent such differences tend to correspond to attitudinal patterns towards welfare policies among the populations in different welfare regimes. Do people living in countries exemplifying the same kind of welfare regime tend to have similar attitudes, and do those who live under different welfare regimes tend to have different attitudes towards welfare state intervention?

The chapter is organised as follows: In the next section, after summarising the main findings that previous research has supplied, a more precise formulation of the issues is provided. The following section describes the data, discusses possible problems of comparing attitudes across countries, and describes the methods applied. After that follows two sections of empirical analysis, one concentrating on aggregate patterns, the other on group differences.

In the concluding section, the main findings are summarised and their implications discussed.

PREVIOUS RESEARCH ON WELFARE REGIMES AND WELFARE ATTITUDES

Our questions about the relationship between welfare state regimes and welfare opinions take as their starting-point the seminal work of Esping-Andersen (1990). His typology is an attempt to classify contemporary western welfare states as belonging to one of three "worlds of welfare capitalism". He argues that welfare states should not be classified according to any continuous measure such as social spending; they are qualitatively different configurations of institutions and distributive outcomes. Different historical actors have been instrumental in creating different welfare states.

Esping-Andersen discerns one "liberal" welfare state regime, in which the market is the primary arena in the distribution of resources and in providing protection for the employed. State provisions are comparatively low and provided as flat-rate benefits or in response to proven need. The second regime type is the "conservative" one, in which state provisions are income-related and encompassing, but distributed strictly according to previous earnings. This regime type strongly emphasises the family in various ways. Women are encouraged to stay at home while their children are small and tax deductions and payment bonuses are used to supplement the bread-winners' income. The last regime type is the "social democratic", in which most of the population is included on a citizenship basis. Provisions are income-related as in the conservative regime, but the floor level under which noone is allowed to fall is set at a higher level. In this regime type, focus is on the individual rather than on the family as the basic unit of society.

As suggested by the labelling of the regime types, Esping-Andersen sees the three regime types as tightly wedded to specific political actors. He also suggests that the various regime types tend to create specific social cleavages and conflicts in the transition from industrial to post-industrial societies, which is of crucial importance for this paper (Esping-Andersen, 1990: Ch. 9). In the liberal regime type, class cleavages tend to dominate other possible sources of inequality and conflict, due to the overwhelming impact of the market as generator of distributional conflict. The conservative regime type creates strong conflicts between "insiders" and "outsiders", between groups with a good labour market position and ensuing adequate protection from social insurance, and a growing surplus population of unemployed and others with a weak labour market attachment or performance. The social democratic regime type tends to create a strong gender and sectoral conflict between a public sector mainly populated by women and a private sector dominated by men. On issues of redistribution, taxation and public services, women in the public sector and men in the private are increasingly likely to take different sides.

Comments and criticisms of Esping-Andersen's theses have been many and variegated. The reworked typology offered by Castles and Mitchell (1992, 1993) is of particular interest in the perspective of this paper. They argue that the label "liberal" in fact covers two sets of welfare states that are fundamentally different both in terms of the political actors behind their development and in their institutional characteristics and distributive outcomes. One is the truly liberal world, which combines low social expenditure, low benefit equality and low level of taxation with a weak position for labour parties and trade unions. The prime example is of course the United States.

The other they denote is the "radical" world, made up of countries like Australia and New Zealand. In these countries, low taxation and small social expenditures are combined with high benefit equality. Incomes and capital taxes are rather high while consumption taxes and social security contributions have been low or non-existent. These countries also have fairly strong labour movements that have been countered by a strong and united right wing, which has made it difficult to translate left electoral strength into government incumbency. In these latter countries, there has been a strong emphasis on "primary welfare", that is, on regulating wages and other work conditions, and less on welfare state redistribution (Castles, 1985, 1988). State intervention has not been regarded as inherently suspect, as in the liberal world, but as preferably targeting the least well off in society.

Previous research on the relationship between welfare regimes and attitudes has reached few firm conclusions.[2] What is common to all studies is that they maintain that large and interpretable differences in attitudes towards welfare and redistribution do exist between different Western capitalist countries. Whether such differences can be interpreted as created by regime differences (Matheson, 1993; Svallfors, 1997), or by quite other factors (Papadakis and Bean 1993; Bean and Papadakis, 1998; Svallfors, 1993), is more controversial. Studies differ, furthermore, in whether they think that common base levels of attitudes co-exist with different lines of conflict (Svallfors, 1993), or if different base levels of support for the welfare state co-exist with similar patterns of group differences (Svallfors, 1997), or whether both aggregate levels and group differences vary (Matheson, 1993).

There are several reasons why previous research has reached so little consensus. One is that the selection of countries has in several of the studies been ill suited to really capture regime differences (Bean and Papadakis, 1998; Papadakis and Bean, 1993; Svallfors, 1993). A second is that some of the analyses suffer from methodological shortcomings – in the construction of indexes or variables or in the analytical strategy applied – which lessen their value (Bean and Papadakis, 1998; Papadakis and Bean, 1993; Svallfors, 1993). A third is that most studies include too few country cases to make interpretations robust; when each regime is represented by only one country it is hard to draw any firm conclusions (Svallfors, 1993; Matheson, 1993). A fourth is that in some of the cases attitudes are analysed that are more related to income distribution than to state intervention proper (Svallfors, 1993, 1997).

In all these respects, the present paper intends to make progress. The attitude questions that are used (see "Data" section) ask for respondents' support for welfare state intervention using a broad set of items. Therefore they avoid some of the problems of interpretation that have marred many of the previous analyses. The selection of countries is intended to capture differences within and between welfare regimes. The analysis will therefore include two countries from the "social democratic" regime (Sweden and Norway), tow countries from the "conservative" regime (Germany[3] and France), two countries from the "radical" regime (Australia and New Zealand) and two countries from the "liberal" regime (Canada and the US).[4] The country cases thus represents four pair of countries which, if welfare regimes structure attitudes and values, should display considerable similarities within pairs and substantial differences in attitudes between the pairs.

In this comparison, focus is set, firstly, on the aggregate levels of support for state intervention: do citizens in the "social democratic" world, with substantial state intervention and extended social citizenship rights, have fundamentally different attitudes towards such measures compared to what is the case in the "liberal" regime, where state intervention is much more circumscribed? And do the citizens of the conservative and radical welfare regimes fall in between? Secondly, the analysis tries to map the class, gender and insider-outsider differences in attitudes: do lines of conflict, as reflected in attitude patterns, follow the conflict scenarios outlined in the discussions of different welfare regimes? Do gender conflicts emerge as especially salient in the social democratic welfare regime, and do class differences come out as especially clear in the liberal regime? And is the insider-outsider split especially clear in the conservative regime?

DATA

The data comes from the *International Social Survey Program* (ISSP), a comparative attitude survey comprised of more than 30 nations to date. The ISSP is an attempt to create a truly comparative data set with which to analyse attitudes and values among the populations of industrialised nations (Davis and Jowell. 1989; Becker et al., 1990). The program was inaugurated in the mid-eighties and now involves more than 30 industrialised countries from five continents. A wide variety of topics have been surveyed, and from 1990 onwards previous modules have been replicated allowing comparison both between nations and through time (Svallfors, 1996b).

While comparative attitude research is potentially very fruitful, it is also fraught with difficulties which may make results and interpretations fragile (see also Jowell, 1998; Küchler, 1987, 1998). The most important problem is probably how to establish the cross-national validity of indicators. Attitudes are by their very nature context-dependent, which is why we want to compare them across nations in the first place. This is of course not a problem in itself. A problem arises if we find that it is not values and attitudes that vary across nations, but the meaning and connotations of various concepts.[5] There is an immanent danger of creating research design artefacts instead of comparing and explaining substantive findings.

This problem has been dealt with as far as possible within the ISSP. The questionnaire design is truly a cross-national exercise involving drafting groups comprised of people from several countries and requiring approval from the whole 30-nation group. The possibility to locate and eliminate problems of cross-national validity has thus been uniquely great within the ISSP. In order to be able to interpret and explain survey findings, something which requires a thorough contextual understanding, researchers are still advised to use a few strategically chosen countries rather than including as many countries as possible in the analysis (Küchler, 1987, 1998).

This is also motivated by the fact that translations of questionnaires pose similar problems when it comes to establishing cross-national validity (Harkness and Schua-Glusberg, 1998). Concepts sometimes cannot be literally translated since they carry nation-specific connotations. Within the ISSP, this has been dealt with both through careful indications in the master questionnaire as to which concept the literal expressions refer and through careful national procedures in translating the questionnaire.[6]

Problems occur also when it comes to samples and non-responses. Samples are in all cases nationally representative probability samples. For six out of eight countries response rates varies between 60% and 70%.[7] Germany has a response rate of 54%, which is an average rate for Germany but still low compared to many other West European countries. The achieved samples are, however, not significantly biased in their age, gender and educational composition (ISSP96: Study descriptions). In short, even if a non-response rate of 30–40% is hardly ideal in itself, non-responses are not likely to substantially bias the comparisons.

When it comes to the French case, however, problems are greater. The French survey was conducted as a one-stage mail-out without reminders or follow-ups. The result is that out of 9500 questionnaires, only slightly more than 1300 were returned. We therefore cannot regard the French sample as a representative one, but one that is to a considerable extent self-selected. How large damage is done to the representativity of the sample is hard to tell. An educated guess is that the French respondents are more interested in politics and have higher education than the French population at large. Exactly what implications this may have for the levels and structure of attitudes towards the welfare state is harder to say. At least considerable caution is required when interpreting the French data.[8]

What the added data difficulties point to is not that comparisons are impossible, but that caution is required in both survey design and in interpretation of the results. Interest should be focused not on small differences in gross percentages on single items, but on larger patterns, on how various groups differ in different countries, using compounded indexes rather than single items. It is also important to carefully establish whether different items really correlate in the same way across national contexts (Küchler, 1987; Scheuch, 1989). The analysis that follows accordingly starts by displaying distributions on the various items and indicators used, and proceeds over the construction of attitudinal indexes, to the use of graphical displays and multiple classification analysis to study group differences in attitudes.

The bulk of the data for the analysis in this paper comes from the 1996 replication of the module on *Role of Government* that was fielded in 25 countries. When choosing what items should be used as indicators of support for government intervention, the ISSP96 offers a range of possibilities. Some of them ask what the government should do for "the economy", which in this case was judged as both being too narrow and too dependent on the actual economic situation of the country in question. A second set of items asks whether more or less should be spent on a range of public activities. This was judged as potentially too difficult to compare between countries, since answers depend much on the actual (or perceived) level of spending. Instead it was decided to use questions which ask respondents if they think *it should be the government's responsibility to* ... and then list a set of items (as displayed in Table I in the next section). In this case, the questions ask about respondents' principal support for government intervention in different respects.

It was felt that this should give a more accurate estimation of levels of support for government redistribution than the other options. In several of thc countries, this question had been posed also in 1990, allowing us to compare the stability of attitudes over time. As shown in the next section, these items also make up summarised indices with appealing technical properties in all eight countries.

ATTITUDES TOWARDS STATE INTERVENTION IN EIGHT COUNTRIES

What responsibility do the citizens of the eight countries think that the state ought to have in securing their livelihoods and redistributing resources? The answer to this question may be said to illuminate the extent to which attitudes towards state intervention differ between different welfare regimes. In Table I, scale means for the different items used in the 1996 survey are displayed for each country. Response scales run in four steps from "should definitely be" to "should definitely not be". They have been recoded into a 0–3 range, with higher values indicating stronger support for state responsibility.[9] In Table II, the items have been summarised to a "Government intervention index".[10]

From the tables a number of interesting observations may be distilled. By and large, the rank order of countries is as we would expect it to be. The social democratic countries display the strongest support for state intervention, followed by the "conservative" and the "radical" worlds, while citizens in the liberal regime have the weakest support for such measures. Differences are particularly clear when it comes to attitudes towards support for unemployed/employment, and towards income redistribution.

However, it is hard to find any clear clustering of countries. For example, Canadians are closer to Australians in their views than they are to citizens of the US; the gap between Norway and Sweden is larger than what is found between Sweden and France; and the gap between France and Germany is bigger than the one between Germany and New Zealand.

In the cases of New Zealand and Canada, Table I shows that their index values are clearly affected by their comparatively high values when it comes to health care. There are good grounds to suspect

TABLE I

Attitudes towards government intervention in eight countries 1996. Scale means

Should it be the government's responsibility to . . .	*Norway*	*Sweden*	*France*	*Germany*	*New Zealand*	*Australia*	*Canada*	*USA*
. . . provide a job for everyone who wants one	2,23	1,89	1,93	1,97	1,55	1,46	1,17	1,25
. . . keep prices under control	2,40	2,26	2,06	1,87	1,94	2,00	1,72	1,82
. . . provide health care for the sick	2,86	2,66	2,37	2,46	2,68	2,36	2,54	2,19
. . . provide a decent standard of living for the old	2,85	2,66	2,42	2,43	2,52	2,31	2,36	2,22
. . . provide a decent standard of living for the unemployed	2,32	2,26	2,10	1,93	1,68	1,70	1,73	1,41
. . . reduce income differences between the rich and the poor	2,06	2,03	2,11	1,76	1,42	1,58	1,46	1,40
. . . give financial help to university students from low-income families	2,06	2,11	2,50	2,11	2,16	2,11	2,15	2,16
. . . provide decent housing for those who can't afford it	1,90	2,05	2,28	1,93	1,96	1,84	1,87	1,78
(n) (minimum)	*(1252)*	*(1236)*	*(1245)*	*(2180)*	*(1095)*	*(2059)*	*(1187)*	*(1026)*

Source: ISSP96

TABLE II

Government intervention index in eight countries 1990 och 1996

	Norway	*Sweden*	*France*	*Germany*	*New Zealand*	*Australia*	*Canada*	*the US*
Government intervention index 1990	*18,91*	—	—	*16,68*	—	*15,15*	—	*14,64*
Cronbachs Alpha	0.80	—	—	0.83	—	0.81	—	0.84
(n)	(1263)	—	—	(2412)	—	(2122)	—	(980)
Government intervention index 1996	*18,76*	*17,96*	*17,82*	*16,49*	*15,82*	*15,42*	*14,94*	*14,20*
Cronbachs Alpha	0.78	0.85	0.83	0.79	0.81	0.82	0.84	0.87
(n)	(1120)	(1092)	(1116)	(1911)	(945)	(1883)	(993)	(1026)

Source: ISSP90; ISSP96.

that this is an institutional effect of the fact that these two countries for a long time had a free and public health care system, in contrast to their in other respects typically "liberal" welfare regimes. The surprisingly low value in Sweden for full employment policies is harder to explain: even if it higher than what is found in the non-European countries it is lower than in Norway, France and Germany. This may indicate that support for welfare state intervention is weaker in Sweden than is sometimes supposed.[11]

The intervention index is very stable between 1990 and 1996 in the four countries that fielded this survey in 1990. Changes are negligible and in no case statistically significant. Neither convergence nor divergence is thus found among the attitudes in different welfare regimes over the course of the 1990s.

The indexes that have now been constructed will in the following section be used to analyse group differences in different countries. There we will find out whether attitudes are structured differently in different welfare regimes.

GROUP DIFFERENCES WITHIN AND BETWEEN COUNTRIES

I this section attitude differences are compared in the eight countries between different classes, between men and women, between public and private sector employees, and between those who receive public support and others. These seem to be the main fault lines that have been emphasised in the discussion about distributional conflicts in different welfare regimes.

What is perhaps the key variable, class, is at the same time the most difficult one to make comparable across countries. The occupational codes applied in different countries have been recoded into a six-class version of the class schema devised by Goldthorpe and colleagues and used in a multitude of empirical studies of social mobility and work. The logic behind this schema is to distinguish classes according to the employment relations that various occupations entail (Erikson and Goldthorpe, 1992: pp. 28–47; Goldthorpe, 2000). The class schema exists in several versions. The version used here distinguishes between unskilled workers, skilled workers, routine non-manual employees, Service class II (lower level controllers and administrators), Service class I (higher level controllers and administrators) and the self-employed (see further appendix). This is the most detailed level for which a classification of data for all eight countries can be achieved.

Three categories of dependants on the welfare state are discerned: the unemployed, the retired and all others. The retired and the unemployed seem to be the main distinct categories of people that are more or less dependent on public benefits, permanently or temporarily, excluded as they are from the labour market. Other categories of people not currently in the labour market are not in the same sense dependent on non-market incomes as the unemployed and the retired. They are therefore brought into the same category as those currently in the labour market.

The question about private or public employment has in several of the countries been posed only to those who currently work. In the US the question has not been included at all. However, this is less of a problem than might have been feared since, as it emerged from the analysis, private vs. public employment is a less important fault line than often has been presupposed.

In Diagram 1, class differences in index values are plotted for the eight countries. As shown, both substantial similarities and interesting differences arise. In spite of the difficulties in constructing comparable class codings (see appendix), the rank order between the classes look very similar in all countries. Workers are the most supportive of state intervention, while Service class I are the most sceptical. Differences between workers and lower level non-manuals are very small, while Service class II and the selfemployed are posed somewhere between lower and higher non-manuals. Some minor exceptions to this pattern occur: in some countries (Canada, France, New Zealand) routine non-manuals are slightly *more* supportive of state intervention than skilled or unskilled workers, and in Australia and Canada the selfemployed are the least supportive of all groups. By and large it is nevertheless the similarities in rank orders that is the main impression.

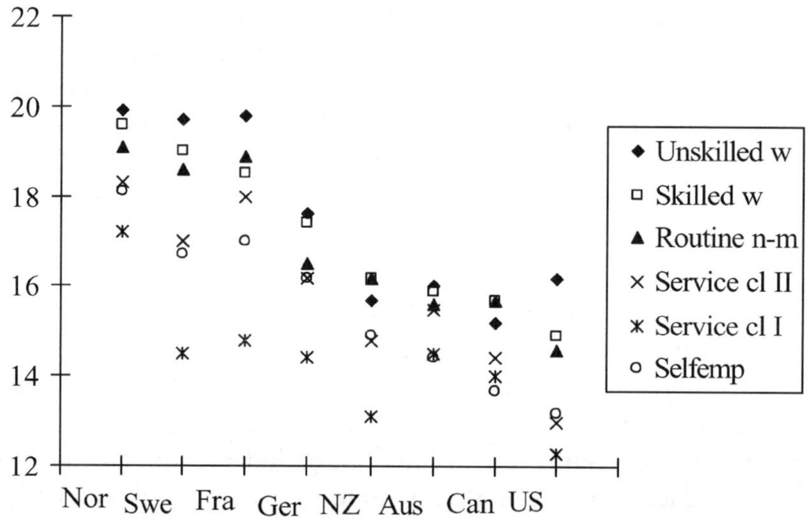

Diagram 1: Index values in different classes.

At the same time we find that the *magnitude* of class differences vary quite substantially between countries. These variations do not follow any demarcations between welfare regimes however. Class differences are comparatively large in Sweden and France and comparatively small in Norway, Australia and Canada. Differences *within* the "regime pairs" are obviously larger than those found *between* them.

What may come across as particularly striking are the large class differences in Sweden, and in particular the low index values among those in Service class I. This indicates that strong support for welfare state measures in Sweden is not extended to this particular group. In fact we have to move to the US and their Service class I to find the only group that is substantially less supportive of state intervention than the higher echelons of employees in Sweden. The contrast to Norway is striking; the differences in aggregate terms between these two Scandinavian countries are more or less an effect of the fact that the higher non-manuals differ so considerably in their attitudes.

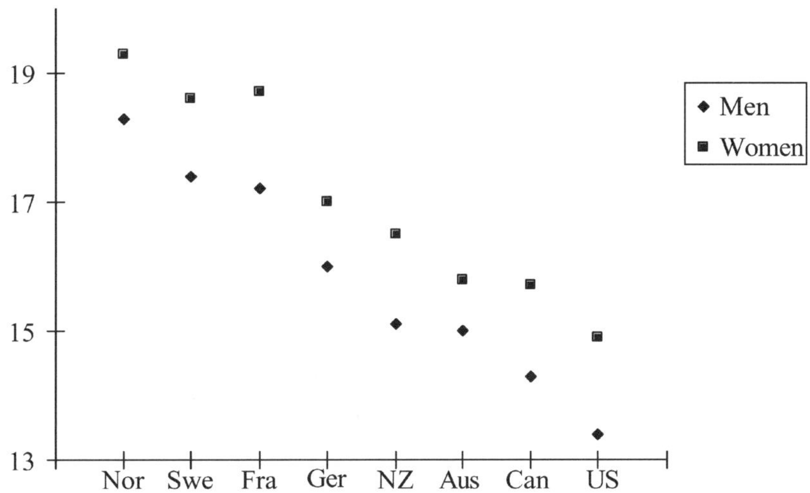

Diagram 2: Index values among men and women.

In Diagrams 2 and 3 we focus on differences between men and women and between groups with different labour market status. As shown, differences between men and women are similar in different countries: women are everywhere more supportive of state intervention than men are. There are no indications that regime differences would create larger gender differences in some places than in others, although gender differences are slightly larger in the "liberal" countries. There is no support for the notion that gender differences would be particularly large in the "social democratic" regime.

In Diagram 3, we find that in all countries those who are neither retired nor unemployed have the weakest support for welfare state intervention. One interesting difference between the countries is that in the two "social democratic" countries pensioners are the most supportive of state intervention while this place is taken by the unemployed in all other countries. There are no signs that the division between "insiders" and "outsiders" should be particularly pronounced in the "conservative" regime; if anything, the opposite is true. Instead we find the largest differences between the unemployed and the "insiders" in New Zealand and the United States.

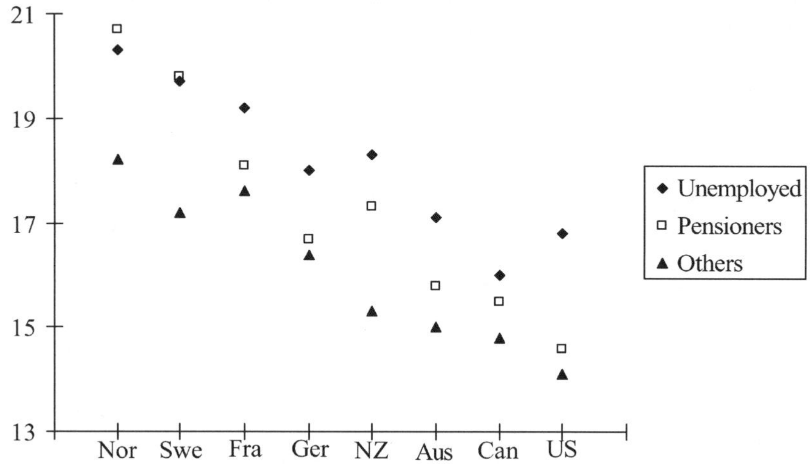

Diagram 3: Index values among unemployed, pensioners and others.

Differences between private and public sector employees (not shown) are completely negligible in most of the countries. It is, as might be expected from the regime discussion, only in Norway and Sweden that some (barely significant) differences occur. Separate analyses for these two countries, where employment sector was included as one variable in multivariate analysis, showed that these sector differences almost disappeared when differences between men and women were held constant. In other respects, results looked virtually identical to those presented in Table III below (cf. Svallfors, 1999a: Table II).

In Table III, then, group differences between men and women, between different classes and between groups with different labour

TABLE III

Government intervention index in different groups in five countries. Multiple classification index. Adjusted means and Betas

	Norway	*Sweden*	*France*	*Germany*	*Australia*	*the US*
Grand mean	18,71	17,89	17,86	16,49	15,19	14,08
Gender	**0,11*****	**0,08****	**0,09****	**0,13*****	**0,11*****	**0,16*****
Men	–0,35	–0.31	–0,32	–0,47	–0,41	–0,87
Women	0,41	0,36	0,50	0,51	0,43	0,82
Class	**0,21*****	**0,35*****	**0,33*****	**0,25*****	**0,13*****	**0,29*****
Unskilled manual	1,04	1,63	1,92	1,13	0,76	2,21
Skilled manual	0,74	1,12	0,77	1,01	0,49	1,33
Routine non-m	0,25	0,42	0,86	–0,26	0,15	0,11
Service class II	–0,32	–0,75	–0,09	–0,38	–0,04	–1,31
Service class I	–1,22	–3,09	–2,87	–1,84	–0,65	–1,62
Selfemployed	–0,51	–1,08	–0,57	–0,03	–0,69	–0,73
Public support	**0,25*****	**0,20*****	**0,07**	**0,06**	**0,11*****	**0,08***
No	–0,45	–0,55	–0,18	–0,06	–0,19	–0,13
Unemployed	1,66	1,05	0,88	1,05	1,82	2,32
Pensioner	1,74	1,60	0,39	–0,05	0,56	0,67
R^2 *(%)*	*13,7*	*19,3*	*13,3*	*8,7*	*4,2*	*10,6*

Levels of significance ***= 0.001-level **= 0.01-level *= 0.05-level

market status have been compared for six of the countries. Because occupation information is missing for those who do not currently work in Canada and New Zealand they have been excluded from the analysis (see appendix).

Table III confirms several of the impressions from the diagrams. The marked class differences in Sweden emerge clearly, just as the comparatively modest ones in Norway, Germany and, in particular, Australia. Clear gender differences are also present in all countries, especially in the US, as are attitude differences between the unemployed and others. That the "public support" variable contributes so much more to the variance in Norway and Sweden than in other countries is because the pensioners display more supportive attitudes towards state intervention here than elsewhere. In Germany and France, differences between groups with different labour market status do not even reach statistical significance.

TABLE IV

Government intervention index in different groups and countries. Multiple classification index. Adjusted means and Betas

Grand mean	16,70
Gender	**0,11*****
Men	–0,45
Women	0,52
Class	**0,24*****
Unskilled manual	1,48
Skilled manual	0,99
Routine non-m	0,25
Service class II	–0,37
Service class I	–1,89
Selfemployed	–0,54
Public support	**0,11*****
No	–0,25
Unemployed	1,41
Pensioner	0,79
Country	**0,35*****
Norway	2,06
Sweden	0,89
France	1,30
Germany	–0,36
Australia	–1,38
USA	–2,53
R^2 (%)	*21,2*

Levels of significance ***= 0.001-level **= 0.01-level *0.05-level

In Table IV all six countries have been included in the same model.[12] Here we find that considerable country differences remain also after taking other factors into account. In fact, country differences are hardly affected at all by holding other variables constant (eta = 0,36; beta = 0,35). The only change is that France, after holding other factors constant emerges as slightly more supportive of welfare policies than Sweden. To give some comparative weight to country differences, we may observe that (the adjusted) differences in scale means between Norway and the US are 4,59, while corresponding differences between unskilled workers and Service class I are 3,37.[13]

To summarise the findings from this section: there is no support for the notion that conflict patterns, as mirrored by attitude differences between different groups should vary in any systematic manner between different welfare regimes. Differences in attitudinal patterns do exist, but they rarely follow the borders between different welfare regimes. Patterns are furthermore quite similar between different welfare regimes. Groups with weaker market position, such as workers, women, and the unemployed are more supportive of welfare state intervention than groups with a stronger market position are.

CONCLUSION

What relevance does the empirical analysis in this paper have for the issue of conflict patterns and group differences in different welfare regimes? Expectations that attitudes towards welfare policies should differ systematically between different welfare regimes receive little support. At an aggregated level large differences are certainly found between the countries. Between the citizens of Norway and those of the US there are considerable differences in the role they want government to play. The rank order between countries is also as could be expected, with "social democratic" countries being the most supportive of state intervention, and "liberal" countries the least with the "conservative" and "radical" countries in between. However, differences within the "regime pairs" are sometimes just as large as between them.

The latter is also the case when we compare group differences across welfare regimes. On the whole, such differences are rather similar in all countries. When interesting differences occur, they rarely follow the demarcation lines between different welfare regimes. Furthermore, such differences hardly ever follow the fault lines suggested by Esping-Andersen and others. Class differences, for example, are larger in Sweden and France than in the "liberal" countries; attitude differences between "insiders" and "outsiders" are smallest in the "conservative" countries; differences between men and women are not larger in the "social democratic" countries than elsewhere. The assertions about how conflict patterns should vary between different welfare regimes get support in one single respect: attitudinal differences between private and public sector employees are larger in Sweden and Norway than in other countries. At the same time these two countries are more marked by class differences and by differences between different labour market statuses than by the gender/sector-based conflict that was suggested as the main fault line.

In relation to previous research the present paper offer both confirmations and refutations. The results that the "social democratic" regime is first and foremost characterised by class differences in attitudes confirm what several other pieces of research has found (Matheson, 1993; Svallfors, 1993, 1997). Matheson's (1993) claim that divisions between "insiders" and "outsiders" are greater in Germany than elsewhere receive no support however. On closer inspection, Matheson's conclusion in this respect receives little support even from his own data and analysis.[14] The results from Svallfors (1997) that patterns of group differences are similar across countries receive support, even if the analysis here has more clearly pointed out that the magnitude of class differences varies across countries.[15]

In conclusion, it seems time to assert that attitudes to welfare policies are only to a very limited extent structured by differences in welfare regimes. A more plausible interpretation is that such differences are structured (a) by general mechanisms, based in the division of labour in capitalist societies, and (b) by nationally specific institutions when it comes to public policies and organised politics. The latter only to a limited extent follow the demarcation lines between different welfare regimes.

In terms of general mechanisms, group differences in attitudes were found to display considerable similarities across nations. Groups with a stronger market position show weaker support for state intervention. Both gender and class differences consistently point in this direction across different welfare regimes. Furthermore, the group with the very weakest market position, the unemployed, displays the very strongest support for state intervention in most of the countries.

In Esping-Andersen (1990) we find perhaps a too strong faith that the welfare state as a stratification system could change such, for a capitalist economy so fundamental, distributional conflict patterns. In relation to the findings here and in other research it would perhaps be more fitting to see the welfare state as one *arena* (among others) where fundamental class and gender conflicts, based in the market stratification and the division of labour, are played out.

This does not, however, mean that the welfare state and other political institutions (as defined in the introduction of the chapter) have no impact in forming attitudes. As shown there are massive differences at an aggregate level between countries in the attitudes towards state intervention. Furthermore, the magnitudes of group differences vary on some points between countries.

In order to understand such country differences, institutions are important to take into consideration. The institutional set-ups of different welfare states lead to different arrangements being perceived as "natural" or "business-as-usual" in, say, the Scandinavian countries compared to the US. These institutional effects are, however, nationally specific in a more complex manner than suggested by the discussion about welfare regimes. The long tradition of free and public health care found in Canada and New Zealand makes these countries different from the US and Australia, and this is something we saw reflected in attitudes among their citizens towards responsibility for health care. The "alternative welfare policy" constituted by the American College system (Hout and Dohan, 1996) makes Americans just as interventionist as citizens of other countries when it comes to economic support for education.

The importance of the institutional heritage also extends beyond welfare policies. The ways in which organised politics have come to mobilise voters, members and sympathisers have important effects for the constitution and dissolution of social divisions. The differences between Sweden and Norway, for example, especially when it comes to attitudes among their higher non-manual employees, can be explained by differences in political articulation. The political right and the employers' federation in Norway have been remarkably low-keyed in their critique of welfare policies. In contrast, their counterparts in Sweden have over the last quarter of a century articulated a far-reaching critique of what is in their view an excessive egalitarianism and over-extended welfare state. Among the higher level employees in Sweden such criticisms have won some support, as shown by their in a comparative perspective strikingly low support for state intervention (Diagram 1).

Differences between the German and the French attitudes may possibly be explained by the peculiarities of the French data (see the Data section). If the French respondents are more interested in political issues than the population at large, this might to some extent explain the clear class differences and comparative strong support for the welfare state found in France.

There are, however, a few key differences between Germany and France in their political organisation and articulation that may give the basis for a more substantive interpretation. In the consensual post-war German model class conflicts and other potential societal divisions have been contained within integrative institutions, in regard to welfare policies, industrial relations and the political system. Furthermore, state intervention has often taken the form of guiding the "social partnership" between interest organisations and other actors in civil society rather than open state intervention (Hancock, 1989; Stjernø, 1995; Streeck, 1997; Jacobi et al., 1998; Weiss, 1998: Ch. 5). The French post-war history instead displays militancy in industrial relations and political party divisions (Gallie, 1983; Levy, 2000), and a long tradition of active state interventionism (Boyer, 1997; Levy, 2000). The relatively strong support for state intervention and the sharp attitude differences we find in the French data may therefore be a contemporary reflection of French political and institutional history.

These arguments are so far only a few brief, and to some extent speculative, examples of the kind of historical and institutional explanations that might lead the way out of the false safety provided by the simplifications of regime typologies. Comparative attitude research needs to become more focussed on how general mechanisms of stratification are modified by nationally specific institutions. The challenge is to be specific enough in analysing national histories and institutions in order to explain attitudinal patterns without getting lost in the multitude of single cases and story-lines. The difficulties of this enterprise are too obvious to merit explication – but who ever said social research should be *easy*?

ACKNOWLEDGEMENT

This chapter is a translated and revised version of "Välfärdsregimer och välfärdsopinioner: en jämförelse mellan åtta västländer", which was published in *Sociologisk forskning*, no. 1, 1999. The research has received economic support from The Board for Social Insurance (RFV), The Swedish Council for Social Research (SFR), The Bank of Sweden Tercentenary Foundation (Riksbankens jubileumsfond) and the Swedish Council for Research in the Social Sciences and Humanities (HSFR). The data used in the paper were made available by Zentralarchiv für empirische Sozialforschung, Köln. Thanks to Francis Castles, Jonas Edlund, Mikael Hjerm, Joakim Palme, Peter Taylor-Gooby and Rune Åberg for their helpful comments, and to Rolf Uher, Janet Harkness, Peter Mohler, Tom Smith, Michel Forse and Sophie Holloway for data and information.

APPENDIX: THE CLASS VARIABLE

The class variable is based on the occupation of the individual, except for those who have never had an occupation, in which case they are given the occupation of their spouse (if any). Pensioners, unemployed, and others who do not presently work are coded according to their last occupation (if any).

In constructing comparable class categories, a number of problems were encountered and strategic decisions made:

- Five different occupational classification schemes were used in the eight countries

Germany, Australia and Canada use the International Standard Classification of Occupations 1988 (ISCO88) on a four-digit level. France uses the same classification, but on a three-digit level (supplemented by a detailed French occupation classification scheme). Norway uses the previous 1968 version of ISCO, on a three-digit level. US uses the same, but on a four-digit level. Sweden uses the Socio-economic Classification (SEI) and the Nordic Occupational Classification (NYK). The former occupation schema is very similar to the Goldthorpe schema, while the latter is a national adaptation of ISCO68.

When reclassifying the ISCO codes into Goldthorpe classes, the reclassifications made by Ganzeboom and Treiman (1996) proved immensely helpful.

These may be downloaded from Harry Ganzeboom's homepage http://www.fsw.ruu.nl/soc/HG. Minor deviations between Ganzeboom's recodings and the ones used here occur, due to national deviancies from the standard ISCO classification or less detailed ISCO information. The deviations seem to be very minor at the level of detail aimed for here. The US data have been recoded from ISCO68 to ISCO88 before creating the class schema. The reclassification from the Swedish occupational classifications were made by Robert Erikson, Jan O Jonsson and Michael Tåhlin at the Swedish Institute for Social Research. The classification used here is not as detailed as theirs, since some of the relevant information is missing from the Swedish ISSP data.

- The question about occupation has in New Zealand and Canada only been posed to those who presently work. These two countries therefore had to be excluded from the multivariate analyses.
- In Germany, all respondents were asked about occupation, but only present occupation (if any) has been reported to the archive. The archived data were therefore matched with data from Zentrum für Umfragen, Methoden und Analysen (ZUMA) in Mannheim, where previous occupation for respondent and spouse were included.
- In the archived file for Australia, no data on spouse's occupation were included. Such information was matched from a file from the Australian National data Archive.

The recoding algorithms that were used can be supplied by the author by e-mail (stefan.svallfors@soc.umu.se).

NOTES

[1] Critiques of the pure rational choice – approach to institutions are found for example in Hall and Taylor (1996) and Rothstein (1996).
[2] In this section, I only summarise the main conclusions and problems of the research on attitude patterns in different welfare regimes. For a more detailed summary of the findings and shortcomings of each individual contribution, see Svallfors, 1999b: pp. 97–99. For a selection of book-length studies on attitudes to welfare policies, see Coughlin (1980); Taylor-Gooby (1985); Svallfors (1989, 1996a); Papadakis (1990); Cook and Barrett (1992); Roller (1992); Jenssen and Martinussen (1994); Borre and Scarborough (1995); Borre and Goul Andersen (1997); Svallfors and Taylor-Gooby (1999).
[3] Here as elsewhere in the paper "Germany" refers to the western Germany, what before 1989 was West Germany. The citizens of former East Germany were exposed to a fundamentally different welfare regime, which is also reflected in the substantial differences between former East Germans and former West Germans in their attitudes to welfare policies and redistribution (Braun and Kolosi, 1994; Roller, 1994).
[4] The selection of countries is identical to the one in Svallfors (1997) with one exception: Austria has been replaced by France. France fielded their first ISSP

survey in 1996 (from which data for this paper is used), while Austria were not able to field the 1996 survey.

[5] For example, anyone interested in comparing attitudes to welfare policies quickly realises that asking about "välfärd" in Sweden and "welfare" in the United States is to pose two entirely different questions. The respondents in Sweden will tell you what they think about pensions, public health care and the social security system. The respondents in the United States will tell you what they think about means-tested programs targeted towards poor people, and they will in most cases also come up with a vague picture of undeserving unwed ghetto mothers or some other highly negative image (Smith, 1987).

[6] The questionnaires may be downloaded from the ISSP page at Zentralarchiv *http://www.za.uni-koeln.de/data/en/issp/* ("ISSP questionnaires in PDF format").

[7] The study description for Australia is missing, but response rates in the ISSP surveys are normally slightly above 60%.

[8] The French data includes a weight variable which makes it possible to make the sample representative in its composition according to gender, age, education level and labour market status. In the analyses, however, unweighted data have been used for the following reasons:

a Such weighting does not guarantee any improvement in *attitudinal* representativity.
b The differences between weighted and

unweighted data are small. On the attitude scale that is used, differences amount to 0,5 on a 24-point scale. Group differences are not affected at all. Indicators of political interest and political participation are not affected by weighting the sample.

c No other country in the paper applies weighting in order to correct bias in non-responses. The only weighting that exists in other countries is to correct differences in sample probabilities (Sweden and Canada, see ISSP96).

[9] "Can't choose" – answers have been excluded. In the original question two items on "provide the industry with the help it needs to grow" and "impose strict laws to make industry do less damage to the environment" were also included. Since these items do not indicate welfare state commitment, and display low correlations with the other items in the table, they have been excluded from further analysis.

[10] The index can vary between 0 and 24 with higher values indicating stronger support for state intervention.

[11] In the literature, Sweden is often presented (mostly by non-domestic observers) as "consensual" or dominated by a "hegemonic Social Democracy'. As will be shown in the analysis, and as have been argued elsewhere, these are labels that would be much more fitting for *Norway* (Svallfors, 1999a).

[12] In order to compensate for the fact that the German and Australian samples are larger than the other ones they have been weighted down to an average (n) of the other four countries. Results for unweighted data are similar to the ones presented

in the table, but class and labour market status differences become somewhat smaller.

[13] The estimates from the table should however not be interpreted quite so precisely, since significant interaction effects occur both between country and class, and between country and labour market status. As shown in Table III, this is because (a) the magnitude of class differences differ between countries and (b) the pensioners attitudes are different in Sweden and Norway compared to other countries.

[14] Labour market status explains only 1,7% of the variance in Matheson's attitude scale, which is less than in the countries he compares with Germany.

[15] Such findings are present also in Svallfors (1997: Table IV) but receive little attention in the text.

Department of Sociology
Umeå University
901 87 Umeå
Sweden

BERNHARD CHRISTOPH and HEINZ-HERBERT NOLL

SUBJECTIVE WELL-BEING IN THE EUROPEAN UNION DURING THE 90S

Welfare is not only a matter of favourable objective conditions – as for example comfortable housing, a healthy environment, good working conditions, educational opportunities and access to public services – but also includes subjective feelings of well-being and appreciation of life: "The quality of life must be in the eye of the beholder" as Angus Campbell (1972) put it once. More recently, Robert E. Lane has emphasised the role of subjective experience as a constitutive element of life quality. "Quality of life is properly defined by the relation between two subjective or person-based elements and a set of objective circumstances. The subjective elements of a high quality of life comprise (1) a sense of well-being and (2) personal development, learning growth. [...] The objective element is conceived as quality of conditions representing opportunities for exploitation by the person living a life" (Lane, 1996: p. 259). Thus there is a consensus among the majority of quality of life researchers to base welfare measurement on both objective and subjective indicators, given the fact "that similar living conditions are evaluated quite differently, that people in bad conditions frequently are satisfied and privileged "persons may be very dissatisfied" (Zapf, 1984: p. 20, authors' translation).

The goal of this chapter is twofold. In the first part there will be a comparative summary description of the development of subjective well-being in EU-countries during the 1990ies. This description will include measures of general life satisfaction as well as data on satisfaction with specific life domains. These are satisfaction with housing, one's job, one's financial situation and with leisure time available. For this analysis we will draw on two databases: several Eurobarometer studies from the nineties provide information on general life satisfaction while data on satisfaction with specific

Social Indicators Research **64:** 521–546, 2003.

life domains are from the ECHP 1996 (a more detailed description of the data is given in the following paragraph).

The second part of the chapter will focus in detail on the two satisfaction items most closely related to individual standard of living: satisfaction with one's housing and with one's financial situation. Throughout this part of the chapter our analysis will mainly concentrate on two questions: first on the relation between subjective well-being and objective conditions on an aggregate (i.e., country-) level and second on the extent to which country differences in subjective well-being might be connected to individual living conditions.

DATA USED

For the analyses on general life satisfaction a series of ten Eurobarometer surveys from the years 1991 to 2000 has been used. Whenever possible we utilised data from the Eurobarometer spring surveys collected sometime between March and May of the respective year. In 1996 and 1999 however, the general life satisfaction item was not available in surveys fielded round this time and therefore other surveys were used.[1]

Since all Eurobarometer surveys include separate samples for Northern Ireland and Great Britain as well as for the eastern and the western part of Germany (in both cases oversampling the smaller of the two), weighted analyses were necessary to obtain representative means for the United Kingdom and Germany. Weighted analyses were also used for calculating overall European means in order to reproduce the actual proportions of the population sizes of all the countries covered.

Examining satisfaction with specific aspects of life we will use the 1996 wave of the European Community Household Panel (ECHP) including 130,693 respondents. This was the most recent panel-wave available for scientific use when the analyses for this article were conducted. We decided to restrict data analyses to this year, since the by then three panel-waves did not seem sufficient to examine developments across time. In addition, no separate results for East and West Germany can be presented, since the ECHP does not include regional (i.e., East/West) information for the Federal Republic of Germany.

THE DEVELOPMENT OF SUBJECTIVE WELL-BEING IN THE 90IES

General Life Satisfaction

Life satisfaction is an indicator that is commonly used to measure general subjective well-being. It is supposed to reflect a cognitive personal evaluation of the total life situation against the background of individual aspirations, expectations and value orientations. Measures of subjective well-being like life satisfaction are by definition only partially determined by external living conditions; they also reflect how the individual citizen perceives and appreciates these circumstances.

In the following, we shall first of all present a descriptive picture of the distribution of general life satisfaction across the EU member states as well as of the respective changes over time. Moreover we shall examine whether specific subgroups of the population are distinctive with respect to their subjective well-being and whether the extent as well as the direction of these subgroup differences deviate from one country to the other.

One underlying question in this volume is to what degree the institutional background in EU-countries influences different aspects of their populations' lifes. In our analysis throughout this chapter we will therefore distinguish three country clusters as described by Vogel (compare chapter 1): the Nordic, the Central and the Southern cluster.

It should be noted that the actual country clustering produced by this classification is comparable to one resulting from a classification that distinguishes welfare state regimes. Therefore it is easy to connect the country groups applied here to those that are constituted according to the four types of welfare state regimes that are usually identified to exist in the European Union (e.g., in European Commission, 2000a): (1) the Nordic cluster is equivalent to the Social-Democratic Welfare States (Denmark, Finland and Sweden), (2) the Central cluster covers (a) the Conservative (Austria, Belgium, France, Germany, Luxembourg and the Netherlands) as well as (b) the Liberal Welfare States (Ireland and the United Kingdom) and (3) the Southern cluster includes the Rudimentary Welfare States (Italy, Greece, Portugal and Spain).

Even though the country groups resulting from both classifications are quite comparable, their theoretical background is somewhat different. The distinction between four different welfare state regimes follows the concept introduced by Esping-Andersen (1990) but supplements the original three regimes by a fourth type for the Southern European countries as discussed by Leibfried (1990) and Esping-Andersen (1999). In contrast to that, the theoretical background of the classification applied here bases the distinction between the clusters on differences in the configuration of welfare delivery systems (market, welfare state and the family) and not on the type of welfare state alone (compare Vogel, 1997).

In the figures provided, the countries of the Nordic cluster are represented by a solid black bar, those of the Central cluster by a black and white one while the bars for the Southern cluster countries are solid grey and the one indicating the EU-average is grey and white.

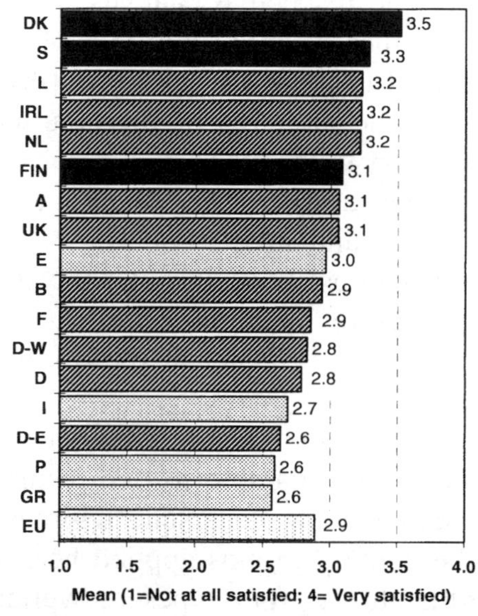

Figure 1. General life satisfaction in EU-countries. Source: Eurobarometer 2000, own calculations.

As can be seen from Figure 1, the differences in life satisfaction across European countries are quite substantial. On average satisfaction scores are highest in Denmark and lowest in Greece.

Figure 1 also shows that no clear-cut association between country clusters and average life satisfaction can be found. While satisfaction in the northern countries, especially in Denmark and Sweden is somewhat higher and the southern countries show amongst the lowest satisfaction levels, no clear inter-group borders can be identified. Thus even though there is a considerable differential in general life satisfaction between northern and southern EU-member states the lines separating country groups appear to be rather weak.

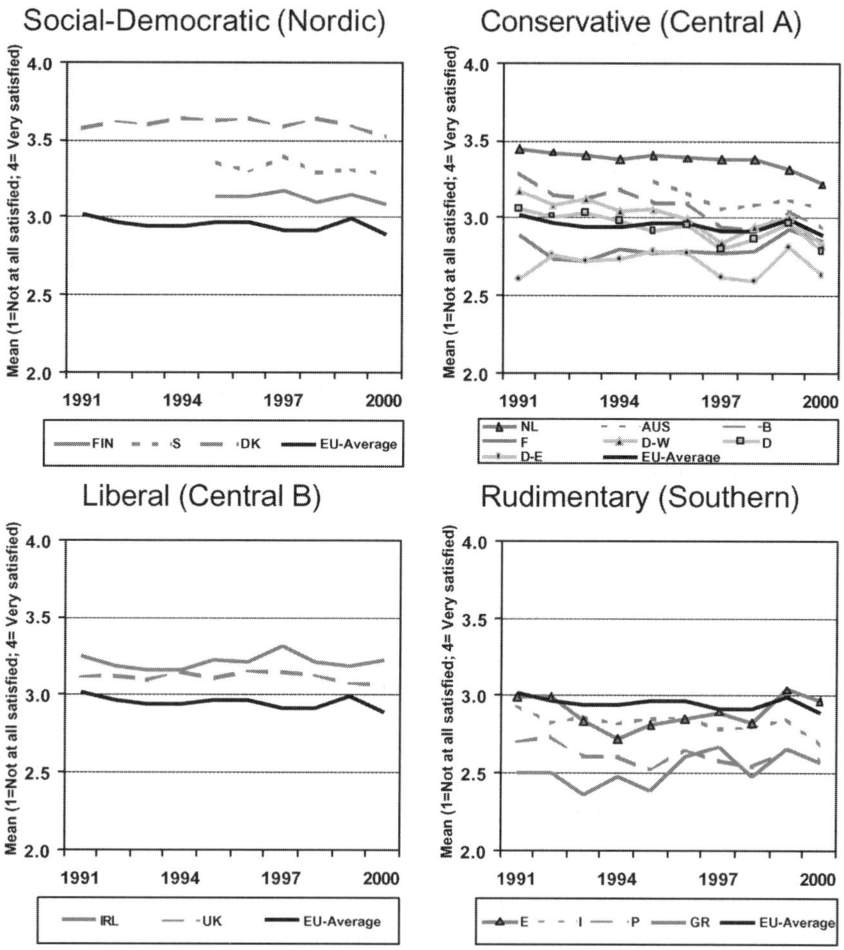

Figure 2. Development of general life satisfaction in the EU. Source: Eurobarometer studies between 1991 and 2000, own calculations.

Comparing developments over time, cluster differences seem to be somewhat more pronounced. Figure 2 displays the national means of general life satisfaction between 1991 and 2000. Since including all data for the Central cluster in one graph would have been somewhat confusing, we decided to arrange this figure by type of welfare state, thus including separate graphs for both groups (the conservative and the liberal welfare states) covered by the Central cluster.

In order to make the results displayed in the four subplots comparable, in each of them the overall mean is indicated by a solid black line. From Figure 2 it becomes obvious that the Social-Democratic and the Liberal welfare states (the latter on a lower level) show above average satisfaction and a rather small variation of values over the entire period.

In contrast to that, general life satisfaction in the Rudimentary Welfare States of the South is generally below average. Only Spain shows some values that are slightly above average, before a steep drop in satisfaction in the early nineties and after a steep rise between 1998 and 1999.[2]

The Conservative Welfare States show a rather heterogeneous pattern with the Netherlands and Austria clearly above, Belgium and Western Germany somewhat around and France and Eastern Germany below the average value.

In sum, a more detailed look at the developments over time leads to the conclusion that the differences in life satisfaction between country groups are more pronounced than they appear considering the 2000 values only. This is not to say however, that there is a causal link between the type of welfare state regime and satisfaction levels. The observed correlation may also be due to other variables, like differences in the general level of living or even cultural differences between the countries in the distinguished clusters.[3]

Differences between Subgroups within Countries

Another important question is whether different population subgroups in the countries at question show different satisfaction levels and whether there are differences with respect to the occurrence or the size of these differences between country clusters.

For general life satisfaction we checked gender differences as well as differences between income quartiles[4] and age groups. As Figure 3 shows, the divergence in satisfaction levels of males and females is almost negligible. Only in Luxembourg and Portugal minor deviations can be found. T-tests show that gender-based differences in the remaining countries are not significant. In contrast to that, the differences in average satisfaction between the top and the bottom income quartiles are particularly high. Life satisfaction obviously increases with the level of income. The highest deviation between income groups is around 0.5 and thus is more than half the size of the maximum distance between country means (which is almost 1.0). However, even though the differences between income quartiles are large, no specific country-pattern can be found.

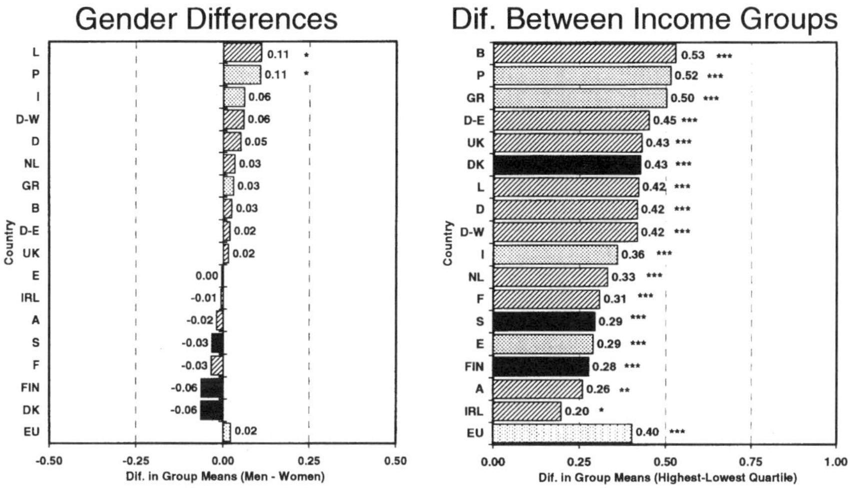

Figure 3. Differences in general life satisfaction between genders and income groups. Source: Eurobarometer 2000, own calculations.

Analysing differences between age groups we compare the most affluent age group (45 to 64) to young adults (20 to 29) and to the elderly (65 and older), following the approach presented by Vogel earlier in this volume (compare chapter 5).

As Figure 4a indicates, the younger respondents show comparably high satisfaction levels in some of the southern countries (Portugal and Greece), but also in France, Finland and Austria. Overall, the young adults seem to be a little bit more satisfied than the reference group of the 45 to 64 olds. In contrast to that, the differences between the reference group and the elderly level off on average. Even though there seems to be a slight tendency for the elderly to be less satisfied than the middle aged in the southern countries, only Portugal shows a significant difference between age groups. On the other side of the scale, the elderly are a little bit more satisfied in Finland, Ireland and France.[5]

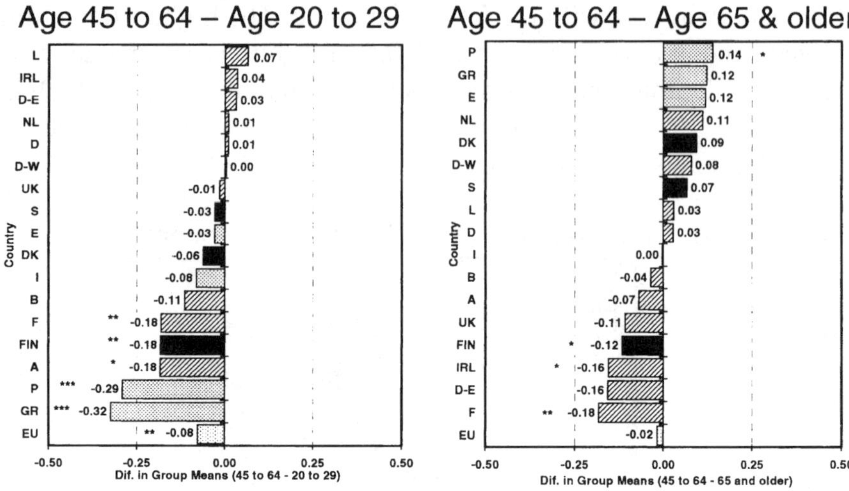

$* = p < 0.05$, $** = p < 0.01$, $*** = p < 0.001$

Figure 4. Differences between age groups. Source: Eurobarometre 2000, own calculations.

Altogether subgroup variations in general life satisfaction are rather small indeed and where some can be found, no specific country patterns are present. The only major differences in life satisfaction appear between the highest and the lowest income quartile, a finding, which demonstrates again that income obviously "does buy satisfaction" as Otis Duncan (1975) put it once.

Satisfaction with Specific Life Domains 1996

After looking at general subjective well-being in terms of life satisfaction, we will now turn to the analysis of satisfaction with four specific life domains: Satisfaction with work, satisfaction with one's own financial situation, satisfaction with housing and satisfaction with leisure time. This analysis will be based on data of the ECHP 1996.[6]

What is most striking about the results presented for all these satisfaction items is that – as in the case of general life satisfaction – the rank orderings for countries all seem to follow the same pattern with North and Central European countries at the top and the southern countries at the bottom end of the scale.

Indeed, as the results for the four satisfaction items displayed in Figure 5 reveal, in three out of four cases the same four countries show the highest average satisfaction: Denmark, Austria, Luxembourg and the Netherlands. Only in the case of satisfaction with leisure time the Netherlands are not among the top four countries, however following closely with a mean-difference of only 0.1. A comparable situation can be found at the bottom end of the scales. For all four satisfaction items the southern countries (Italy, Spain, Portugal and Greece) show the lowest values among all EU countries.

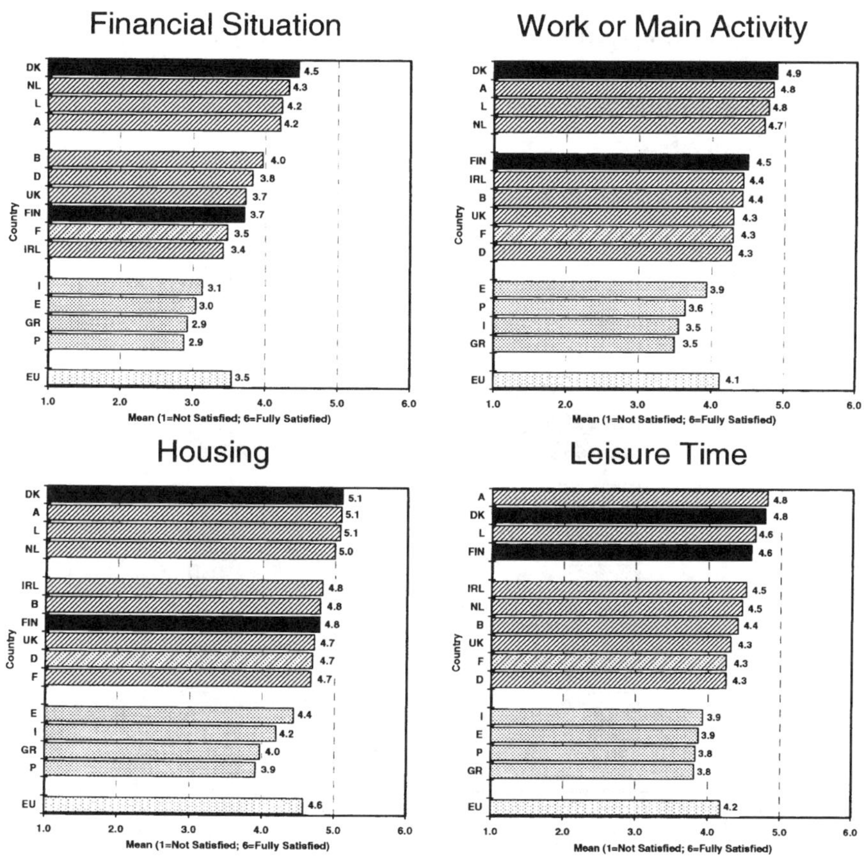

Figure 5. Satisfaction with specific aspects of life. Source: ECHP 1996, own calculations.

The remaining countries (Belgium, Finland, Ireland, the UK, Germany and France) are usually found between these two groups. Values in these countries are generally close to one another, however with the exception of satisfaction with the financial situation, the UK, France and Germany usually make up the bottom end. In the case of Germany one should bear in mind the rather large satisfaction differences between the eastern and the western part of the country which, however, cannot be represented using ECHP data.[7]

Overall Europeans are much more satisfied with their housing, their leisure time and their work than they are with their financial situation. In addition to that, the difference between the most and the least satisfied population is largest in case of satisfaction with the financial situation. It should also be noted that with the exception of the Finnish case, the distinction between a Nordic cluster characterised by high, a Central cluster showing average and a Southern group displaying low satisfaction values adequately reflects the data displayed in Figure 5.

Subgroup Differences in Life Domains

Gender differences in satisfaction are comparably low for all four domains. They are particularly low in the case of satisfaction with housing.

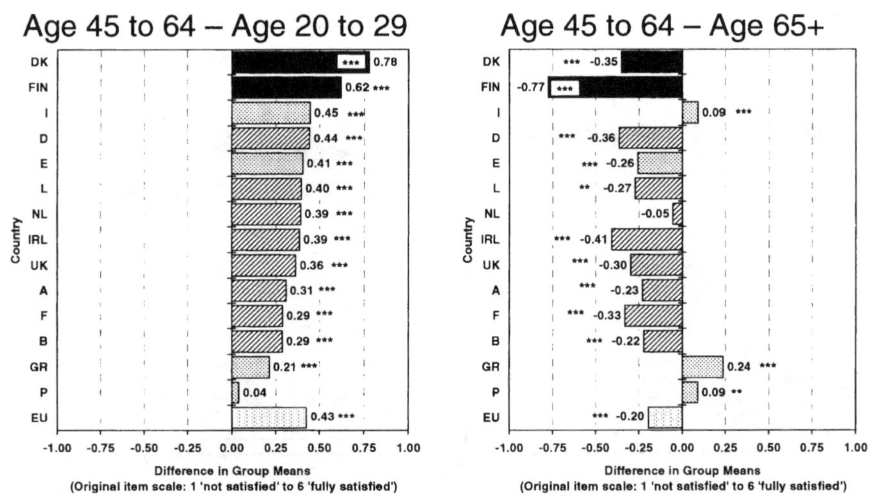

* = $p < 0.05$, ** = $p < 0.01$, *** = $p < 0.001$

Figure 6. Age differences in satisfaction with the financial situation. Source: ECHP 1996, own calculations.

In general there is a tendency for males in the southern countries, especially in Italy, to be somewhat more satisfied than their female counterparts. For some domains higher satisfaction values among females can be found in countries like the UK, Finland (work and financial situation) and Denmark (leisure) (results not displayed).

Differences between age groups turn out to be domain specific. As one would have expected, the persons in the most affluent age group (45 to 64 years of age) are more satisfied with their financial situation than younger people (aged 20 to 29). As Figure 6 displays, this applies to all countries except Portugal (the positive value shown in the figure is not statistically significant). Comparing the former age group to persons at pension age (65 and older) the situation changes. In all countries but in Italy, Greece and Portugal persons in the older age group are more satisfied with their financial situation than the 45 to 64 year olds.

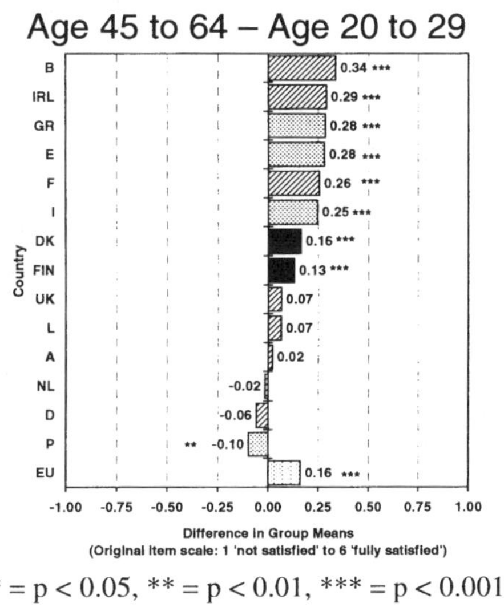

Figure 7. Age differences in satisfaction with work or main activity. Source: ECHP 1996, own calculations.

The fact that elderly persons in these three countries are less satisfied with their financial situation is puzzling, since it has been shown by Vogel (chapter 5) that the income gap between this age group and the middle aged is particularly low in the southern countries. One has to keep in mind however, that satisfaction does not simply reflect objective conditions. As Vogel pointed out, this comparably favourable financial situation of the elderly in the southern countries is mainly due to the fact that people with poor pensions are likely to live in their childrens' home. In that case the affected persons might not consider their own financial situation to be a favourable one, even though their objective financial needs are adequately taken care of in the family context.

Regarding satisfaction with work or main activity we restrict the analysis to a comparison between the two younger generations, since it can be assumed that persons in the oldest age group are already retired. Therefore their answers are not directly comparable to those of people in the working ages.

Looking at the difference between the two remaining age groups displayed in Figure 7 it can be seen that in most of the countries the age group of the 45 to 64 year olds is more satisfied with their work or main activity than the youngest cohort. In the UK, Luxembourg, Austria, the Netherlands and Germany no significant difference can be found while in Portugal the younger cohort shows higher average satisfaction.

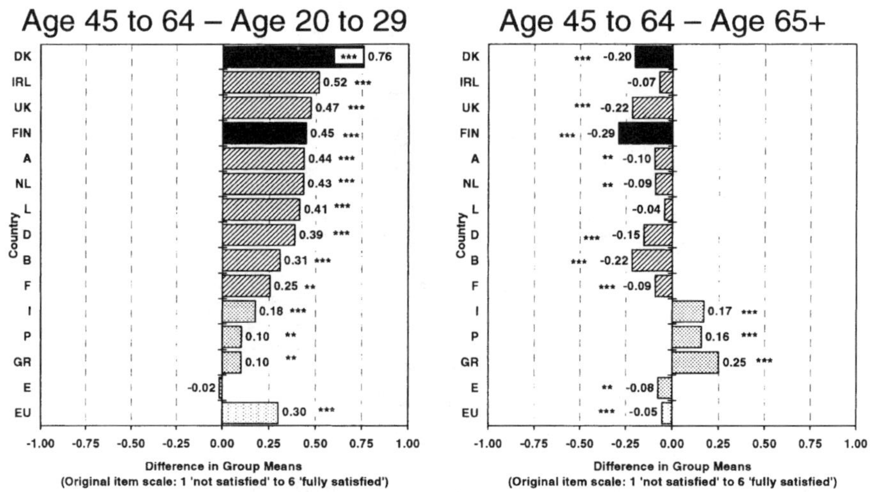

* = p < 0.05, ** = p < 0.01, *** = p < 0.001

Figure 8. Age differences in satisfaction with housing. Source: ECHP 1996, own calculations.

Satisfaction with housing is highest among the elderly in most countries of the European Union (see Figure 8) while the youngest age group usually shows the lowest satisfaction level. Only Italy, Portugal and Greece depart from this general pattern. For all these three countries satisfaction levels of the oldest cohort are lower than those for the 45 to 64 year olds. In the case of Portugal and Greece satisfaction of the elderly is even below that of the youngest age group. This result may at least in part reflect the more rapid improvement of living conditions in these countries, from which the younger generations may have profited most.

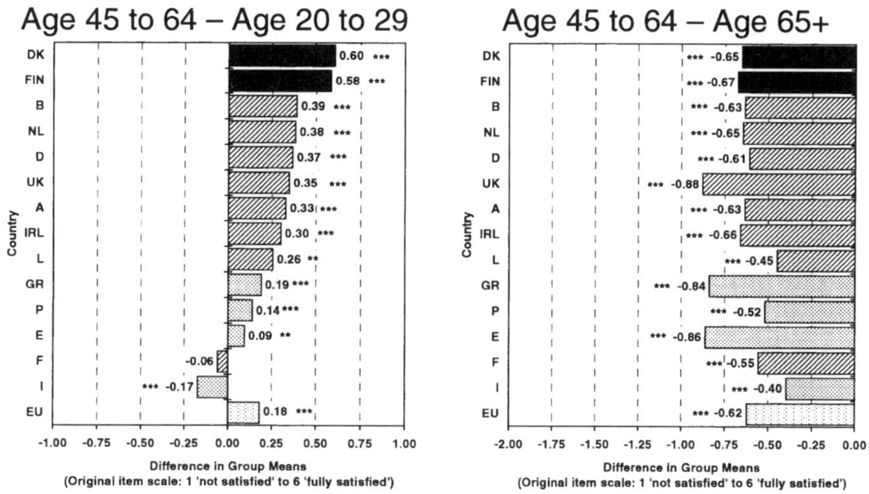

* = p < 0.05, ** = p < 0.01, *** = p < 0.001

Figure 9. Age differences in satisfaction with amount of leisure time. Source: ECHP 1996, own calculations.

In comparison to the age group 45–64 the younger people are less satisfied with the amount of leisure time that is available to them (Figure 9). Only the young Italians are somewhat more satisfied with leisure time than the middle aged and no significant difference between both age groups can be found in France.

The highest satisfaction with the amount of leisure time available is found, however, among people aged 65 and over. This result comes not surprisingly since normally people in this age group are retired and thus the amount of leisure time they have at their discretion should in fact be larger than that available to people in the working ages.

As far as the differences between the well-off and the poorer people in a society are concerned, it can be shown, that in most cases the former display larger satisfaction levels than the latter. Since the satisfaction items are either directly (as in case of the financial situation) or at least closely (work and housing) connected to the respondents' material circumstances this is not much of a surprise. Only in the case of satisfaction with leisure time there is no obvious theoretical connection to a person's material standing and, as we will see, this fact is also reflected by the empirical results.

Using income quintiles of disposable income, average satisfaction of the people in the highest quintile can be compared to the corresponding values of respondents in the lowest quintile.[8]

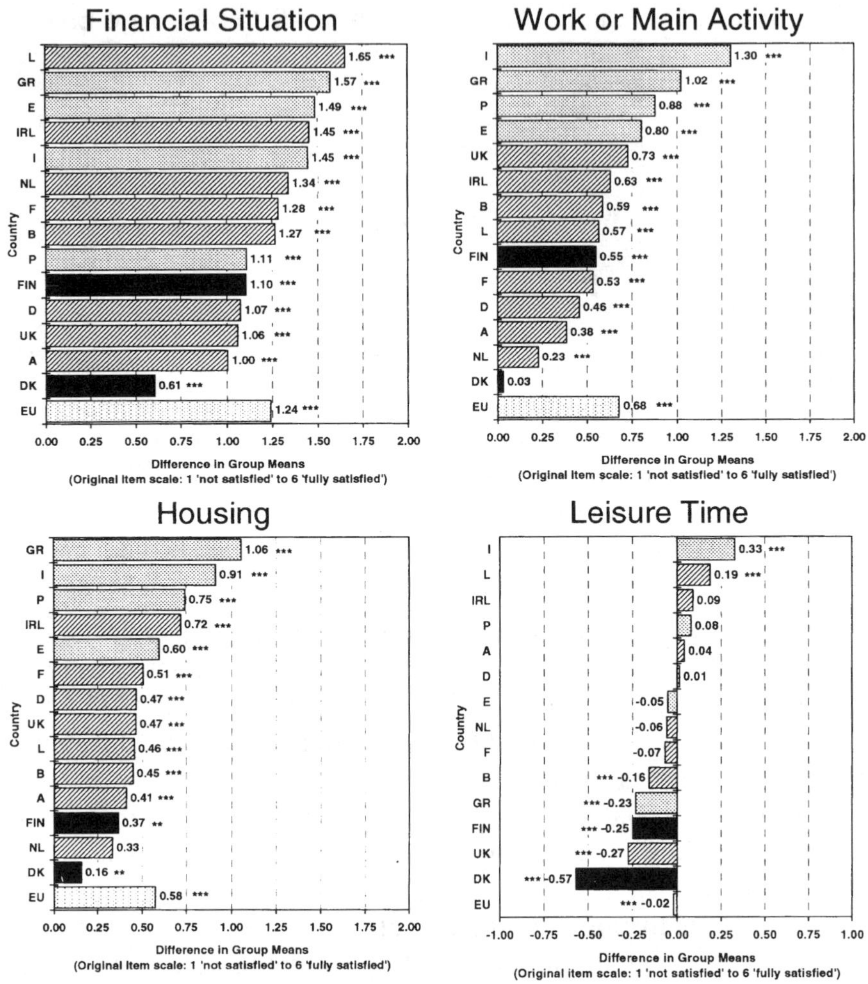

* = p < 0.05, ** = p < 0.01, *** = p < 0.001

Figure 10. Differences in satisfaction between income quintiles. Source: ECHP 1996, own calculations.

Figure 10 exhibits the rather large differences in average satisfaction between high and low income respondents. Looking at satisfaction with work, housing and the financial situation, people in the highest quintile are on average much more satisfied than their less well-off fellow citizens. The actual size of the difference however varies greatly from a (non-significant) 0.03 in the case of satisfaction with work in Denmark to a difference as large as 1.65, that can be found in the case of satisfaction with the financial situation in Luxembourg. In all three cases the differences between income groups are smaller in northern and central European countries like Denmark, Austria or the Netherlands and larger in the southern states Greece, Spain, Italy and Portugal. Nevertheless differences are not at all clear-cut and exceptions from this rule are to be found as well, like e.g., the comparatively low differences in Portugal or the pronounced ones in Luxembourg in case of satisfaction with the financial situation.

The situation is somewhat different for satisfaction with the amount of leisure time. In this case, in most of the countries satisfaction of the lower income group is either higher than among persons in the upper quintile or the difference is statistically not significant. Only in Italy and Luxembourg the better-off persons are also more satisfied with the amount of leisure time they have at their discretion.

Summing up there are clear differences in satisfaction with life domains between country clusters. With the exception of Finland on the level of general means the values follow the expected rank ordering, with the countries of the Nordic cluster showing the highest satisfaction, the Central cluster being in between and the Southern cluster having the lowest average satisfaction.

Examining the disaggregations however, no clear-cut distinction between country clusters is possible. In the case of gender differences there are hardly any and in the case of age groups and income quintiles rank orderings are by and large item specific.

HOW TO EXPLAIN SATISFACTION DIFFERENCES IN THE EUROPEAN UNION?

Looking at the diversity in satisfaction levels between countries within the European Union and the respective, rather stable patterns, the question arises, how these differences might be explained. The respective literature offers various explanations for satisfaction-differences between the populations of different countries: they might first of all be caused by unequal objective living conditions, but could also reflect specific national characteristics, like e.g., cultural traits and value orientations or could even be due to a particular kind of national response behaviour (for an overview of arguments compare Veenhoven, 1997). Thus one related question is, whether between country differences might be connected either with aggregate measures of the countries' characteristics or with distinctive attributes of the individual respondents, in particular their objective situation measured at the micro level.

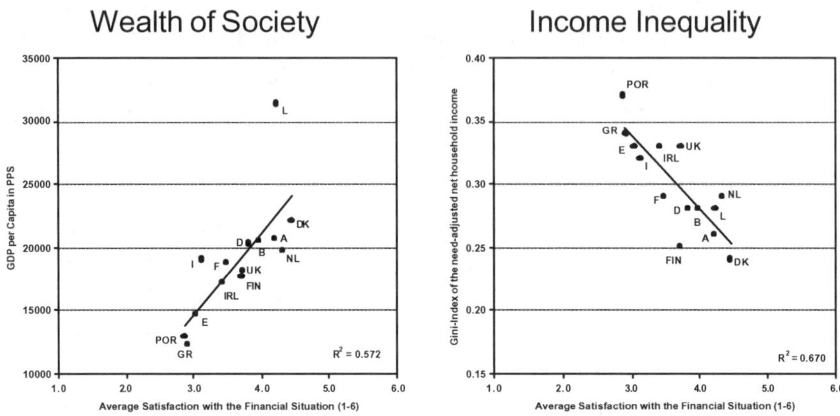

Figure 11. Aggregate level determinants of satisfaction with the financial situation. Source: ECHP 1996, own calculations/European Commission 2000.

Analysing aggregate data we observe a clear correlation between satisfaction levels in life domains and measures of the prosperity as well as the level of income inequality encountered in a society. Figures 11 and 12 exemplify this relationship for satisfaction with the financial situation and satisfaction with housing. It can be seen that satisfaction levels are usually higher in more wealthy countries (wealth being measured by the GDP per capita[9]) and lower in societies that are characterised by a higher level of income inequality (measured by the Gini-coefficient of disposable income).

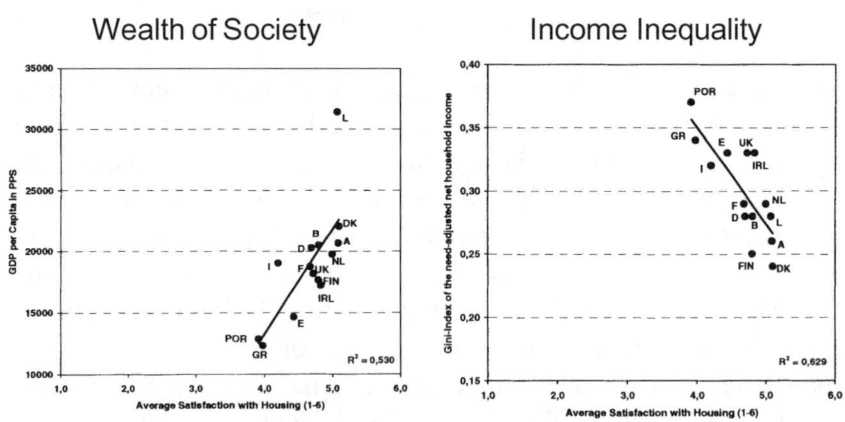

Figure 12. Aggregate level determinants of satisfaction with housing. Source: ECHP 1996, own calculations/European Commission 2000.

In general the association between satisfaction measures and the Gini-coefficient is larger than that found between satisfaction and the Gross Domestic Product. One reason for that are the comparably high GDP figures in Luxembourg that influence results.

It can also be seen from the figures that the association with both aggregate measures is considerably stronger in the case of satisfaction with the financial situation. Results for the other two satisfaction items are close to those presented here and are therefore not displayed separately.

However, looking at aggregate measures does not provide information on the associations existing at the individual level. Even though persons in wealthier countries tend to be more satisfied, this does not necessarily imply that within each country wealthier persons are more satisfied than those being less well-off. Thus the question arises, whether the relationships observed at the aggregate level hold true at the individual level as well. In order to receive a more accurate idea of the processes taking place at the individual level, multivariate microdata-analysis will be applied. As in the case of aggregate measures this analysis will be restricted to satisfaction with housing and satisfaction with the financial situation.

Influences of Objective Living Conditions on Satisfaction at the Individual Level

Evaluating the results of individual level analysis, the major question is, to what extent differences in objective living conditions in EU member states as well as in the composition of their population might have an influence on the differences in satisfaction found between them. In order to answer this question, in a first step several groups of possible determinants will be identified. In a second step we will examine the extent to which these influence variables contribute to the diversity of satisfaction levels found throughout Europe. This is done by comparing the country effects of a series of multiple regression models.

In the context of the following analyses we will distinguish three possible groups of determinants: First we will look at general social and demographic background variables. These are age, gender, marital status, education, employment status, foreign nationality (relative to the country of residence) and the presence of dependent children in the household. Since disposable income should have a particularly strong influence on both satisfaction items it is analysed as a separate 'group' of influence variables along with a quadratic income term that takes into account that – according to the law of diminishing returns – the positive influence of income on the two satisfaction items is supposed to become smaller for larger incomes. In a third step specific variables determining either satisfaction item will be controlled.

Influences on Satisfaction with Housing

In addition to the variables discussed above the following were assumed to influence satisfaction with housing. First of all there is the living space available and the quality of housing conditions. The former is measured by the number of rooms per person in the household. The latter comprises two indices, one for housing amenities like e.g., that there is a bath or a place to sit outside (e.g., a terrace) and a second one for the amount of problems the respondents have with their present accommodation.[10]

In addition it is controlled, whether respondents live in a single house (rather than in an apartment), own the housing they live in, whether they consider housing costs to be a financial burden for them and whether they perceive crime or vandalism in the area.[11]

Figure 13 shows the estimated differences in satisfaction with housing in comparison to the French values if different groups of influence variables are controlled for.[12] There are two important results that can be drawn from the figure. First, looking at the Coefficients of Determination (R^2) we see that the control variables employed in the models explain much more of the variance in the individuals' satisfaction with housing than the country variables alone. While the latter explain roughly 10 percent of this variation, the last model which controls for all the determinants explains about 30 percent.

It can also be seen from the figure that the overall differences between countries are significantly reduced by controlling for the different groups of influence variables. The maximum difference decreases from an initial value of 1.22 (between Denmark and Portugal) to 0.81 (between Austria and Greece) after controlling for all the variables included into the fourth model.

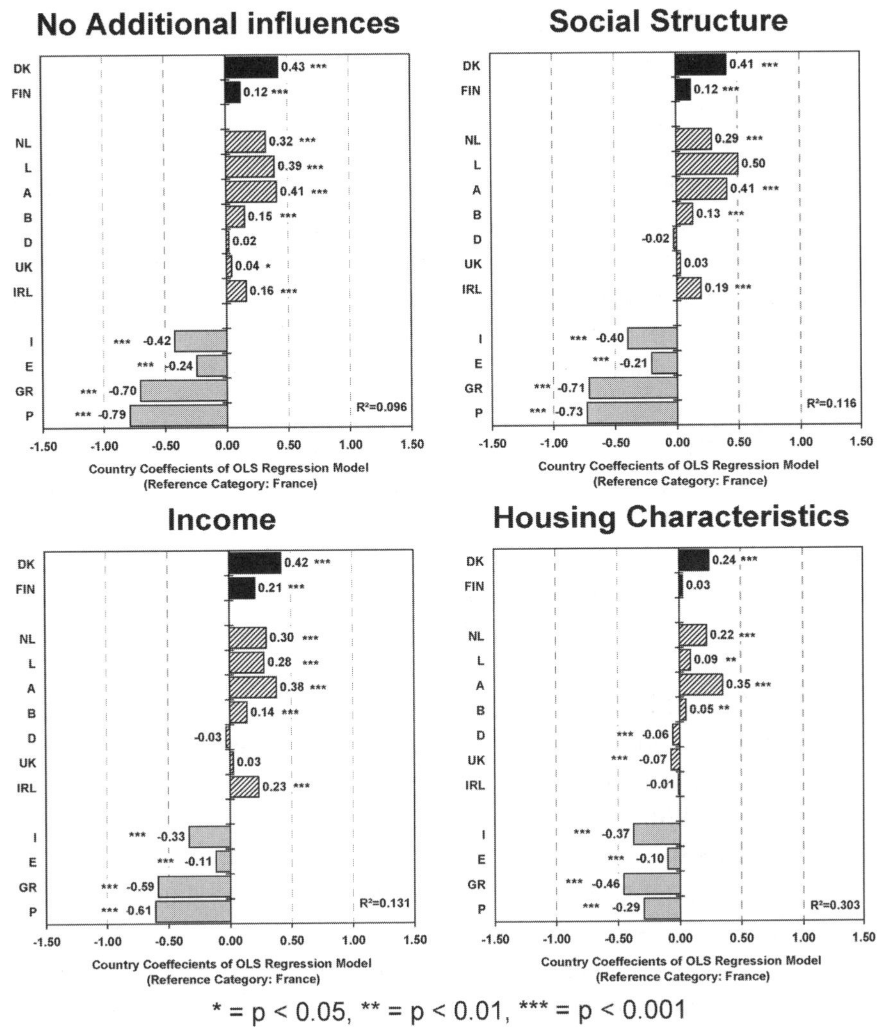

Figure 13. Estimated country-differences in satisfaction with housing controlling for selected influence variables. Source: ECHP 1996, own calculations.

In some countries like for example Portugal or Luxembourg a particular high amount of the difference to the comparison group is explained by income and housing characteristics. Others however, like for example the Netherlands or Austria show almost stable differences in all four models. Thus, even though it seems that some aspects of satisfaction with housing can be explained by objective differences between EU-countries, a quite significant level of intra-country differences prevails.

Influences of Objective Living Conditions on Satisfaction with the Financial Situation

It seems to be quite plausible to assume that subjective satisfaction with the financial situation is strongly related to the objective material situation of the respondents,[13] which is mainly made up by two components, the respondents' income and their material living circumstances. The latter are measured using three indices, one for (consumer-)goods owned by the household, one for its standard of living in terms of items of everyday life the household can afford and a third one indicating, whether the household faces financial problems or not.[14]

All three indices are included in the fourth model. In addition it is controlled, whether the household was able to save some money in the preceding year. The other three models are comparable to those calculated for satisfaction with housing. The first one includes no additional control variables, in the second the social structure variables are added and the third additionally includes the two income terms.

Figure 14 displays the results of the regression models. As in the case of satisfaction with housing, a much larger part of the variation in the individuals' satisfaction with their financial situation (37.4 percent) is explained by considering all possible influences than by including only the country variables (12.9 percent).

Focusing on country differences we see that the distance between the most and the least satisfied country is almost cut in half (from 1.61 to 0.81) when controlling for all possible determinants. Especially the relative position of the southern countries is significantly improved when controlling for income and the material situation indices, particularly in the case of Greece.

The enormous increase in this latter case can be explained by the exceptionally high percentage of people in Greece that have a low standard of living or that face financial problems of one or the other kind. 50.3 percent of the Greek population can only afford two or less items of the standard of living index. Only Portugal has comparably low values (37.3 percent) while for the rest of the countries the percentage is between 10 and 16 (Finland, Italy and Spain) or below 10 percent (other countries). Likewise 46.6 percent of the Greeks have a value of one or higher on the index for financial problems. In comparison to that almost 21.4 percent of the Finnish population are in a comparable situation, whereas the percentages for all other countries are below 13 percent.

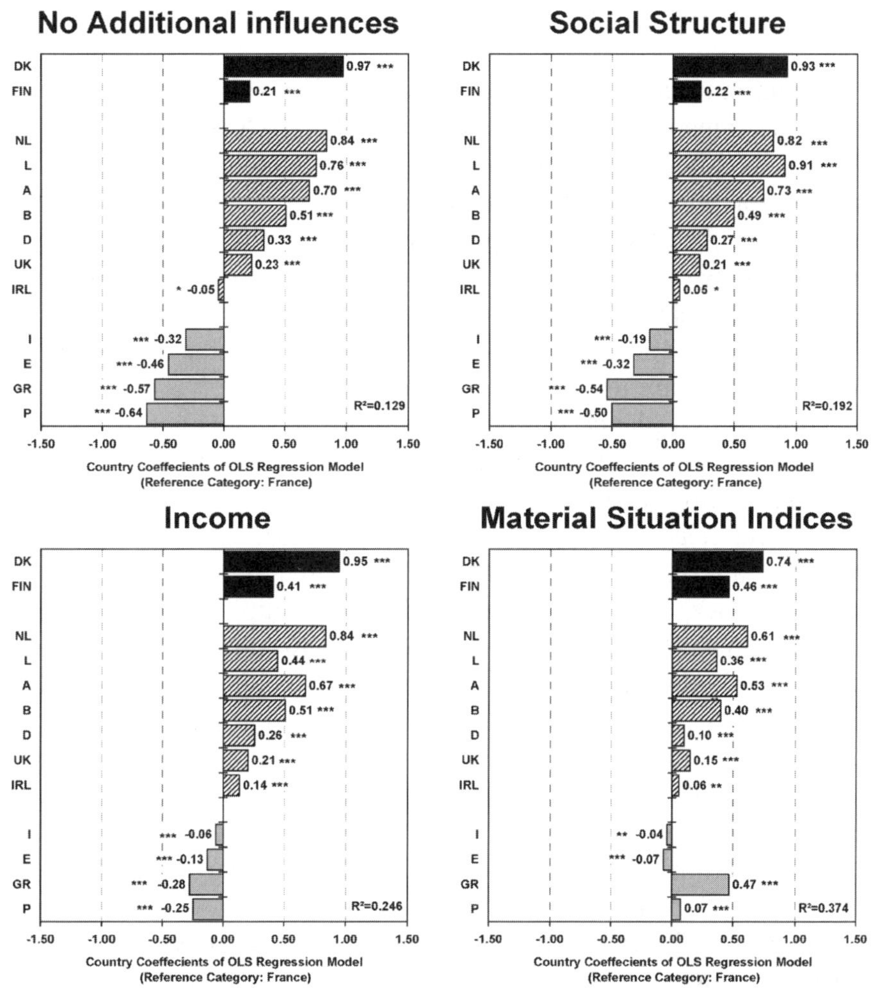

$* = p < 0.05$, $** = p < 0.01$, $*** = p < 0.001$

Figure 14. Estimated country-differences in satisfaction with the financial situation controlling for selected influence variables. Source: ECHP 1996, own calculations.

Thus, the particularly low satisfaction with the financial situation in Greece and to a lesser extent in the other countries of the Southern cluster largely resembles the bad objective conditions encountered by the population in these countries. However, the differences in satisfaction in the EU that remain even after controlling for deviations in objective conditions are still considerable.

SUMMARY AND CONCLUSIONS

There are substantial differences in subjective well-being across the member states of the European Union. This is true in the case of general well-being – as measured by life satisfaction – as well as for satisfaction with specific life domains.

Overall, these differences observed within the European Union are following a pronounced pattern with northern European countries usually showing the highest and countries in the South displaying the lowest satisfaction scores, while the countries of central Europe are usually found in between.

Thus, at first glance it seems that subjective satisfaction follows the pattern of country clusters as it was introduced by Vogel. However, taking a second look this assertion might be questioned for several reasons: first of all, there are clear exceptions to that general pattern, Finland being a quite obvious example, in the case of general satisfaction as well as regarding domain specific satisfaction values. Secondly, differences between subgroups follow hardly any consistent pattern. Thus, it might be doubted whether the observed country differences reflect common characteristics of country clusters.

The final part of this chapter focused on causes of differences in satisfaction across societies at the individual level. Analysis revealed that satisfaction levels are to a large extent due to the objective living conditions of the individual citizens in the respective country, since satisfaction differences diminish substantially after controlling for corresponding variables. On the other hand a considerable amount of the differences in subjective well-being remains unexplained. Thus there is good reason to assume that both, objective living conditions as well as factors like value orientations, national characteristics or cultural traits are needed to explain differences in satisfaction.

NOTES

[1] In 1996 the Eurobarometer 44.2_bis study, fielded in February, has been used. In 1999 the only data set available including general life satisfaction

was fielded in October/November. Results covering these years should thus be interpreted cautiously, since seasonal effects might occur. In addition it should be mentioned that the 44.2_bis study is different from the rest of the surveys used, to the extent that it has a much larger sample size (overall it includes 65,178 respondents while the respective number for the other surveys is between 13,121 and 19,477). Detailed information on Eurobarometer surveys is available at the Central Archive for Empirical Social Research (ZA) in Cologne (http://www.gcsis.org/en/data_service/eurobarometer/index.htm).

[2] Please note that the time between these two surveys is 18 months rather than a year, since the 1999 data were collected in October/November, while most of the other data (including those for 1998) have been collected in spring (compare the data description above for details). Thus assuming a continuous process, 1999 spring time data might have shown a somewhat lower incline.

[3] On attempts to explain European differences in life satisfaction see for example Inglehart and Rabier (1986), Inglehart (1989), Veenhoven (1994), Noll (1997), Inglehart and Klingemann (2000).

[4] In our analyses of Eurobarometer data we used the harmonised household income quartiles included in the datasets. We preferred this to the alternative, which would have been to calculate quintiles from a grouped income variable. Since this variable covered only 10 income groups we did not consider this an appropriate procedure. Please note that the Eurobarometer household income figures are not need adjusted.

[5] Please note that during the weighting procedure the number of cases for the East German subsample is weighted down in order to put the number of cases in the right proportion to that of its West German counterpart (which is roughly 1:4). This might have an influence on the results of statistical significance testing. If unweighted analysis of the data is performed the t-test for this age difference in East Germany renders significant results.

[6] Please note that the questions discussed here were not covered by the Nordic surveys used to supplement ECHP data in other parts of this volume. Therefore it was not possible to cover Sweden and Norway in the ECHP-based analyses in this chapter, since there are no data available for these countries in the ECHP waves 1 to 3.

[7] For detailed results on life satisfaction and satisfaction with various life domains in West- and East-Germany based on the German Welfare Surveys see Habich et al. (1999) and the respective articles in Datenreport 1999 and Datenreport 2002: on general life satisfaction see Bulmahn (2000, 2002), an overview of satisfaction with life domains is given in Habich and Noll (2000) and in Christoph (2002), for differences concerning the labour market see Noll (2000), information on satisfaction with housing conditions can be found in Berger-Schmitt (2000a, b) and on satisfaction with amount of leisure time see Schöb (2000). A good documentation of differences regarding income-related measures is included in Hanesch et al. (2000).

[8] Speaking of disposable income we refer to a need adjusted net household income. Household income is computed by summing incomes from all sources (such as e.g. work, social transfers etc.) and of all persons in the household. Need adjustments are made using the OECD modified scale, weighting the first adult

in the household by 1, further persons aged 14 or older by 0.5 and children under 14 years of age by 0.3. All income quintiles have been calculated relative to the respective countries' income distributions.

[9] Data Source for GDP-figures: European Commission (2000b: p. 215).

[10] The index for housing amenities has values from 0 to 5. One is added for each of the following features that is present in the dwelling: a separate kitchen; a bath or a shower; an indoor flushing toilet; hot running water; a place to sit outside. The item 'heating or electric storage heaters' was not included in the index since its importance varies greatly between northern and southern member countries. The index for problems with the accommodation has values from 0 to 7. It was coded in a manner that high values indicate a positive situation. Therefore one is added for each of the following problems that is **not** present: shortage of space; noise from neighbours or from outside; not enough light; lack of adequate heating facilities; leaky roof; damp walls, floors etc.; rot in window frames or floors.

[11] Another question whether there is pollution by traffic or industry was also tested. Since it did not show a significant influence on housing satisfaction, the variable was not included in the model.

[12] Results shown are the country coefficients of four OLS-Regression models. Countries were coded as dummy variables. If a set of dummy variables is used in regression analysis, it is necessary to drop one of them from the model so that it can be used as a reference category. We decided to use France, because the French values were in both cases closest to the European average (compare Figure 5). The first model includes no control variables. In the other models the groups of control variables discussed above are consecutively added to the model (thus that the fourth model includes all control variable discussed).

[13] Parts of this paragraph have been published previously in German (Christoph, 2001).

[14] The index for consumer-goods available to household members has values from 0 to 7. One is added for each of the following goods owned by the household: a car; a colour TV; a video recorder; a microwave oven; a dishwasher; a telephone; a second home.

The index for the standard of living has values from 0 to 6. One is added to the index for each of the following items the household can afford: keep the home adequately warm; a week's annual holiday away from home; replace worn-out furniture; buy new, rather than second-hand clothes; eat fish, meat or chicken every second day; have friends or family for drink/dinner once a month.

The index for financial problems has values from 0 to 4. One is added if during the preceding year the household was unable to pay any of the following: rent for the accommodation; mortgage payments; utility bills; installments or other loan repayments.

REFERENCES

Berger-Schmitt, R.: 2000a, 'Wohnen', In: Statistisches Bundesamt in Zusammenarbeit mit WZB und ZUMA (eds.), Datenreport 1999 (Bundeszentrale für politische Bildung, Bonn), pp. 500–511.

Berger-Schmitt, R.: 2000b, 'Wohnqualität in Ostdeutschland 1990–1998. Annäherung an westdeutsches Niveau bei nur geringen Verbesserungen für einkommensschwache Haushalte', Informationsdienst Soziale Indikatoren (ISI) 23, p. 11–13.

Bulmahn, T.: 2000, 'Globalmaße des subjektiven Wohlbefindens', In: Statistisches Bundesamt in Zusammenarbeit mit WZB und ZUMA (eds.), Datenreport 1999 (Bundeszentrale für politische Bildung, Bonn), pp. 420–430.

Bulmahn, T.: 2002, 'Globalmaße des subjektiven Wohlbefindens', In: Statistisches Bundesamt in Zusammenarbeit mit WZB and ZUMA (eds.), Datenreport 2002 (Bundeszentrale für politische Bildung, Bonn), pp. 431–441.

Campbell, A.: 1972, 'Aspiration, satisfaction and fulfilment', In: A. Campbell and P.E. Converse (eds.), The Human Meaning of Social Change (Russell Sage Foundation, New York), pp. 441–446.

Christoph, B.: 2001, 'Wohlstand wichtiger als Einkommen für die Zufriedenheit mit der finanziellen Situation. Untersuchungen zur Zufriedenheit mit der finanziellen Situation im europäischen Vergleich', Informationsdienst Soziale Indikatoren (ISI) 26, pp. 12–15.

Christoph, B.: 2002, 'Zufriedenheit in Lebensbereichen', In: Statistisches Bundesamt in Zusammenarbeit mit WZB und ZUMA (eds), Datenreport 2002 (Bundeszentrale für politische Bildung, Bonn), pp. 442–452.

Duncan, O.D.: 1975, 'Does money buy satisfaction?', Social Indicators Research 2, pp. 267–274.

Esping-Andersen, G.: 1990, The Three Worlds of Welfare Capitalism (Polity Press, Cambridge).

Esping-Andersen, G.: 1999, Social Foundations of Postindustrial Economies (Oxford University Press, Oxford).

European Commission: 2000a, The Social Situation in the European Union 2000 (Office for Official Publications of the European Communities, Luxembourg).

European Commission: 2000b, Eurostat Yearbook. A Statistical Eye on Europe. Data 1988–1998 (Office for Official Publications of the European Communities, Luxembourg).

Habich, R., H.-H. Noll: 2000, 'Zufriedenheit in Lebensbereichen', In: Statistisches Bundesamt in Zusammenarbeit mit WZB und ZUMA (eds.), Datenreport 1999 (Bundeszentrale für politische Bildung, Bonn), pp. 431–442.

Habich, R., H.-H. Noll, W. Zapf: 1999, 'Subjektives Wohlbefinden in Ostdeutschland nähert sich westdeutschem Niveau. Ergebnisse des Wohlfahrtssurveys 1998', Informationsdienst Soziale Indikatoren (ISI) 22, pp. 1–6.

Hanesch, W., P. Krause, G. Bäcker, M. Maschke, B. Otto: 2000, Armut und Ungleichheit in Deutschland. Der neue Armutsbericht der Hans-Böckler-Stiftung, des DGB und des paritätischen Wohlfahrtsverbands (Rowohlt, Hamburg).

Inglehart, R.: 1989, Kultureller Umbruch. Wertewandel in der westlichen Welt (Campus Verlag, Frankfurt a.M./New York).

Inglehart, R., H.D. Klingemann: 2000, 'Genes, culture, democracy, and happiness', In: E. Diener and E.M. Suh (eds.), Culture and Subjective Well-being (The MIT Press, Cambridge, MA), pp. 165–183.

Inglehart, Ronald, J.-R. Rabier, 1986, 'Aspirations adapt to situations. But why are the Belgians so much happier than the French? A cross-cultural analysis of the subjective quality of life', In: F.M. Andrews (ed.), Research on the Quality of Life (University of Michigan, Ann Arbor), pp. 1–56.

Lane, R.E.: 1996, 'Quality of life and quality of persons: A new Role for government', In: Avner Offer (ed.), In Pursuit of the Quality of Life (Oxford University Press, Oxford), pp. 256–293.

Leibfried, S.: 1990, 'Sozialstaat Europa? Integrationsperspektiven europäischer Armutsregimes', Nachrichtendienst des Deutschen Vereins für öffentliche und private Fürsorge 70, pp. 295–305.

Noll, H.-H.: 1997, 'Wohlstand, Lebensqualität und Wohlbefinden in den Ländern der Europäischen Union', In: S. Hradil and S. Immerfall (eds.), Die westeuropäischen Gesellschaften im Vergleich (Leske + Budrich, Opladen), pp. 431–473.

Noll, H.-H.: 2000, 'Arbeitsmarkt und Erwerbstätigkeit', In: Statistisches Bundesamt in Zusammenarbeit mit WZB und ZUMA (eds.), Datenreport 1999 (Bundeszentrale für politische Bildung, Bonn) pp. 480–489.

Schöb, A.: 2000, 'Gesellschaftliche Beteiligung und Freizeit', In: Statistisches Bundesamt in Zusammenarbeit mit WZB und ZUMA (eds.), Datenreport 1999 (Bundeszentrale für politische Bildung, Bonn), pp. 480–489.

Veenhoven, R.: 1994, 'Is happiness a trait? Test of the theory that a better society does not make people any happier', Social Indicators Research 32(2), pp. 101–160.

Veenhoven, R.: 1997, Advances in Understanding Happiness. [http://www.eur.nl/fsw/research/happiness/97c-ab.htm]. (Previously published in French in: Revue Québécoise de Psychologie 18, pp. 267–293).

Vogel, J.: 1999, 'The European 'welfare mix': Institutional configuration and distributive outcome in Sweden and the European Union. A longitudinal and comparative Perspective', Social Indicators Research 48(3), pp. 245–297.

Zapf, W.: 1984, 'Individuelle Wohlfahrt: Lebensbedingungen und wahrgenommene Lebensqualität', In: Wolfgang Glatzer and Wolfgang Zapf (eds.), Lebensqualität in der Bundesrepublik. Objektive Lebensbedingungen und subjektives Wohlbefinden. (Frankfurt a. M., Campus, pp. 13–26).

Centre for Survey Research and Methodology (ZUMA)
P.O. Box 122155
68072 Mannheim
Germany

JOACHIM VOGEL

TOWARDS A TYPOLOGY OF EUROPEAN WELFARE PRODUCTION: SUMMARY AND DISCUSSION

The research agenda of this report sets out from the tradition of the social indicator movement, focussing on the distribution of living conditions at micro level. With access to new comparative welfare surveys (ECHP and Nordic databases) the variation of living conditions within as well as between nations can be studied in more detail, and for a complete set of EU member states, for some nations even in a longitudinal perspective. Likewise is recent *regime research* drawing on new comparative data on the institutional context behind individual living conditions. Combining these data on 'welfare production' provide insight into the way living conditions are monitored by the labour market, welfare state and family at national level, and on the combined 'welfare efficiency' of these institutions.

While social indicator research is rich and faceted, with long tradition at national level, with respect to aspects of welfare outcome and distributive features, regime research is young, and has but recently expanded from its early focus on welfare *state* arrangements towards characteristics of other welfare institutions. In the tradition of Titmuss (1958) and Marshall (1975) several typologies of welfare state models have been developed by Esping-Andersen (1991, 1999), Castles and Mitchell (1992), Korpi and Palme (1994) and others. This line of thinking in terms of national characteristics identifies *welfare state regimes* as ideal types. The regimes tradition originally focussed on the relation between the labour market and welfare state, and in particular on the provisions of the welfare state. Research along these lines is expanding, exposing inconsistencies between these ideal types and empirical reality, and adding new dimensions. In the same vein models of *employment regimes, gender regimes and family regimes* have been proposed (Lewis, 1992; Duncan, 1995; Hirdman, 1990, and others), expanding the institutional background of the variation of living conditions. These new perspectives will be incorporated in a new typology integrating

Social Indicators Research **64:** 547–572, 2003.

the contributions of the welfare state, of the labour market as well as the family, towards a typology of *European welfare production strategies*.

We have combined these two research traditions. The new perspective in this report is an empirical-exploratory and integrated approach matching institutional performance and living conditions. First, we have explored the general character of national welfare production by integrating labour market, welfare state and family characteristics in the European union. Second, the corresponding distributive features have been identified, and included in the typology. Hence, this approach is not exclusively looking at one institution or one distributive characteristic, but on the configuration of institutions in conjunction with various distributive features.

We have abandoned the tradition of using nations as single illustrations to idealtypical categories. Instead we use the new comparative databases to utilize the full set of EU-member states to explore the variation of institutional features and distributive outcomes. This strategy builds on the conception that there should be a limited number of logical welfare production strategies (or 'welfare mix') in modern society, each with its own characteristic profile of welfare distribution. In order to locate such ideal types empirically, we needed to explore the full set of EU nations, and utilise a larger set of data sources with full coverage for all EU member states. Providing empirical evidence for such a larger set of nation cases, instead of just illustrating them by single cases, will underscore the theoretical argument.

There is a wide variation of institutional forms between the European Union member states, which also should produce logical variation in the distributive patterns of living conditions. In fact, the European Union can be seen as a natural laboratory for the institutional-individual link. We have explored this link in a *comparative* perspective as well as *longitudinal* perspective. The comparative approach is aiming at the identification of similarities and dissimilarities between EU member states with respect to institutional configuration and corresponding distributive outcomes in the mid 1990s. The longitudinal approach follows the Swedish case over a period of some 35 years, for two reasons. Sweden has a special role as a forerunner towards a general expansion of the welfare state, as well as towards the 'inclusive labour market', and towards a general breakdown of traditional family bonds. The 'Swedish model', or rather Nordic model, has been recognised for its egalitarian policies, its special features in reducing poverty and class inequality, and for promoting equal opportunities for women. Furthermore, Sweden is one of very few countries with access to excellent long time series data, which just recently are beginning to be built up in Europe.

The indicators have been selected from available data sources and recent research experience. The labour market is represented by indicators of *enrolment, inclusion (employment rates of youth, women, elderly), social and work relations, work ethic, and earnings*. Welfare state performance is measured by *social protection expenditure, reduction of income equality, and policies regulating/modifying the two other institutions* (labour market policies, family policies). The family as a welfare institution was identified by the *timing/spacing of exit from the parents home, partnering, fertility, de-partnering, and household size and structure*. Distributive outcomes are measured as *inequality of disposable income, poverty, wealth, and inequality of material living standards by social class, gender, generation and family characteristics*.

The basic assumptions of this approach are as follows. There is a *functional division of responsibility for welfare delivery* between the labour market, welfare state and family. The character of the distributive outcome (level of inequality and impact of social cleavages) will correspond to the institutional mix. The division of responsibility, as well as the provisions of each of the three institutions, can be evaluated with respect to *welfare efficiency* to improve living conditions and reduce poverty, social exclusion and general inequality. In various proportion, the overall distributive structure carries the imprint of each of the three institutions, reflecting the distributive principles of the labour market (competition, competence), welfare state (collective solidarity) and family (reciprocity).

The institutional configuration should be reduced to a limited number of logical combinations or *welfare productions models*. We should designate the major role to the labour market; malfunctioning of the labour market will exhaust the welfare state as well as the family and produce larger levels of inequality. Welfare state and family are two alternative correctives. 'Efficient' labour markets (full employment, equality of earnings) will relieve the welfare state as well as the family. In reverse, the generous welfare state requires the efficient labour market; and further: generous welfare states and efficient labour markets promote emancipation from the family.

The *driving forces* behind the current welfare mix are external and internal factors, such as global competition, national resources, infrastructure, the historical and ideological tradition, power relations and ideological struggle. The 'welfare mix' will accommodate to economic change, political cleavages and power relations, and accordingly change over time, and differ between nations.

At micro level, people will adapt to available opportunities. *Coping behaviour* serves to avoid poverty and social exclusion, and to maximise general living conditions; it relates to the labour market (e.g., job seeking, training), welfare state (utilising/adjusting to available transfers and services), as well as the family (exit from parental home, partnering, fertility, separations).

Recent economic change involves major malfunctions of the welfare mix, related to the labour market (global competition, mass unemployment, job and wage flexibilization), the welfare state (recovery policies), as well as the family (fragmentation), implying a changing institutional configuration as well as decreased overall institutional efficiency in providing good and equal living conditions.

The agenda of this report concerns the following questions:

1. Can we identify clusters of EU countries with similar welfare production models?
2. Is there an 'optimal' model of welfare production with higher welfare efficiency, with respect to the reduction of inequalities?
3. Are there deviant cases from the dominant welfare mix of institutional configuration and distributive outcome? How can these be explained?

A SUMMARY OF EMPIRICAL FINDINGS

The Interrelationship of European Welfare Institutions

Chapters 2–4 have sufficiently demonstrated that there are considerable similarities *within* clusters of EU member states, and dissimilarities *between* them, with respect to the configuration of welfare institutions. There is a Nordic region (Sweden, Denmark,

Finland and Norway) and a Southern European region (Greece, Italy, Spain, Portugal), which are counterparts with respect to all three welfare delivery institutions. The central region, including the remaining EU member states (Germany, France, Belgium, Netherlands, Luxembourg, UK, Ireland) is usually in intermediate position. The member states in each of these three clusters almost exclusively fall into the same institutional categories, which applies to all three institutions. This means that the member states *within* each cluster exhibits about the same 'welfare mix', with rather few exceptions from this general pattern.

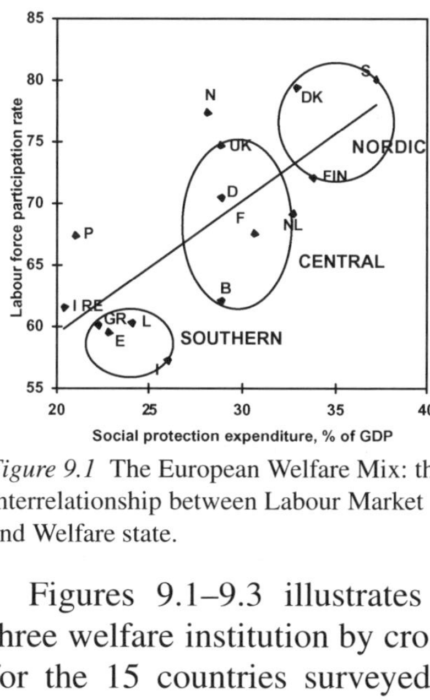

Figure 9.1 The European Welfare Mix: the interrelationship between Labour Market and Welfare state.

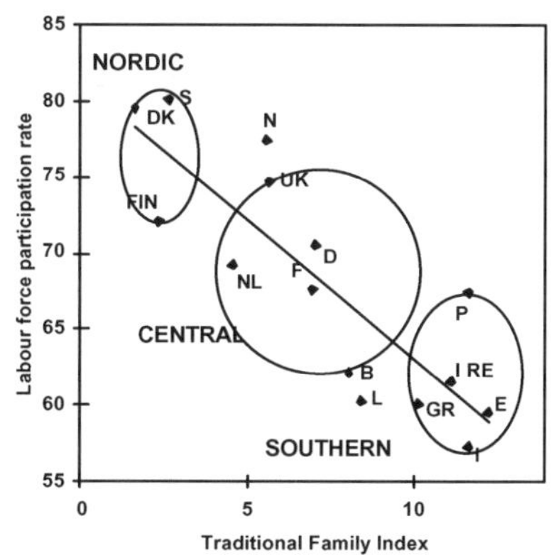

Figure 9.2 The European Welfare Mix: the interrelationship between Labour Market and Family.

Figures 9.1–9.3 illustrates the interrelationship between the three welfare institution by crossing three key indicators pair-wise, for the 15 countries surveyed.[1] First, Figure 9.1 orders the EU nations the *labour force participation* (market) and *social protection expenditure* (welfare state); see definitions in chapters 2 and 3. Portugal is an outlier when it comes to labour force participation, and belongs in this respect to the central cluster; this also applies to female employment and unemployment. Sweden and Finland were in a deep recession in the early 1990s, and 1995 which these data refer to is therefore not representative for their employment situation in a longer time perspective. Around 1990 as well as again at the end of the 1990s both countries are located at much higher enrolment levels.

Next, in Figure 9.2 we relate *labour force participation* (market) to the *Traditional Family Index* (as defined in chapter 4), again displaying three homogenous clusters of similar welfare mix. The outliers are again Portugal, which has already been discussed, and Ireland. Ireland seems to be close to the southern cluster when it comes to female employment as well as the role of family. The Netherlands is again close to the Nordic cluster with respect to family formation. Finally, Figure 9.3 orders the nations by *social protection expenditure* (welfare state) versus the *'traditional family' index* (family). Again the Netherlands is located close the Nordic cluster.

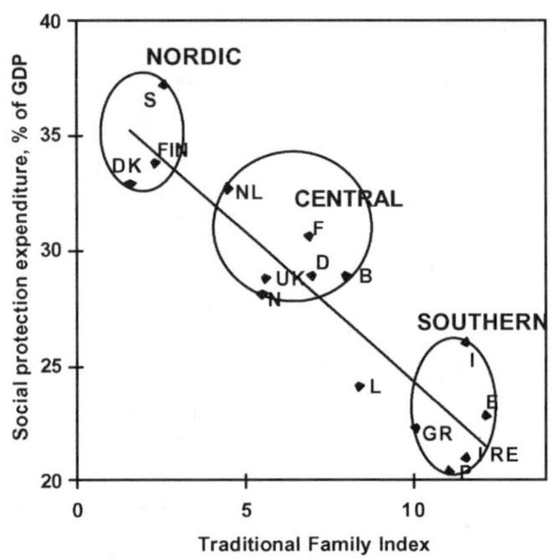

Figure 9.3 The European Welfare Mix: the interrelationship between Welfare State and Family.

In summary, these findings based on one global indicator for each institution underscore the interrelationship between the three welfare delivery institutions. A larger set of further indicators providing details paints about the same picture (see chapter 2–4 and Vogel, 1997). There are three rather distinct clusters of EU nations, with two distinct models of welfare production (Nordic and Southern) and one intermediate model (central EU region).

The welfare state has the largest impact in the Nordic region. The Nordic welfare states also have the most efficient labour markets when it comes to its role in providing jobs and earnings. Hence, the Nordic welfare production model combines a generous welfare state with extensive passive and active labour market policies promoting full employment, equal opportunities and maximum dispersion of earnings. In fact, it is in the Nordic region the market plays its major role as a welfare delivery institution. In the Nordic countries the market also supports generous welfare state arrangements, since it widens the tax base as well as limits the needs for social intervention. These data also indicate that all of the Nordic countries rate low on the traditional family support. This can be seen as a consequence of the strong welfare state and market, opening for a pluralisation of family forms.

In the same vein, the southern cluster combines a weak welfare state and a weak labour market, with strong family tradition. There is certainly need for social network support and strong families, to compensate for weak market and welfare state support.

Figures 9.1–9.3 demonstrate that the institutional configuration consists of is rather few combinations. The Nordic strong welfare states are also characterised by inclusive labour markets with respect to the role of the labour market as a welfare delivery system, and they also have weak family institutions. The southern cluster includes only weak welfare states, as well as 'weak' labour markets (with respect to welfare delivery), but all of them are on the other hand characterised by strong traditional families. All members of the remaining central cluster are in intermediate position concerning all three institutions, with just a few exceptions.

This uniformity within clusters underlines the division of responsibility for welfare production between institutions, and in particular, their compensatory role. Strong welfare states exclusively also have strong labour markets which mobilise a comparatively large part of the working age population and deliver earnings to a larger share of adults. This symbiosis between welfare state and market is a precondition for the battle against poverty, social exclusion and general inequality. The 'inclusive' labour market produces a larger tax base able to finance a larger welfare state, as well as limits the need for social intervention. Consequently, active and ambitious labour market policies play a major role in advanced welfare states. Looking at our data we can conclude that there are no national cases which rate high on only one of these two institutions and not the other. In the case of Sweden we have a strong combination of a compressed structure of earnings, due to high employment levels as well as an egalitarian distribution of working hours, and in addition a larger volume of tax/transfer corrections of market income, as compared to other EU-member states (Björklund and Freeman, 1997).

In the southern cluster we find weak labour markets (with the exception of Portugal). Again, exclusively in all of these member states the traditional family plays a major role as a welfare institution. The household size is much larger, a larger proportion of the population lives in extended households, the exit of youth comes later, larger shares of the aged move in with their children, divorce rates are much lower, and lower shares are living as singles. Hence, the traditional family is the functional alternative when market and welfare state fail to deliver basic living standards. In reverse, traditional family formation and gender roles may also lead to lower employment rates, and consequently to a weak welfare state.

The Link Between European Welfare Institutions and Distributive Outcome

The level and character of inequality of material living standards within each of the member states is related to the unique configuration of the three major welfare delivery systems, i.e., the labour market, the welfare state and the family. Similar institutional arrangements and performance should produce similar welfare outcomes at individual level. The empirical findings again suggest there are three distinct clusters of member states (the Nordic, the Southern, and the intermediate central cluster), with distinct distributive features related to labour market performance, welfare state arrangements and family patterns.

The following series of graphs will give the final picture by integrating the institutional mix and its distributive outcome. Again, this graphic presentation is not complete but focuses on the most crucial indicators; further indicators provide about the same general picture (Vogel, 1997). Figure 9.4 displays the market/welfare state mix in the European Union with respect to the level of **inequality of disposable equivalent income** (as measured by Gini-coefficients), where the Gini-levels are displayed inside the graph next to the country code (high Gini levels indicating higher inequality are underlined and in italics; low 'Gini levels are bold). Figure 9.4 again underlines the general pattern in the European Union: We can see that strong welfare states (Sweden, Denmark, in normal years also Finland) are *always* combined with strong labour markets (higher labour market enrolment rates), and this combination produces significantly lower income inequality. High levels of income inequality are normally found in the Southern cluster, generally combining lower levels of labour market mobilisation with low social protection expenditure. The exception is UK with higher level of income inequality than expected from its institutional configuration.

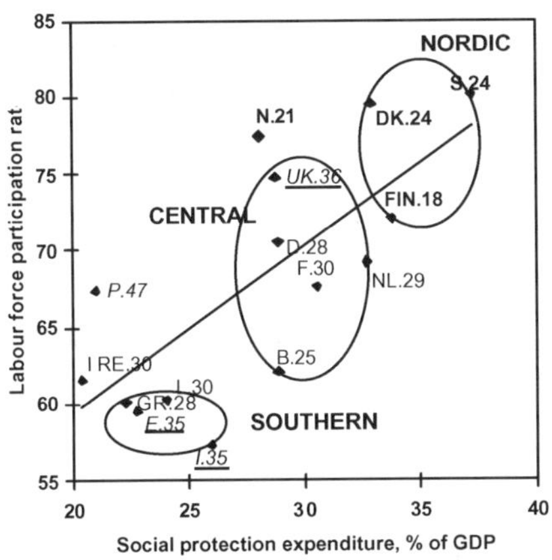

Figure 9.4 Inequality of disposable income (Gini-coefficients), by labour market enrolment and welfare state provisions.

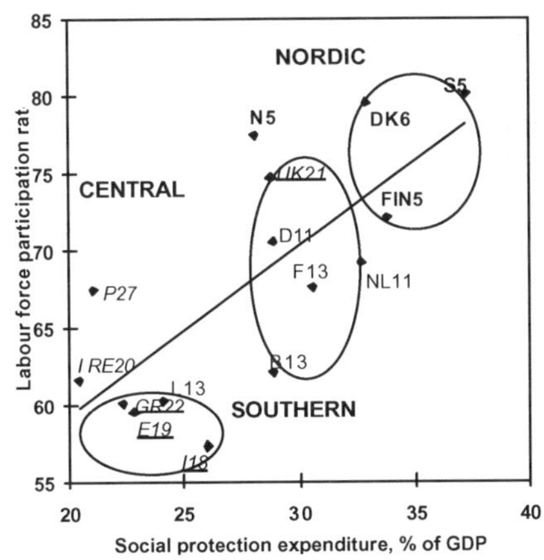

Figure 9.5 Poverty rates (<50% of average disp. income), by labour market enrolment and welfare state provisions.

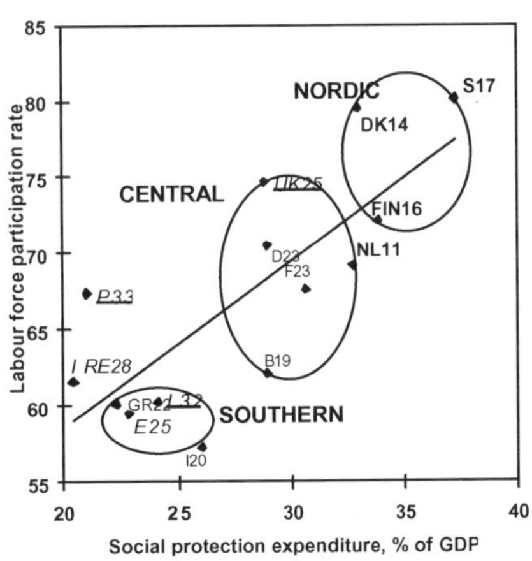

Figure 9.6 IClass inequality (index), by labour market enrolment and welfare state provisions.

Figure 9.5–9.6 show the corresponding structure for the **poverty rate**[2] and the class inequality **index**.[3] The deviants from the dominant picture are first of all UK, exhibiting higher poverty rates as well as larger levels of class inequality, which is consistent with other recent statistics.

The next two figures (9.7–9.8) concern inequality between generations, this time seen in the welfare state/family institutional context. Here is the *reversed* regional differences are demonstrated. Higher generational inequality[4] is exhibited in the Nordic countries. The role of the family is rather obvious. The traditional family in the southern cluster incorporates larger proportions of youth as well as elderly; larger households utilise the scale effect as well as support family members will lower personal resources (youth, elderly). These graphs underline that the family and the welfare state are functional alternatives, with its distributional features.

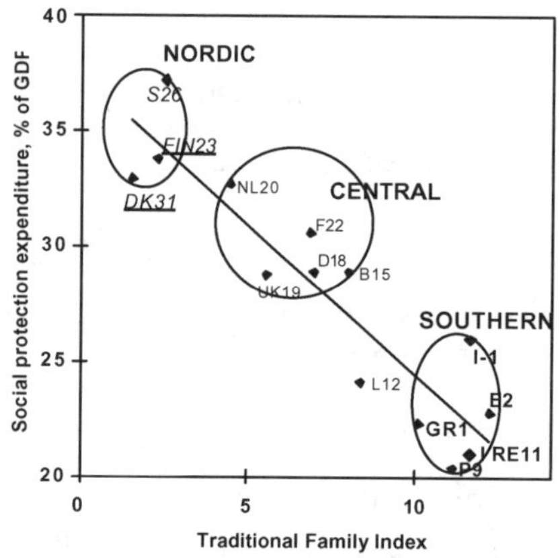

Figure 9.7 Inequality between generations (20–29 vs 45–64 years), by welfare state provisions and family characteristics.

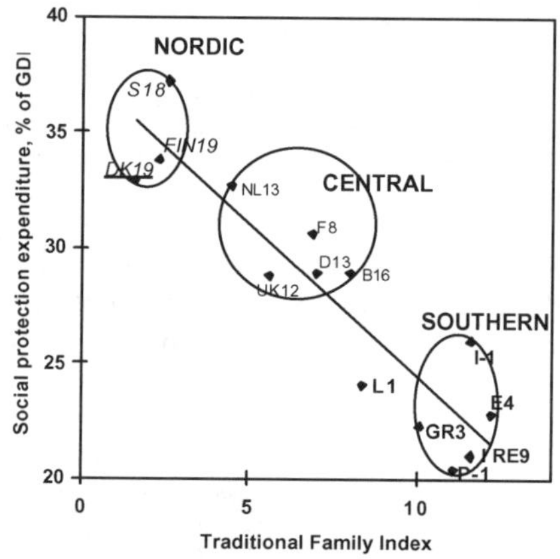

Figure 9.8 Inequality between generations (65–84 vs 45–65 years), by welfare state provisions and family characteristics.

In summary, these data indicate that the distribution of income and material living standards in each of the member states is related to the unique configuration of the three major welfare delivery institutions, i.e., the labour market, the welfare state and the family; similar institutional arrangements and performance produce similar welfare outcomes at individual level as well. Furthermore, there are in fact three rather distinct clusters of EU-nations, each with similar institutional performance as well as similar distributive outcome; and we observe there are distinct dissimilarities between the three clusters. These findings indicate there are *three different national strategies of welfare production*, which only can become visible with a larger set of nations, in this case the 15 EU member states compared in this report.

This similarity within clusters, and dissimilarity between clusters, also extends beyond the income distribution addressed in this report. Other studies focusing on the distribution of material living conditions in a wider sense (Vogel, 1997, 1999, 2000a), and on coping behaviour related to family formation (Vogel, 1998, 1997, 2001b) also demonstrate the link to the welfare mix. Less distinct though, we have shown that health disparities are related to the institutional context (Vogel and Theorell, chapter 6, 2002).

Further on we will demonstrate that the longitudinal study of the Swedish welfare mix during the past 3 decades displays the same co-variation between institutional configuration and distributive outcome.

Towards a Typology of European Welfare Production Models

The data for the European Union, around 1995, are further summarised in Figure 9.9. In summary, our findings suggest the following typology:

There is **a Nordic cluster** (Sweden, Denmark, Finland and Norway) with (close to) full employment for men as well as for women, and with generous levels of universal welfare state provisions. This is the combination of a rather successful co-operation between the labour market and welfare state in sharing the responsibilities for welfare delivery, equality and income security. Our data exhibit several favourable distributive features, including lower levels of general income inequality, poverty, as well as class and gender inequality (reported in Vogel, 1997, 1999, 2000b; see also chapter 5).

The combination of the *'inclusive labour Market'* (full employment, larger female enrolment, lower unemployment rates, equality in earnings, co-determination traditions, larger levels of intrinsic work orientation) and *generous welfare state* arrangements (transfers, services) support economic security and independence for men as well as women, youth and the elderly. Consequently, this experience of security also reduces the traditional welfare function of the family. Accordingly, our data for the Nordic cluster (Vogel, 1998) indicate early exit from the parental household, early partnering, larger volumes of single adults, mobility between partnerships, consensual unions, and extra-marital childbearing. The welfare role of the traditional large family is rather limited in the Nordic countries, and the drift towards fragmentation and diversity has proceeded farther, towards very small household size. On the other hand, recent Nordic fertility levels have been much higher than the Southern levels (Vogel, 2001a), which is explained by generous family policies (public child care, paid parental leave).

It should be noted that the uniqueness of the Nordic cluster extends far beyond the indicators displayed in this summary, including left-wing political dominance, high levels of labour union enrolment, strong political support for egalitarian income policies and extensive public services, high levels of voting rates and general participation in collective organisations, as well as rather homogeneous value patterns. However, it should be added that, in the Swedish case, some of this uniqueness was lost over the last decade.

There is **a Southern cluster** (Italy, Greece, Spain, and in most aspects Portugal) with poor labour market performance in providing earnings and economic independence (low employment rates, high unemployment rates, larger inequalities in earnings), as well as welfare state provisions (lower social protection expenditure, poor child care provisions and lower options of paid leave and family subsidies). The distributive structure in the Southern cluster displays much higher levels of income inequality and poverty. Other studies indicate that this also applies to higher levels of class inequality.

On the other hand, the southern cluster displays lower levels of inequality between generations. The family plays a major role as a welfare delivery institution, supporting weak family members, in particular young adults (larger volumes of youth unemployment), women (inactivity on the labour market) and the elderly (lower pension rights). Hence, our data (Vogel, 1998, 2001c, see also chapter 4) indicates larger family size, later exit from the parental home, later partnering, lower separation rates, lower rates of singlehood, and frequent multi-generation families, as compared to the Nordic cluster. Partnerships tend to be more stable, but the volume of economical dependants (young adults, housewives, elderly) is higher. In a longitudinal perspective, there should be an *increasing mismatch* between the opportunity structure defined by institutional context and the secular demand of economic independence and for a full life including both work and family life among younger women. Recent data indicate an increase of coping behaviour, such as postponed partnering and very low and late fertility, as compared to the Nordic cluster.

The **Central European cluster** (Germany, France, the Netherlands, Belgium, Luxembourg, UK and Ireland) generally falls in intermediate position between the Nordic and Southern clusters, on the institutional mix as well as the distributive outcome and coping behaviour. Some countries are closer to the Nordic cluster or the Southern cluster. For instance, Germany displays a rather Southern pattern of lower child care provisions and lower female employment rates; UK has a pattern of higher income inequality and poverty level, rather similar to the Southern cluster; both countries without the support of the traditional family. The structure of these findings is summarised in Figure 9.9 (precise estimates are given in chapter 2–5).

THE SWEDISH CASE

Institutional Configuration in Sweden 1963–1998

The corresponding analysis for the Swedish case provides a second perspective to the institutional mix, namely a longitudinal account of the establishment of the Swedish model of welfare production reaching back to 1963 (Figure 9.10). Looking at the Swedish trends we clearly see that labour market efficiency (light grey lines) and welfare state provisions (dark grey line) are positively correlated, while the role of family (doted lines) is negatively related to labour market as well as welfare state performance. From the early 1960s to early 1990s Sweden had a parallel increase of employment rates,[5] female labour market enrolment6 and constant low unemployment rates, indicating increasing labour market efficiency. Concurrently, male employment declined slowly due to reduced pension age and liberal opportunities for premature retirement. In summary, the demographic burden decreased, while it increased in most other European countries. Towards the end of the 1980s there were 2,2

	WELFARE INSTITUTIONS			DISTRIBUTIVE OUTCOME		
	the inclusive labour market	the extensive welfare state	the inclusive family	income inequality	poverty rate	class inequality
statistical indicators:	*labour force participation*	*social expenditure*	*'traditional family index'*	*Gini-coeff.*	*<50 % of mean*	*inequality index*
NORDIC CLUSTER						
Sweden	***HIGH***	***HIGH***	***LOW***	***LOW***	***LOW***	***LOW***
Denmark	***HIGH***	***HIGH***	***LOW***	***LOW***	***LOW***	***LOW***
Finland	***HIGH***	***HIGH***	***LOW***	***LOW***	***LOW***	***LOW***
Norway	***HIGH***	*medium*	*medium*	***LOW***	***LOW***	***n.a.***
SOUTHERN CLUSTER						
Italy	***LOW***	***LOW***	***HIGH***	***HIGH***	***HIGH***	*medium?*
Spain	***LOW***	***LOW***	***HIGH***	***HIGH***	***HIGH***	***HIGH***
Greece	***LOW***	***LOW***	***HIGH***	***HIGH***	***HIGH***	*medium?*
Portugal	*medium*	***LOW***	***HIGH***	***HIGH***	***HIGH***	***HIGH***
CENTRAL CLUSTER						
Germany	*medium*	*medium*	*medium*	*medium*	*medium*	*medium*
France	*medium*	*medium*	*medium*	*medium*	*medium*	*medium*
Netherl.	*medium*	*medium*	*medium*	*medium*	*medium*	***LOW***
Belgium	*medium*	*medium*	*medium*	*medium*	*medium*	*medium*
Luxembg	*medium*	*medium*	*medium*	*medium*	*medium*	***HIGH***
UK	*medium*	*medium*	*medium*	***HIGH***	***HIGH***	***HIGH***
Ireland	*medium*	***LOW***	***HIGH***	*medium*	***HIGH***	***HIGH***

Figure 9.9 European welfare production.

persons in employment for each adult (20–84 years). The growth in female employment equals the size of the new service jobs in the public sector created in this period, amounting to an overall increase in gainful employment by some 10 percent. Hence, a large volume of unpaid work in the household sector has been transferred to the public sector.

These long-term Swedish trends, between 1960 and 1990, are outstanding in a comparative perspective. There was a gradual shift in the welfare mix, with responsibilities transferred from families to labour market and welfare state. In a period of stagnation in Western labour markets, Sweden managed to increase female employment, keep unemployment low, expand the public sector's transfers and services, and balance the public budgets as well. During this period social protection expenditure expanded from about 10 to 40 percent of GDP. Meanwhile, the role of the family declined, with decreasing household size and increasing rates of single households (Figure 9.10). Here we see the gradual erection of the Swedish model. In other words, the interrelationship between the three welfare institutions we have located in the comparative analysis also prevails in the longitudinal Swedish case.

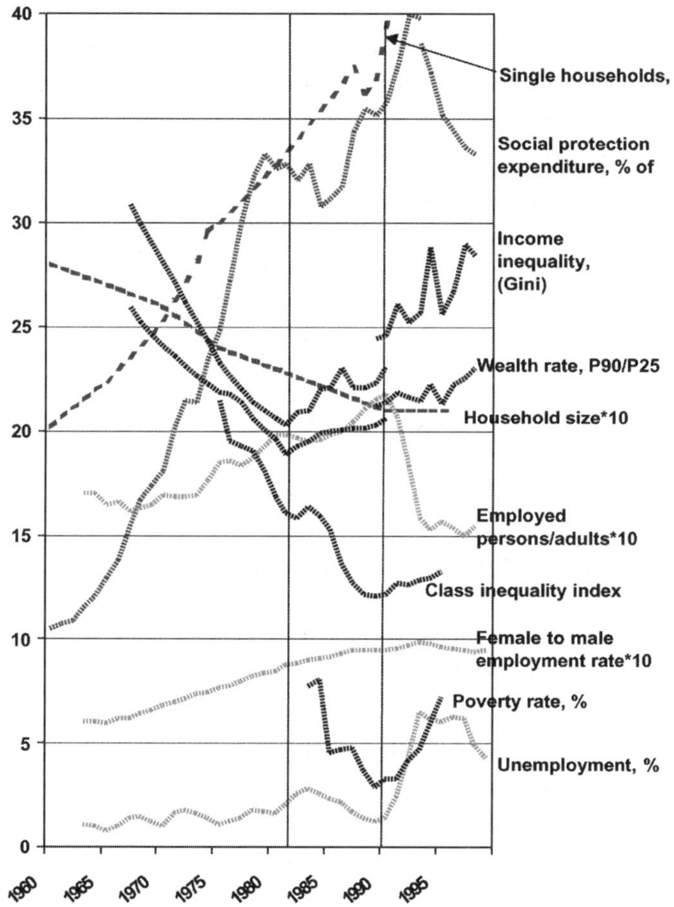

Figure 9.10 The Swedish welfare mix 1960–1999 and its distributive outcome. Sources: Labour Force Surveys, SNA, Censuses, Income surveys.

However, these policies came to an end around 1990 with the coincidence of general deregulation, large non-financed tax reductions, in unfortunate timing with a deep recession and subsequent decline in domestic demand. Sweden faced a new situation, with severe reduction in the overall welfare efficiency of the labour market as well as the welfare state, which is also reflected in Figure 9.10. There was a sharp decline of employment among men as well as women (by 12 percent points), along with a rapid growth of unemployment. This had severe consequences for the youngest generation as well as immigrants (entrants to the labour market). The sudden increase in unemployment also had a strong impact on the budget balance in Sweden. Income maintenance systems were exhausted and eventually reduced in coverage, entitlements and compensation levels. In other words, Sweden had to face a new regressive shift in the 'welfare mix': the responsibility shifted from the labour market to the welfare state, and consequently back to the household sector. Swedish trends for social protection expenditure (GDP-share) indicate a strong increase up to the early 1990s, but then followed a decade of decline (see Figure 9.10). Recovery policies hit most of the public transfer systems and services during the 1990s. Sweden combined what has been called a 'breathtaking' consolidation of the budget reducing a 12,3 percent deficit to a 2,1 surplus in 5 years (1993–1998), which included a 'dramatical' reduction of the social protection expenditure from 37 to 33 percent of GDP (Scharpf, 1999).

In summary, the Swedish welfare state comes out less generous at individual level towards the end 1990s; but in a comparative perspective public provisions are still larger than most industrial nations, as indicated in chapter 3. In mid 1990s as well as throughout the past 30 years, however, the Swedish labour market contributed more to the individual living standards than in most other EU member states. From 1995 there was again a recovery of earlier levels of labour market participation and welfare state generosity. Today, Sweden and the other Nordic countries still have the highest employment rates, as well as the most evenly distributed command over resources (earnings) relevant on other arenas as well.

The corresponding longitudinal analysis of Swedish family formation indicates there is a long-term change towards a fragmentation of family ties in Sweden over the last 20 years (see also chapter 4). The household size is declining, the proportion of singles and consensual unions are increasing, formal marriages are declining, and pregnancies are postponed after the establishment on the labour market. This is a combined consequence of delayed family formation related to prolonged youth education and later entry in the labour market, and a trend towards a pattern of interruption in cohabitation, i.e., higher mobility between relationships. Old people moving in with mid-aged children are almost non-existent, and there is only a minor delay of exit from the parental home. In summary, the traditional family is gradually loosing ground. Sweden seems to be the leading country in this process deviating much in this respect from the southern EU member states, where in fact we can observe increased mobilisation of family networks.

Swedish Welfare Institutions and Distributive Outcome 1963–1998

The link between the institutional configuration and distributive outcome established in the comparative study of EU-member states is also found in the longitudinal study of the Swedish case (see Figure 9.10). Figure 9.10 includes four indicators of income structure and material living standards (black lines). In general terms, the change in institutional performance displayed here is accompanied by change in distributive features, going in the same direction as already found in the comparative analysis, strengthening our argument.

The data indicate that poverty and class inequality declined until the early 1990s, accompanied by increased labour market enrolment and social protection expenditure, as well as fragmentation of the family. Figure 9.10 also indicates that the wealth rates already began to expand in the early 1980s, as the overall political and union control over income formation was weakened. This contributed to an increase in Gini-coefficients for income inequality starting in the early 1980s. However, around 1991 a parallel international recession and an unsuccessful tax reform (further reducing the marginal income tax rate and kapital taxation, as well as the overall tax level) produced an unemployment choc as well as a rapid 12 percent decline of the work force. Domestic demand declined and huge budget deficits followed, along with subsequent heavy reductions in public transfers and services. The consequences, which are going in the expected direction, are indicated by increased poverty rates and (further) increasing Gini-coefficients for disposable income, taking Sweden back to the level of the early 1970s.

Hence, the 1990s saw a major regression from the egalitarian income structure characterising the Swedish model. However, in a relative sense, as compared with the central and Southern EU member states, Sweden as well as the other Nordic countries still constitute a separate cluster of rather successful welfare mix.

DISCUSSION

The central message of our findings concerns the role of the institutional context in shaping the distribution of material living conditions, as well as coping behaviour such as the timing of the move from the parental household, partnering, de-partnering, and fertility.

There are distinct *dissimilarities between three clusters of EU-countries* (Nordic, Southern and Central member states), concerning the national configuration of three welfare institutions (*'welfare mix');* including the *labour market* (employment, earnings), *welfare state* (general social protection expenditure, income redistribution, labour market and family policies), and *family* (family network support); as well as the *distributive outcome* (income distribution, poverty, inequality of material living standards) and *coping behaviour*. Likewise, there are distinct *similarities within these three clusters of EU-countries* concerning the institutional configuration as well as distributive outcome and coping behaviour.

Our findings indicate there are *two distinct national strategies of welfare production and one intermediate strategy*, which only can become visible with a larger set of nations, in this case 15 EU member states studied in this report, as well as in a longitudinal analysis of single nations, as in the Swedish case. This analysis demonstrates the obvious: inequality is a social consequence of inadequate institutional performance.

The Interdependence of Labour Market and Welfare State

National welfare delivery institutions are responsive to external forces (general economic development, global competition), infrastructure (natural resources, technological development, democratic rule), historical traditions, and power relations between various interests (ideological dominance, unionism, economic policies). There is a large variation in this respect within the European union, which over the past decades has decreased. The statistics presented in this report demonstrates that the institutional configuration measured in the European context consist of only three models, two distinct models and one intermediate. All of the extensive Nordic welfare states are also characterised by 'inclusive' labour markets. Furthermore, all of them have weak family institutions. The Southern cluster includes only rudimentary welfare states, as well as 'weak' labour markets, but all of them are on the other hand characterised by strong traditional families. The members of the remaining central cluster are in intermediate position concerning all three institutions, with just a few exceptions.

This restriction to only two models and one intermediate model, and the uniformity within clusters underlines the functional interrelationship between institutions and the division of responsibilities for welfare production, as well as the limitations of their compensatory role. Strong welfare states exclusively also have efficient labour markets which mobilise a comparatively large part of the working age population and deliver earnings to a larger share of adults. This symbiosis between welfare state and labour market is a precondition for the battle against poverty, social exclusion and general inequality. The inclusive labour market provides higher levels of individual opportunities, which reduces the need for welfare state intervention, as well as produces a larger tax base, able to finance a larger welfare state. Consequently, ambitious active as well as passive labour market policies play a major role in advanced welfare states. In other words: the inclusive labour market is required for the generous welfare state. Accordingly, it is in the Nordic region the labour market plays its most efficient role as a welfare delivery institution. Much of the welfare efficiency and egalitarian distributive structure of the Nordic welfare state is in fact a consequence of its capacity to engage the labour market as a welfare delivery institution.

Looking at our data we can also conclude that there are no national cases which rate high on only one of these two institutions and not the other. We can see no exception from this rule among the EU member states; all nations displaying high tax and social expenditure levels, also have achieved high employment levels; and all member states with low employment levels, accordingly, have low levels of welfare state provisions. Hence, here is no empirical evidence here that lower welfare state intervention, or 'flexibility' ('incentives' such as lower levels of job security, lower social security provisions, inequality of earnings) buy higher employment levels. Lower welfare state intervention and larger levels of inequality does not seem to be a requirement for high employment levels.

The Southern cluster illustrates the logic of poor labour market performance and its consequences for the other welfare institutions. Lower labour market enrolment, larger volumes of unemployed and larger inequality of earnings will preclude generous welfare state arrangements, for three reasons. First, the mere volume of the needy will not allow generous public provisions. Second, such provisions will have to be targeted and restricted to the most needy, excluding the middle class. Hence, redistribution will only affect extreme poverty and exclusion, not inequality in a wider sense. Thirdly, with such an imbalance between needs (low employment, high unemployment, unequal earnings) and resources (the potential tax base), it will be difficult to mobilise political support for public provisions. Accordingly, in all of the southern member states the traditional family will have to take on a major role as a welfare institution. The household size is much larger, a larger proportion of the population lives in extended households, the exit of youth from their parent's household comes later, larger shares of the aged move in with their mid-age children, divorce and separation rates are lower, and lower shares are living as singles. Hence, the traditional family is the functional alternative when labour market and welfare state fail to deliver basic living standards. This is also clearly indicated by recent increase in coping behaviour with respect to family formation (further delayed exit, partnering and fertility).

The lesson from these findings are clearly that welfare and equity has to be earned on the market; family and welfare state can only correct the contribution of the labour market. Further, the combat of poverty and social exclusion should not be the exclusive responsibility of the welfare state. The findings of this report underline that equity is accomplished best when responsibilities are shared between labour market, welfare state and family. *Distributive efficiency*; in contrast to economic efficiency, or even financial efficiency, lies in the productive skill of politics to mobilise and fine tune the labour market and the family towards this goal. Hence, the prominent mission of politics is to engage all three welfare institution towards the common goal of jobs and welfare for all, which includes extensive labour market policies, as well as family policies such as family transfers, collective care of children and the elderly, and support of the combination of family and career.

The Traditional Family as a Resort When Market and Welfare State Fail

Family support is the functional alternative when the labour market and welfare state are poor performers in their welfare delivery role. Our data indicate that the traditional family cannot reduce income inequality and poverty, on a general level, as efficient as the welfare state. Income inequality and poverty rates are much higher in the Southern cluster.

Nevertheless, the traditional family plays an important role in reducing inequality and poverty. Our data indicate that the traditional family also reduces certain dimensions of inequality more efficient, namely inequality between generations. This outcome is explained by the very different role of the family in the South as compared to the North. Young adults are staying on longer with their parents in Italy, Greece, Spain and Portugal, especially when they are in education and before they are permanently established on the labour market, or in a stable partner relationship. This means that they share the economic resources of the larger parental home, including the pooled household income, housing conditions and consumer durables, by utilising the economy of scale. The same applies to the elderly, which are frequently moving in with their middle-aged children in the Southern countries (see chapter 4). It can be assumed that this patterns is also selective with respect to personal income: elderly with low pensions tend to be included in larger households, which leaves a positively selected group of elderly in their own small households.

Hence, our data indicate that the generational differences are more efficiently reduced in the South, as compared to the Nordic institutional welfare states. However, this advantage is at the expense of personal dependence on the larger household, husbands, fathers and grown-up children; for women, young adults and the elderly. However, in the Southern countries this pattern is a necessity in the light of the market/welfare state configuration. The corresponding values are rooted in historical tradition, which hardly can be said about the Nordic countries rating low on the status of the traditional family. In the Nordic countries the strong welfare state and inclusive labour market are instead perceived as a precondition and opening for personal independence as well as social rights, in particular with respect to equal opportunities.

The Changing Family

We have seen a long-term change in family formation in Europe, with fundamental effects on the role of the family as a welfare institution, as well as a resort for emotional support, affection and security. Our data indicate that there is a vast variation in family forms within the European union, and that the change goes in different direction in Europe. Current family formation can be interpreted from two perspectives; first, as rational coping behaviour in reaction to available opportunities in the search for optimal living conditions; and second, as consequences of traditional norms and social practise for household formation and care giving.

In the Nordic countries we have seen strong fragmentation, diversification and emancipation of young adults, women and the elderly from the traditional patriarchy of the one-breadwinner family. This emancipation is driven by the long-term improved welfare efficiency of the labour market (increased employment opportunities) and welfare state (care and parental leave). The Nordic cluster forms a vanguard moving towards full employment for women and a transfer of domestic work onto the public service sector.

It could be assumed that the corresponding values go in the same direction in the South, but with the current lower welfare efficiency of market and welfare state, responsibilities are returned to the family, thereby preserving traditional family patterns. There are important trends supporting the Northern two-breadwinner model. First and from an individual perspective, the levels of general education for women as well as men are rapidly increasing; second, there is the influence of the Nordic prototype of equal opportunities, offering a career and economic independence; and third, there is an understanding of the economic advantages of the two breadwinner model.

From a societal perspective, the two breadwinner model is in line with the overall strategy to stimulate 'self service' welfare production: it reduces poverty, buffers the problem of temporary income loss in one-earner families, increases the tax base and relaxes public spending. On the other hand, the two-earner model also demands heavy public investments to support female and maternal employment, including care facilities for children and the elderly, paid parental leave and regulation for time off. These investments pay off in additional job creation and increased employability, as well as increased tax base and reduced family and child poverty. This will in turn relieve public finances and give space for other pressing public expenses.

Inadequate Labour Market and Welfare State Performance Will Disturb and Delay Reproduction and Family Formation, and Relocate Responsibility to the Family

Our data also indicate the importance of the welfare mix, and its corresponding distributive outcome, in shaping individual coping behaviour serving to master opportunities offered by the market, welfare state and family. The transitions to adulthood are the crucial test case of the efficiency of the welfare mix. There is good evidence that the Southern welfare mix is increasingly in conflict with the aspirations of young adults (and in particular women) towards a career, economic independence and the two-breadwinner model (see Vogel, 2001b, and chapter 4). Data are indicating that the age of exit from the parental home has increased, partnering occurs later, and fertility rates are decreasing in the southern cluster. This should be interpreted as reactions to poor labour market performance as well as scanty family provisions.

Looking at the Nordic data it should be obvious that we are facing a cluster of generous institutional arrangements (good job opportunities for men as well as women; publicly financed child care facilities, paid maternal/paternal leave and liberal family policies), which support the reconciliation between work and maternity as well as the two-breadwinner model. The Nordic countries have seen no increased exit age, no delayed partnering and in recent times display increased fertility. The different fertility levels in Europe (see chapter 4) demonstrate that there are indeed two divers patterns prevailing: fertility and employment are *negatively* correlated in the South, which indicates that the preconditions for combining career and childbearing are poor. Female employment and fertility are *positively* correlated in the North, which shows that the institutional conditions for consolidation of maternity and career are available (public child care, paid parental leave, job opportunities).

CONCLUDING REMARKS

The overall message concerning the combat of inequality and social exclusion in Europe points at the importance of a co-ordination of all three major welfare delivery institutions towards that goal. The winning welfare production strategy, with respect to equity, builds on full employment, which in turn will produce complementary and generous welfare provisions. The European experience also indicates that there are no short cuts to equity, or towards full employment, by reduced welfare state engagement, or by increased 'market flexibility' via incentives creating decreased job and income security and larger wage differentials. Instead, the data indicate a stronger role for politics in shaping the distributive structure, by stimulating and controlling the labour market and the family.

Over the past two decades, it has become increasingly difficult to preserve shared responsibility for welfare production between labour market and welfare state, based on informal agreements at the national level. We have seen a gradual drift away from the post-war welfare mix: the roles of the labour market and the family as welfare providers have been reduced, creating increasing problems for public welfare production. Statistics indicate a corresponding trend in distributive outcome in most EU-member states towards larger inequality of material living conditions.

A new welfare mix is emerging, in similar direction but various pace in different parts of Europe. Modern capitalism has been deliberated from its national dependence, as well from much of its responsibility for national welfare production. Concurrently, this creates a new pressure on the other welfare institutions to fill the gap, and subsequent negative features in the distributive structure.

With the lost community of interest in welfare production within the *national* context, there is a new conflict between the various driving forces within market economy; between short-term interests of global shareholders and far-off management on one side, and long-term sustainability of consumption, domestic human relations based on face-to-face contacts, and local co-operation and responsibility on the other.

The new independence from the informal contract of co-operation between welfare institutions writes a new chapter in the history of welfare production in most European countries. With persistent mass unemployment, stagnating employment, and even dramatically declining employment rates (Sweden, Finland), accelerated skill requirements, flexible work arrangements, income insecurity and increased work related stress; the balance between politics and market has changed in favour of market forces. While this process has been slow in central and Southern Europe, it was sudden and strong in the North.

Whether this transition is the end of history, or yet another chapter in the history of market economy and the welfare state remains to be seen. Mainstream thinking seems to accept this development as inevitable, adapting to the new global economy by further privatisation, de-centralisation, flexible work relations, low-pay jobs, decreased taxes, and limited public transfers and services. Such prescriptions can only increase inequality; which in fact, in this line of thinking, sometimes is perceived as a goal in itself to promote flexibility and work incentives.

Within the European union there is another option, which is to recapture control over market forces within the larger context of the European union. Reclaiming the commitment of the market forces and returning to *inclusive* labour markets appears to be the only route in defence of equity. In fact, today's Europe is at a cross-road between a liberal and social-democratic pathway, pointing at increased poverty, social exclusion and class and multidimensional inequality, or, at best, towards status quo.

NOTES

[1] Further indicators are presented in chapters 2–4.
[2] Below 50 percent of the average equivalent disposable household income.
[3] The inequality index in Figures 9.6–9.8 measures deprivation in material living conditions, based on a basket of households assets; see technical comments in chapter 5 and Vogel.
[4] To the disadvantage of youth and elderly, respectively; see further technical comments in chapter 5.
[5] Defined as the ratio between employed adults (20–84 years) to not employed adults (to fit this graph multiplied by 10).
[6] Defined as the ratio between female and male employment rates.

SCB Statistics Sweden
Welfare Analysis Program
and
University of Umeå
P.O. Box 24300
10451 Sweden

REFERENCES

Aaberge, Björklund, Jäntti, Pedersen, Smith and Wennemo: 2000, 'Unemployment shocks and income distribution: How did the nordic countries fare during their crisis?', Scandinavian Journal of Economics 102(1).

Atkinson, A.B.: 1997, 'Bringing income distribution in from the cold', The Economic Journal, March 1997.

Atkinson, A.B.: 1998, Poverty in Europe (Blackwell).

Atkinson, A.B.: 1999, Increased Income Inequality and the OECD Countries and the Redistribution Impact of the Government Budget. Contribution to Wider conference.

Atkinson, A.B.: 1996, 'The changing distribution of income: Evidence and explanation', German Economic Review 1.

Atkinsson, R. and Smeeding: 1993, Income Distribution in OECD Countries (OECD, Paris).

Bean, C. and E. Papadakis: 1998, 'A comparison of mass attitudes towards the welfare state in different institutional regimes', 1985–90 International Journal of Public Opinion Research 10, pp. 211–236.

Becker, J.W., J.A. Davies, P. Ester and P. Ph Mohler (eds.): 1990, Attitudes to Inequality and the Role of Government (Sociaal en Cultureel Planbureau, Rijswijk).

Berger-Schmitt, R.: 2000a, 'Wohnen', In: Statistisches Bundesamt (ed.), Datenreport 1999 (Bundeszentrale für politische Bildung, Bonn), pp. 500–511.

Bernardes, J.: 1997, Family Studies: An Introduction (Routledge, London).

Bettio, F. and S. Prechal: 1998, Care in Europe. European Commission, DG5.

Björklund, A. and R.B. Freeman: 1997, Generating Equality and Eliminating Poverty: The Swedish Way (Swedish Institute for Social Research, Stockholm).

Boh, K. et al.: 1989, Changing patterns of European Family Life. A Comparative Analysis of 14 European Countries (Routledge, London).

Borre, O. and E. Scarbrough (eds.): 1995, The Scope of Government (Oxford University Press, Oxford).

Borre, O. and J.G. Andersen: 1997, Voting and Political Attitudes in Denmark (Aarhus University Press, Aarhus).

Social Indicators Research **64:** 573–584, 2003.

Bosma, H., Appels, A., Sturmans, F., Grabauskas, V. and Gostautas, A.: 1994, 'Differences in mortality and coronary heart disease between Lithuania and the Netherlands: Results from the WHO Kaunas-Rotterdam intervention study (KRIS)', Int J Epdemiology 23, pp. 12–19.

Boyer, R.: 1997, 'French Statism at the crossroads', In: C. Crouch and W. Streeck (eds.), Political Economy of Modern Capitalism (Sage, London).

Bozon, M. and O. Kontula: 1997, 'Initiation sexuelle et genre-comparison des évolution de douze pays Europeans', Population 6.

Braun, M. and T. Kolosi: 1994, 'Wandel der Einstellungen zu sozialer Ungleichheit in Deutschland und Ungarn', In: M. Braun and P. Ph Mohler (eds.), Blickpunkt Gesellschaft 3. Einstellungen und Verhalten der Bundesbürger London (Westdeutscher Verlag, Opladen).

Buhlmahn, T.: 2000, 'Subjektives Wohlbefinden', In: Statistisches Bundesamt in Zusammenarbeit mit WZB und ZUMA (eds.), Datenreport 1999 (Bundeszentrale für politische Bildung, Bonn), pp. 420–430.

Burniaux, D., F. Fore, M. d'Ercole and Oxley: 1998, Income Distribution and Poverty in Selected OECD Countries. Economic Department Working Papers, No. 189 (OECD, Paris).

Campbell, A.: 1972, 'Aspiration, satisfaction and fulfilment', In: A. Campbell and P.E. Converse (eds.), The Human Meaning of Social Change (Russell Sage Foundation, New York), pp. 441–446.

Castles, F.G. and D. Mitchell: 1992, 'Identifying welfare states regimes: The links between politics, instruments and outcomes', Governance 5, pp. 1–26.

Castles, F.G. and D. Mitchell: 1993, 'Worlds of welfare and families of nations', In: F.G. Castles (ed.), Families of Nations. Patterns of Public Policy in Western Democracies (Dartmouth, Aldershot).

Castles, F.G.: 1985, The Working Class and Welfare (Allen & Unwin, Sydney).

Castles, F.G.: 1988, Australian Public Policy and Economic Vulnerability (Allen & Unwin, Sydney).

Cherlin, J.C., E. Scabini. and G. Rossi: 1997, 'Still in the nest: Delayed home leaving in Europe and the United States', Journal of Family Issues 6.

Christoph, B.: 2001, 'Wohlstand wichtiger als Einkommen für die Zufriedenheit mit der finanziellen Situation. Untersuchungen zur Zufriedenheit mit der finanziellen Situation im europäischen Vergleich', Informationsdienst Soziale Indikatoren (ISI) 26, pp. 12–15.

Cook, F.L. and E.J. Barrett: 1992, Support for the American Welfare State. The Views of Congress and Public (Columbia University Press, New York).

Cordon, J.A.F.: 1997, 'Youth, residential independence and autonomy: A comparative study', Journal of Family Issues 6.

Coughlin, R.M.: 1980, Ideology, Public Opinion and Welfare Policy (Institute of International Studies, Berkeley).

Davis, J.A. and R. Jowell: 1989, 'Measuring national differences. An introduction to the International Social Survey Programme (ISSP)', In: R. Jowell, S. Witherspoon and L. Brook (eds.), British Social Attitudes. Special International Report (Gower, Aldershot).

Devin F., S. Inglis, P. Moss and P. Petrie: 1997, State of Art Review of the Reconciliation of Work and Family Life for Men and Women and the Quality of Care Services. Final Report for the European Commission Equal Opportunities Unit (DGV).

Duncan, O.D.: 1975, 'Does money buy satisfaction?' Social Indicators Research 2, pp. 267–274.

Duncan, S.: 1995, 'Theorising European gender systems', Journal of European Social Policy 5(4).

Ebbinghaus, B. and J. Visser: 2000, Trade Unions in Western Europe since 1945 (Macmillan).

Erikson, R. and J.H. Goldthorpe: 1992, The Constant Flux. A Study of Class Mobility in Industrial Societies (Clarendon Press, Oxford).

Esping-Andersen, G.: 1990, The Three Worlds of Welfare Capitalism (Polity Press, Cambridge).

Esping-Andersen, G.: 1999, Social Foundations of Postindustrial Economies (Oxford University Press, Oxford).

Esping-Andersen, G. (ed.): 1996, Welfare States in Transition. National Adaptations in Global Economies (UNRISD and Sage).

European Commission: 1998, Reconciliation between Work and family Life in Europe. DG5, Brussels.

European Commission: 2000a, The Social Situation in the European Union 2000 (Office for Official Publications of the European Communities, Luxembourg).

European Commission: 2000b, Eurostat Yearbook. A Statistical Eye on Europe. Data 1988–1998 (Office for Official Publications of the European Communities, Luxembourg).

EUROSTAT: 1994, Poverty Statistics in the late 1980s. Research Based on Micro Data. Statistical Document.

EUROSTAT: 1995, Europe in Figures.

EUROSTAT: 1995, Women and Men in the European Union. A Statistical Portrait.

EUROSTAT: 1995, Yearbook 1995. A Statistical Eye on Europe 1983–1993.

EUROSTAT: 1996, European Community Household Panel (ECHP, Methods, Vol. 1, Survey Questionnaires, Waves 1–3.

EUROSTAT: 1998, Social Protection Expenditure and Receipts 1980–95.

EUROSTAT: 2000, European Social Statistics: Income, Poverty and Social Exlusion (Luxembourg).

EUROSTAT: 2000, Key Data on Health 2000 (Luxembourg).

Evans, G.: 1992, 'Testing the validity of the goldthorpe class schema', European Sociological Review 8, pp. 211–232.

Förster, M.F.: 2000, Trends and Driving Factors in Income Distribution and Poverty in the OECD Area. OECD: Labour Market and Social Policy Occasional papers no 42.

Gallie, D.: 1983, Social Inequality and Class Radicalism in France and Britain (Cambridge University Press).

Gallie, D. and S. Paugam: 2001, Welfare Regimes and the Experience of Unemployment in Europe (Oxford).

Ganzeboom, H.B.G. and D.J. Treiman: 1996, 'Internationally comparable measures of occupational status for the 1988 International Standard Classification of Occupations', Social Science Research 25, pp. 201–239.

Ginter, E.: 1995, 'Cardiovascular risk factors in the former communist countries. Analysis of 40 MONICA populations', Eur J Epidemiol 11, pp. 199–205.

Goldthorpe, J.: 2000, 'Social class and the differentiation of employment contracts', In: J.H. Goldthorpe (ed.), On Sociology: Numbers, Narratives and the Integration of Research and Theory (Clarendon Press, Oxford).

Gorski, P.A.: 1998, 'Perinatal outcome and the social contract: Interrelationships between health and society', Acta Paediatr Jpn 40(2), pp. 168–172.

Gottschalk, P. and T. Smeeding: 1997, 'Cross-national comparisons of earnings and income inequality', Journal of Economic Literature XXXV, June 1997.

Gottschalk, P. and T. Smeeding: 1999, Empirical Evidence on Income Inequality in Industrialised Countries. Luxembourg Income Survey Working Paper No. 154.

Gual, A. and J. Colom: 1997, 'Why has alcohol consumption declined in countries of southern Europe?', Addiction 92 Suppl 1, pp. 21–31.

Gustafsson, B. and M. Johansson: 1999, 'In search for smoking guns: What makes income inequality vary over time in different countries?', American Sociological Review 24.

Gustafsson, B. and P. Pedersen: 1999, Poverty and Low Income in the Nordic Countries. NORD 1999, 6.

Habich, R. and H.-H. Noll: 2000, 'Zufriedenheit in Lebensbereichen', In: Statistisches Bundesamt in Zusammenarbeit mit WZB und ZUMA (ed.), Datenreport 1999 (Bundeszentrale für politische Bildung, Bonn), pp. 431–442.

Habich, R. and H.-H. Noll, W. Zapf: 1999, 'Subjektives Wohlbefinden in Ostdeutschland nähert sich westdeutschem Niveau. Ergebnisse des Wohlfahrtssurveys 1998', Informationsdienst Soziale Indikatoren (ISI) 22, pp. 1–6.

Hall, P.A.: 1992, 'the movement from keynesianism to monetarism: Institutional analysis and british economic policy in the 1970s', In: S. Steinmo, T. Kathleen and F. Longstreth (eds.), Structuring Politics. Historical Institutionalism in Comparative Analyses (Cambridge University Press, Cambridge).

Hall, P.H. and R. Taylor: 1996, 'Political science and the three new institutionalisms', Political Studies 44, pp. 936–957.

Hallqvist, J.: 1998, Socioeconomic Differences in Myocardial Infarction Risk. Academic thesis, Karolinska Institutet, Stockholm.

Halman, L.: 1997, European Images and Discourses on the Family. Exploring Value Differences and Similarities in the Domain of Primary Relations in Eastern and Western Europe. WORC Paper 97.09.009/1. Tilburg.

Hancock, M.D.: 1989, West Germany. The Politics of Democratic Corporatism (Chatham House Publishers, Chatham, NJ).

Hanesch, W., P. Krause, G. Bäcker, M. Maschke and B. Otto: 2000, Armut und Ungleichheit in Deutschland. Der neue Armutsbericht der Hans-Böckler Stiftung, des DGB und des paritätischen Wohlfahrtsverbands (Rowohlt, Hamburg).

Hantrais, L.: 1995, Social Policy in the European Union.

Harkness, J.A. and A. Schua-Glusberg: 1998, 'Questionnaires in translation', In: J.A. Harkness (ed.), Cross-Cultural Survey Equivalence (ZUMA, Mannheim).

Hauser, R.: 1997, 'Soziale Sicherung in westeuropäischen Staaten', In: S. Hradil and S. Immerfall (eds.), Die westeuropäischen Gesellschaften im Vergleich (Opladen, Leske+Budrich).

Hirdmann, Y.: 1988, 'Genussystemet' (The Genus System), in Demokrati och makt i Sverige (SOU, Stockholm).

Hoem, B.: 1998, Barnafödande och sysselsättning. Upp- och nedgången i fruktsamheten 1985–1997 (Childbearing and female employment. The fertility rise and fall in Sweden 1985–1997). Demographic reports 1998.1. Statistics Sweden.

Holdsworth, C.: 2000, 'Leaving home in Britain and Spain', European Sociological Review 16(2).
Höpflinger, F.: 1997, Haushalts- und Familienstrukturen im intereuropäischen Vergleich.
Hout, M. and D.P. Dohan: 1996, 'Two paths to educational opportunity: Class and educational selection in Sweden and the United States', In: R. Erikson and J.O. Jonsson (eds.), Can Education be Equalized? The Swedish case in Comparative Perspective (Westview Press, Boulder).
Inglehart, R.: 1989, Kultureller Umbruch. Wertewandel in der westlichen Welt (Campus Verlag, Frankfurt a.M./New York).
Inglehart, R. and H.D. Klingemann: 2000, 'Genes, culture, democracy, and happiness', In: E. Diener and E.M. Suh (eds.), Culture and Subjective Well-being (The MIT Press, Cambridge, MA), pp. 165–183.
Inglehart, R. and J.-R. Rabier: 1986, 'Aspirations adapt to situations. But why are the Belgians so much happier than the French? A cross-cultural analysis of the subjective quality of life', In: Frank M. Andrews (ed.), Research on the Quality of Life (University of Michigan, Ann Arbor), pp. 1–56.
ISSP: 1990, International Social Survey Program 1990 – Role of Government II. Datafile compiled at Zentralarchiv, Universität zu Köln.
ISSP: 1996, International Social Survey Program 1996 – Role of Government III. Datafile compiled at Zentralarchiv, Universität zu Köln.
Jacobi, O., B. Keller and W. Müller-Jentsch: 1998, 'Germany: Facing new challenges', In: A. Ferner and R. Hyman (eds.), Changing Industrial Relations in Europe (2nd ed.) (Blackwell, Oxford).
Jäntti, M. and S. Danziger: 1991, Income Poverty in Advanced Countries. Institute for Economic Research, Discussion papers 151, Helsinki.
Jenssen, A.T. and W. Martinussen (eds.): 1994, Velferdsstaten i våre hjerter (Ad Notam Gyldendal, Oslo).
Józan, P.E. and R. Prokhorskas: 1997, Atlas of Leading and "Avoidable" Causes of Death in Countries of Central and Eastern Europé (Budapest, Hungarian CSO Publishing House).
Juel, K., P. Bjerregaard and M. Madsen: 2000, 'Mortality and life expectancy in Denmark and in other Euopean countries: What is happening to middle-aged Danes', European J Public Health 10, pp. 93–100.
Kautto, M., J. Fritzell, B. Hvinden, J. Kvist and H. Uusitalo (eds.): 2001, Nordic Welfare States in the European Context (Routledge).
Kawachi, I., B.P. Kennedy and R. Glass: 1999, 'Social capital and self-rated health: A contextual analysis', Am J Public Health 89(8), 1187–1193.

Keys, A., C. Aravanis, H.W Blackburn, F.S. Van Buchem, R. Buzina, B.D. Djordjevic, A.S. Dontas, F. Fidanza, M.J. Karvonen, N. Kimura, D. Lekos, M. Monti, V. Puddu, H.L. Taylor: 1966, 'Epidemiological studies related to coronary heart disease: Characteristics of men aged 40–59 in seven countries', Acta Med Scand Suppl. 460, pp. 1–392.

Kolberg, J.E.: 1992, The Study of Welfare State Regimes (M.E. Sharpe, London).

Korpi and Palme (eds.): 1997, Contested Citizenship. A Century of Social Policy Development in the Western World.

Kristensson, M.: 1998, The Li Vicordia study. Possible causes for the differences in coronary heart disease mortality between Lithuania and Sweden. Linköping University Medical Dissertations. Linköping.

Küchler, M.: 1998, 'The survey method: An indispensable tool for social science research everywhere?', American Behavioral Scientist 42, pp. 178–200.

Küchler, M.: 1987, 'The utility of surveys for cross-national research', Social Science Research 16, pp. 229–244.

Kunst, A.: 1997, Cross-national Comparisons of Socio-Economic Differences in Mortality. Doctoral thesis, Erasmus University of Rotterdam, Holland.

Kunst, A.E., F. Groenhof, J.P. Mackenbach and E.W. Health: 1998, 'Occupational class and cause specific mortality in middle aged men in 11 European countries: Comparison of population based studies', EU Working Group on Socioeconomic Inequalities in Health BMJ 316, pp. 1636–1642.

Lane, R.E.: 1996, 'Quality of life and quality of persons: A new role for government', In: Avner Offer (ed.), In Pursuit of the Quality of Life (Oxford University Press, Oxford), pp. 256–293.

Leibfried, S.: 1990, 'Sozialstaat Europa? Integrationsperspektiven europäischer Armutsregimes', Nachrichtendienst des Deutschen Vereins für öffentliche und private Fürsorge 70, pp. 295–305.

Leibfried, S.: 1993, 'Towards a european welfare state? On integrating poverty regimes into the european community', In: C. Jones (ed.), New Perspectives on the Welfare State in Europe (Routledge, London).

Levi, M.: 1990, 'A logic of institutional change', In: K.S. Cook and M. Levi (eds.), The Limits of Rationality (University of Chicago Press, Chicago).

Levy, J.: 2000, 'France: Directing adjustment?', In: F. Scharpf and V.A. Schmidt (eds.), Welfare and Work in the Open Economy: Volume II: Diverse Responses to Common Challenges (Oxford University Press, Oxford).

Lewis, J.: 1992, 'Gender and the development of welfare regimes', Journal of European Social Policy 2(3).

Linking Welfare and Work: 1999, European Foundation for the Improvement of Living and Working Conditions.

Löfström, Å: 1996, Variation in Female Activity and Employment Patterns: Th case of Sweden. Umeå Economic Studies No. 407.

Löfström, Å: 2000, Att sätta barn till världen – en förstudie. Umeå Economic Studies No. 529.

Marshall, T.H.: 1950, Citizenship and Social Class (Cambridge University Press).

Matheson, G.: 1993, The Decommodified in a Commodified World. Unpublished PhD thesis, University of New England, Armidale.

Molarius, A., J.C. Seidell, S. Sans, J. Tuomilehto, and K. Kuulasmaa: 2000, 'Educational level, relative body weight, and changes in their association over 10 years: An international perspective from the WHO MONICA Project', Am J Public Health 90(8), pp. 1260–1268.

Muntaner, C. and J. Lynch: 1999, 'Income inequality, social cohesion, and class relations: A critique of Wilkinson's neo-Durkheimian research program', Int J Health Serv. 29(1), pp. 59–81.

Nilsson, P. and K. Orth-Gomér (eds.): 2000, 'Self-rated health in a European perspective', FRN, p. 2, Uppsala.

Noll, H.-H.: 2000, 'Arbeitsmarkt und Erwerbstätigkeit', In: Statistisches Bundesamt in Zusammenarbeit mit WZB und ZUMA (ed.), Datenreport 1999 (Bundeszentrale für politische Bildung, Bonn), pp. 480–489.

Noll, H.-H.: 1997, 'Wohlstand, Lebensqualität und Wohlbefinden in den Ländern der Europäischen Union', In: Stefan Hradil und Stefan Immerfall (eds.), Die westeuropäischen Gesellschaften im Vergleich (Opladen, Leske + Budrich), pp. 431–473.

North, D.C.: 1990, Institutions, Institutional Change and Economic Performance (Cambridge University Press, Cambridge).

O'Connor, J.: 1996, 'From women in the welfare state to gendering welfare state regimes', Current Sociology 44(2).

OECD: 1995, Education at a Glance. OECD Indicators.

OECD: 1998, Income distribution and poverty in selected OECD-countries. OECD, Economics Department Working Papers 189.

Papadakis, E. and C. Bean: 1993, 'Popular support for the welfare state: A comparison between institutional regimes', Journal of Public Policy 13, pp. 227–254.

Papadakis, E.: 1990, Attitudes to State and Private Welfare: Analysis of Results from a National Survey. Sydney, SPRC Reports and Proceedings no. 88.

Pierson, P.: 2000, 'Coping with permanent austerity: Welfare state restructuring in affluent democracies', In: P. Pierrson (ed.), The New Politics of the Welfare State (Oxford University Press, Oxford).

Pinelli, A.: 1998, Determinants of Fertility. New Family Forms and Context Characteristics. Council of Europe.

Ribe, M.: 1987, A Multivariate Approach to Social Inequality. Statistics Sweden.

Roller, E.: 1992, Einstellungen der Bürger zum Wohlfahrtsstaat der Bundesrepublik Deutschland Opladen: Westdeutscher Verlag.

Roller, E.: 1994, 'Ideological basis of the market economy: Attitudes toward distribution principles and the role of government in western and eastern Germany', European Sociological Review 10, pp. 105–117.

Rosseneu, M., J.C. Fruchart, J.M. Bard, V. Nicaud, N. Vinaimont, F. Cambien and G. De Backer: 1994, 'Plasma apolipoprotein concentrations in young adults with a parental history of premature coronary heart disease and in control subjects. The EARS Study. European Atherosclerosis Research Study', Circulation 89(5), pp. 1967–1973.

Rothstein, B.: 1996, 'Political institutions – An overview', In: R.E. Goodin and H.-D. Klingemann (eds.), A New Handbook of Political Science (Oxford University Press, Oxford).

Rothstein, B.: 1998, Just Institutions Matter: The Moral and Political Logic of the Universal Welfare State (Cambridge University Press, Cambridge).

Rubery, J., C. Fagan and M. Smith: 1994, Changing Patterns of Work and Working-Time in the European Union and the Impact of Gender Divisions. Report to the Equal Opportunities Unit, DG5. Commission of the European Communities.

Scharpf, F.: 1999, 'Economic changes, vulnerabilities, and institutional capabilities', In: F. Sharpf and V. Schmidt (eds.), Welfare and Work in the Open Society, vol. 1 (Oxford University Press).

Scheuch, E.K.: 1989, 'Theoretical implications of comparative survey research: Why the wheel of cross-cultural methodology keeps on being reinvented', International Sociology 4, pp. 147–167.

Schöb, A.: 2000, 'Gesellschaftliche Beteiligung und Freizeit', In: Statistisches Bundesamt in Zusammenarbeit mit WZB und ZUMA (ed.), Datenreport 1999 (Bundeszentrale für politische Bildung, Bonn), pp. 530–540.

Sgritta, G.: 2001, Family and Welfare Systems in the Transition to Adulthood: An Emblematic Case-Study. Paper presented at the Conference on Family Forms and the Young Generation in Europe, Milano, 20–22 September 2001.

Smith, T.W.: 1987, 'That which we call welfare by any other name would smell sweeter', Public Opinion Quarterly 51, pp. 75–83.

Statistics Netherlands: 1996, European Social Indicators. A Review of the Extended Short Eurostat List of Social Indicators.

Statistics Sweden: 1996, The Swedish Survey of Living Conditions: Design and Methods. Appendix 16, series Living Conditions.

Steinmo, S. and J. Watts: 1995, 'It's the institutions, stupid! Why comprehensive national health insurance always fails in America', Journal of Health Politics 20, pp. 329–372.

Steinmo, S., K. Thelen and F. Longstreth (eds.): 1992, Structuring Politics. Historical Institutionalism in Comparative Analysis (Cambridge University Press, Cambridge).

Stjernø, S.: 1995, Mellom kirke og kapital (Scandinavian University Press, Oslo).

Streeck, W.: 1997, 'German capitalism: Does it exist? Can it survive?', In: C. Crouch Colin and W. Streeck (eds.), Political Economy of Modern Capitalism (Sage, London).

Sussman, M., S. Steinmetz and G. Peterson: 1999, Handbook of Marriage and the Family (Plenum Press).

Svallfors, S. and P. Taylor-Gooby (eds.): 1999, The End of the Welfare State? Responses to State Retrenchment (Routledge, London).

Svallfors, S.: 1989, Vem älskar välfärdsstaten? Attityder, organiserade intressen och svensk välfärdspolitik (Arkiv, Lund).

Svallfors, S.: 1993, 'Policy regimes and attitudes to inequality: A comparison of three European nations', In: T.P. Boje and S.E.O. Hort (eds.), Scandinavia in a New Europe (Scandinavian University Press, Oslo).

Svallfors, S.: 1996a, Välfärdsstatens moraliska ekonomi. Välfärdsopinionen i 90-talets Sverige (Boréa, Umeå).

Svallfors, S.: 1996b, 'National differences in national identities: An introduction to the International Social Survey Program', New Community 22, pp. 127–134.

Svallfors, S.: 1997, 'Worlds of welfare and attitudes to redistribution: A comparison of eight western nations', European Sociological Review 13, pp. 283–304.

Svallfors, S.: 1999a, 'Political trust and attitudes towards redistribution: A comparison of Sweden and Norway', European Societies 1, pp. 241–268.

Svallfors, S.: 1999b, 'Välfärdsregimer och välfärdsopinioner: en jämförelse mellan åtta västländer', Sociologisk Forskning 1, pp. 93–119.

Svallfors, S. (ed.): 1995, In the Eye of the Beholder. Opinions on Welfare and Justice in Comparative Perspective (Scandbook, Umeå).

Taylor-Gooby, P.: 1985, Public Opinion, Ideology and State Welfare (Routledge & Kegan Paul, London).

Värnik A, W.D. and G. Eklund: 1994, 'Suicides in the Baltic countries 1968–1990', Scand J Soc Med 22, pp. 166–169.

Värnik, A., D. Wasserman, M. Dankowicz and G. Eklund: 1998, 'Age-specific suicide rates in the Slavic and Baltic regions of the former USSR during perestroika, in comparison with 22 European countries', Acta Psychiatr Scand 98 (Suppl.394), pp. 20–25.

Veenhoven, R.: 1994, 'Is happiness a trait? Test of the theory that a better society does not make people any happier', Social Indicators Research 32(2), pp. 101–160.

Veenhoven, R.: 1997, Advances in Understanding Happiness. [http://www.eur.nl/fsw/research/happiness/97c-ab.htm]. (Previously published in French in: Revue Québécoise de Psychologie 18, pp. 267–293).

Vogel, J.: 1991, Social Report for the Nordic Countries: Living conditions and Inequality in the Late 1980s. Statistical Reports of the Nordic Countries. Copenhagen.

Vogel, J.: 1994, 'Social indicators and social reporting. traditions and options for the development of comparative social indicators for the European Union', Statistical Journal of the United Nations ECE 11.

Vogel, J.: 1996, 'The future direction of social indicator research. Key note speech, World Conference on Quality of Life, August 22.25, 1996, Prince George, Canada', Social Indicators Research 42.

Vogel, J.: 1997, Living Conditions and Inequality in the European Union. Eurostat: Population and Social Conditions E/1997-3. Luxembourg.

Vogel, J.: 1998a, Coping with the European Welfare Mix. Welfare Delivery Systems, Family Formation and Material Inequality between Types of Families in the European Union. Paper presented at the 1998 Siena Group Meeting on Families at the End of the Twentieth Century; Sidney, Australia, 7–9.12.1998.

Vogel, J.: 1998b, Three Types of European Society. Internet: Nordic News Network; WWW@NNN.SE.

Vogel, J.: 1999, 'The European welfare mix: Institutional configuration and distributive outcome in Sweden and the European Union. A longitudinal and comparative perspective', Social Indicators Research 48.

Vogel, J.: 2000a, Inequality in Material Living Standards in Europe: A Lesson for Developing Countries? Paper prepared for the Conference on "North- South Relationships in the in the World Economy in the XXI Century: Inequalities, Well-Being, Opportunities", L'Aquila, Abruzzo, Italy, September 6–8 2000.

Vogel, J.; 2000b, Welfare Production Models and Income Structure. A Comparative and Longitudinal Perspective: European Union: mid 1990s and Sweden 1963–1998. Paper prepared for the Rich-Poor Conference of ISA working group 6; Berlin 20–21 October 2000.

Vogel, J.: 2001c, European Welfare Regimes and the Transition to Adulthood: Comparative and Longitudinal Perspective. Paper prepared for the Conference on Family Forms and the Young Generation in Europe, Milano, Italy, 20–22 September 2001.

Vogel, J.: 2001d, Ageing and Living Conditions of the Elderly: Sweden 1980–1998. Paper presented at the 5th conference of the International Society for Quality of Life Studies, Washington, November 28–August 1, 2001.

Vogel, J.: forthcoming 2002, 'Towards a typology of European welfare production: Summary and conclusions', In: K.U. Mayer, R. Habich and W. Glatzer (eds.), Sozialstaat und Sozialberichterstattung. Festschrift zum 65. Geburtstag von Wolfgang Zapf (Leske + Budrich, Leverkusen).

Vogel, J. and L. Häll (eds.): 1997, Välfärd och ojämlikhet i 20-årsperspektiv 1975–95 (Living Conditions and Inequality in Sweden 1975–95). Report 91, series Living Conditions. Statistics Sweden.

Vogel, J., L. Häll, S.E. Johansson and C. Skjöld: 2000, Äldres levnadsförhållanden 1980–1998 (Living Conditions of the Elderly 1980–1998). Report 93, series Ling Conditions. Statistics Sweden, Swedish Social Ministry, and Swedish Board for Health and Social Affairs.

Vogel, J. and T. Theorell: 2001, European Welfare Production Models and their Health Outcome.

Vogel, J. et. al.: 1988, Inequality in Sweden: Trends and Current Situation. Series Living Conditions, Statistics Sweden.

Weiss, Linda: 1998, The Myth of the Powerless State: Governing the Economy in a Global Era (Polity Press, Cambridge).

Whelan, C., R. Layte, B. Maitre and B. Nolan: 2000, 'Poverty dynamics', European Societies 2(4).

Wilkinson, R.G.: 1998, 'Mortality and distribution of income. Low relative income affects mortality', BMJ 23; 316(7144), pp. 1611–1612.

Wilkinson, R.G.: 1996, Unhealthy Societies: The Afflictions of Inequality (London, Routledge).

Zapf, W.: 1984, 'Individuelle Wohlfahrt: Lebensbedingungen und wahrgenommen Lebensqualität', In: W. Glatzer and W. Zapf (ed.), Lebensqualität in der Bundesrepublik. Objektive Lebensbedingungen und subjektives Wohlbefinden (Frankfurt a. M, Campus), pp. 13–26.

APPENDIX

SELECTED TABLES

Social Indicators Research **64:** 585–598, 2003.

TABLE 5.1

Annual disposable household income (ECU, in PPP). Calculated per consumer unit equivalent (OECD-modified scale), and for all subgroups expressed as a percentage of the *national* average. Persons 20–84 years. Source: ECHP/NSS 1994

	Nordic				Central							Southern				
	EU14	FIN	S	DK	N	B	D	F	UK	I	IRL	L	NL	P	GR	E
Average for all 20–84 years	*11831*	*10922*	*11229*	*12406*	*11474*	*13154*	*13660*	*12513*	*13333*	*10014*	*10048*	*23148*	*12446*	*7625*	*7764*	*9090*
Index for all 20–84 years	100.0	100.0	100.0	100.0	100.0	100.0	100.0	100.0	100.0	100.0	100.0	100.0	100.0	100.0	100.0	100.0
Sex																
Men	103.0	102.2	101.0	103.4	102.4	102.6	104.9	101.7	104.3	102.1	102.1	103.0	102.2	102.7	102.5	101.1
Women	97.2	97.9	99.0	96.7	97.7	97.5	95.5	98.4	95.9	98.0	98.0	97.1	97.9	97.5	97.7	99.0
AGE																
20–24 yr.	87.8	84.2	47.4	85.2	92.2	95.1	87.5	81.9	94.7	88.5	94.8	94.8	80.0	101.4	94.3	89.5
25–44 yr.	104.7	101.7	99.0	100.3	95.6	107.9	103.8	101.1	105.5	105.4	105.7	105.1	102.1	107.9	111.0	109.3
45–64 yr.	106.0	109.1	119.4	115.1	113.9	103.0	107.2	108.9	109.2	101.7	104.7	100.9	111.5	102.9	100.8	97.0
65–84 yr.	86.2	86.5	93.2	80.7	92.3	81.1	83.6	93.0	76.7	92.6	81.1	88.3	85.9	77.6	80.6	91.3
Household composition																
Single adult 65+ yr.	74.5	70.9	79.9	75.2	76.8	74.6	76.4	82.5	61.9	81.1	62.3	78.9	80.8	53.7	63.8	78.5
Single adult 30–64 yr.	109.7	95.3	109.5	98.2	96.9	105.3	110.1	100.4	110.9	118.2	101.3	112.1	118.8	93.3	121.7	128.0
Single adult –30 yr.	82.5	76.9	69.6	71.2	72.0	96.1	84.1	72.7	92.8	127.2	109.9	89.9	65.5	92.7	94.5	120.0
Single parent	90.3	91.0	70.7	82.3	89.8	88.5	83.6	85.6	77.2	105.9	84.8	—	85.7	95.3	105.3	104.2
Couple 65+ yr., no ch	88.8	99.0	108.6	88.1	99.5	78.6	87.4	100.0	83.1	94.1	81.0	88.8	87.1	68.4	72.2	78.8
Couple –65 yr., no ch	122.9	117.3	131.6	122.6	119.0	115.0	118.6	115.6	128.6	130.2	149.3	121.8	129.5	121.2	113.8	130.4
Couple with childr.	99.6	103.4	93.0	101.7	101.5	103.3	99.6	101.4	99.5	96.7	100.5	97.6	90.4	109.3	106.2	100.0
Other households	93.7	86.0	41.7	115.0	105.0	105.8	89.9	86.1	98.8	93.6	101.3	92.4	93.7	90.2	96.5	95.6
Type of family																
Lives w parents	99.9	104.9	—	112.4	110.1	102.3	103.2	96.3	105.8	97.4	103.1	101.7	97.6	110.6	102.3	99.9
Marr/CU, with Ch	99.6	103.3	99.7	100.4	100.8	103.1	99.0	102.0	97.9	97.5	99.4	96.7	89.3	108.1	107.0	100.5
Marr/CU, no Ch	109.8	111.7	122.0	113.0	110.0	99.5	108.9	109.4	113.2	112.4	120.8	111.1	114.8	93.0	93.1	103.9
Single, with Ch	84.0	91.6	77.1	79.5	87.6	85.9	77.5	83.7	70.2	103.4	74.7	—	78.7	93.3	106.7	103.8
Single, no Ch	89.7	83.1	89.5	83.6	83.4	92.1	91.4	88.0	83.8	98.5	83.2	95.3	91.6	69.5	88.4	98.6
Other Households	93.7	86.0	41.7	115.0	105.0	105.8	89.9	86.1	98.8	93.6	101.3	92.4	93.7	90.2	96.5	95.6

TABLE 5.1

Continued

	Nordic				Central							Southern				
	EU14	FIN	S	DK	N	B	D	F	UK	I	IRL	L	NL	P	GR	E
No of Children 0–17 yrs																
No childr.	102.9	100.1	101.1	101.9	104.5	100.3	102.9	100.8	105.1	103.7	107.1	105.3	106.2	102.7	99.6	102.4
1	99.7	104.4	101.6	98.2	98.9	101.7	99.7	103.2	94.2	99.2	103.1	93.1	88.5	103.9	105.3	100.4
2	91.6	100.4	98.8	94.6	90.7	100.1	85.7	98.3	91.2	87.8	93.6	89.6	82.4	93.2	100.7	92.5
3+	76.3	88.3	85.8	76.9	83.3	90.9	79.6	86.4	64.8	66.5	77.7	75.7	72.3	64.2	79.5	77.3
With childr. 0–6 yr.	93.3	99.3	94.8	93.8	89.0	100.0	87.6	98.4	83.8	96.8	90.4	81.2	80.2	100.2	109.6	101.8
Education level																
3rd level	137.8	140.5	125.1	117.1	111.6	124.9	125.0	139.6	141.3	150.6	159.5	147.5	133.1	247.8	149.8	152.4
Post compulsory	104.7	103.9	90.2	101.7	99.2	103.2	100.8	101.4	104.3	115.4	114.7	112.9	98.7	139.1	113.0	113.9
Compulsory	87.4	97.6	102.8	93.7	100.4	87.1	93.3	83.6	86.9	87.9	78.9	83.1	86.3	85.1	82.9	83.5
Labour market position																
Self-employed	102.4	100.0	103.6	110.7	113.2	106.4	103.5	109.1	116.2	100.1	113.0	116.4	118.3	79.9	97.4	91.9
Employed	114.9	114.9	109.5	109.6	106.8	116.9	112.0	110.5	115.4	119.1	123.8	109.5	110.8	122.9	123.9	126.1
Unemployed	78.4	85.7	87.9	90.7	83.1	79.0	78.5	80.5	75.3	70.0	73.2	—	82.3	92.0	87.7	79.1
In education	89.2	81.5	55.7	68.8	86.8	98.3	84.8	82.9	85.6	101.4	103.8	88.8	72.2	123.7	97.7	96.0
Retired	87.8	88.3	99.0	81.9	89.9	83.3	84.1	95.1	77.7	94.1	80.6	88.4	88.0	81.5	85.7	91.3
Doing housework	84.7	91.3	90.2	83.4	94.0	83.2	91.7	83.2	76.0	81.3	83.5	88.5	88.2	79.5	91.0	86.7
Other	79.5	82.3	79.1	82.7	—	72.5	69.9	88.0	81.2	75.3	69.7	82.7	88.6	68.0	96.1	79.8
Working hours																
Men 30+ h/w	112.9	113.6	109.2	113.8	108.0	115.7	113.9	109.5	117.5	110.6	118.7	109.0	111.1	110.0	110.8	112.4
Women 30+ h/w	119.6	113.2	111.0	108.4	111.3	122.1	111.8	116.8	125.0	122.5	138.1	120.7	132.2	113.2	115.1	139.0
1–29 h/w	104.8	99.1	101.3	106.1	96.2	106.5	107.8	100.9	95.2	114.7	117.6	96.3	108.6	119.4	119.2	111.3
Total work load in households																
Couple, both full-time	126.9	127.1	120.8	115.9	117.2	126.9	120.4	123.9	130.9	128.7	144.1	130.0	145.0	120.7	118.7	152.0
Couple, full+part	107.5	108.9	108.0	116.4	100.2	107.5	111.0	105.4	99.5	115.9	121.1	100.3	104.6	117.5	113.4	112.6

TABLE 5.1

Continued

	Nordic				Central							Southern				
	EU14	FIN	S	DK	N	B	D	F	UK	I	IRL	L	NL	P	GR	E
Couple, full+non-act.	98.3	102.1	106.5	104.5	102.8	101.3	101.5	99.6	104.3	93.5	108.9	92.7	94.0	92.6	98.6	92.7
Couple, both part-time	109.6	98.0	100.4	107.3	101.9	108.4	114.0	108.5	98.2	123.7	117.6	102.5	109.2	119.8	124.9	114.5
Couple, part+non-act.	93.2	98.4	112.2	97.0	94.0	96.9	92.9	88.2	99.6	97.6	87.6	88.5	88.8	72.5	90.7	81.8
Couple, both non-act	87.5	90.3	98.5	90.3	89.5	82.0	87.6	92.9	82.6	88.2	82.5	89.5	86.9	82.5	88.6	85.2
Single, full-time	113.7	105.7	92.1	103.1	106.3	116.5	109.7	103.7	120.3	118.9	122.2	111.6	121.9	106.3	118.2	122.4
Single, part-time	91.3	83.9	75.1	80.9	82.2	92.5	83.8	80.9	82.7	108.6	111.8	76.8	104.1	121.4	109.3	102.3
Single, non-act.	80.4	77.5	68.2	74.3	82.9	83.8	78.8	82.7	67.4	86.3	75.4	83.0	80.2	84.8	87.7	88.4
Socio-economic group																
Upper non-man/empl.	134.4	128.5	125.3	131.5	—	126.2	135.0	146.7	135.4	119.9	151.5	147.7	132.7	145.9	131.5	144.6
Top managers	155.4	145.4	151.6	150.0	—	139.5	135.4	174.0	157.4	157.0	178.9	—	127.5	261.4	239.9	213.0
Professionals	153.3	133.1	125.5	129.9	—	132.6	143.7	164.3	150.8	150.6	174.1	154.5	136.5	247.6	176.6	206.0
Lower non-manual	116.9	110.0	113.1	107.6	—	120.8	113.0	111.3	110.5	129.9	125.5	119.1	116.3	136.1	128.7	133.9
Lower managers	112.8	133.6	108.6	112.9	—	122.6	113.4	101.7	111.7	141.0	121.8	—	123.7	132.7	118.8	101.4
All manual workers	93.6	102.0	94.9	100.3	—	100.2	91.2	88.6	96.5	98.6	100.0	77.5	90.9	86.9	98.4	93.1
Skilled man./foremen	97.2	104.2	96.0	106.1	—	104.6	94.4	92.1	100.8	103.9	108.2	79.9	93.5	88.4	102.0	97.1
Unskilled manual	89.6	100.4	92.7	96.0	—	97.3	85.7	85.2	92.7	92.0	94.4	75.5	88.1	85.3	94.3	89.4
Small farmers	74.3	90.6	—	76.9	—	60.8	—	71.1	117.0	68.8	96.8	—	104.5	52.6	68.8	71.1
Sector																
Private sector	110.2	107.0	108.0	112.4	106.3	114.5	109.8	107.1	115.1	110.2	116.8	101.9	113.2	99.8	104.7	109.4
Public sector	123.3	110.1	111.4	107.6	106.9	120.6	118.2	119.4	121.1	126.0	138.2	134.7	120.7	163.2	138.2	157.9

TABLE 5.2

Adjusted annual disposable income (OECD-modified scale), by gender, age, labour market status and household type. Relative income levels for subgroups are compared with a reference group (=0) within each classification

	Nordic			Central							Southern			
	DK	FIN	S	B	D	F	IRE	UK	L	NL	I	GR	E	P
Sex														
Women	–283	–214	–17	184*	–549*	275	749*	–121	–183	767*	334*	272*	542*	95
Men	0	0	0	0	0	0	0	0	0	0	0	0	0	0
Age														
20–29 yr.	3004*	–1992*	–2991*	–1002	–2534*	2614*	–904*	–1272*	–2012	–3296*	–575*	179*	–558*	–450
30–44 yr.	1142*	–736*	–547*	–332*	–731*	–803*	–417	–282	–475	–1360*	–65	371*	456*	–342
45–64 yr.	0	0	0	0	0	0	0	0	0	0	0	0	0	0
65–84 yr.	3540*	–2031*	–2806*	–3224*	–2582*	–886*	–2828*	–3608*	–145	–3316*	–1071*	–320*	–312	–394
Labour market status														
Manual worker	0	0	0	0	0	0	0	0	0	0	0	0	0	0
Upper non-man	4123*	3335*	2881*	3691*	5727*	7028*	5129*	5288*	14893*	4947*	2586*	3428*	4783*	4816*
Lower non-man	1634*	1363*	1733*	3030*	3054*	2859*	2315*	2071*	8526*	2819*	3515*	3139*	3795*	4088*
In education	1820*	–1012*	–2749*	54	–1042	107	281	–579	2128	–2679*	552	833*	880*	2911*
Unemployed	–372	–1327*	–1027*	–2885*	–1680*	1024*	–2956*	–3360*	–858	–1364*	–2207*	–288*	–1254*	–119
Retired	1963*	–1173*	–693	–1498*	–2085*	102	–350	–515	585	1626*	407	1802*	725	602
Homeworker	1067	–50	–779	–2358*	–239	1232*	–2031*	–1439*	1316	–1025*	–1554*	138*	–835*	–444
Misc	–669	–1394	–2575*	–3225*	–3486*	1238*	–3025*	–1213*	–1107	–668	–1730*	1249*	–952*	–1014*
Household type														
Couple, w ch	0	0	0	0	0	0	0	0	0	0	0	0	0	0
Couple, no ch	2893*	1891*	3620*	1470*	2715*	1755*	2629*	3263*	3776	4245*	2198*	–254*	989*	–59
Single, w ch	2088*	–610	–1814*	–1282*	–2757*	2584*	–1623*	–2513*	–1689*	–1258	635	–521*	494	–1272*
Single, no ch	150	–856*	670*	518	729*	–831*	–623*	626	319	2093*	745*	–784*	195	–1785*
Staying w par	4554*	3014*	–5376*	919	3359*	1963*	775*	2179*	2549	4898*	783*	–72*	481*	350
Other h'holds	1648*	327	–2553*	1401*	1079*	1110*	1019*	1160*	1057	4198*	323	–210*	186	–698*
R^2	0.20	0.18	0.38	0.13	0.16	0.11	0.20	0.13	0.19	0.19	0.09	0.08	0.12	0.13

TABLE 5.3

National poverty rates. Poverty line = 50 percent of the national average adjusted disposable income. Persons aged 20–84 years, excluding full-time students and young adults living with their parents. Percent. Source: ECHP/NSS

	Nordic			Central							Southern					
	EU14	B	DK	D	GR	E	F	I	IRL	L	NL	P	FIN	S	UK	N
All 20–84 years	15.3	12.6	6.5	10.9	21.8	19.1	13.1	17.9	20.0	12.9	11.4	26.8	4.6	5.5	20.6	5.0
Sex																
Men	14.1	11.5	5.4	9.4	20.7	18.9	12.4	17.0	18.0	11.8	10.7	24.9	4.8	5.6	18.2	4.2
Women	16.3	13.6	7.6	12.2	22.7	19.3	13.8	18.6	21.9	13.9	12.0	28.4	4.4	5.4	22.8	5.9
Age																
20–24 yr.	22.8	22.6	17.6	20.1	20.5	26.7	24.8	21.4	22.6	13.6	32.7	24.7	14.4	25.9	22.3	14.2
25–44 yr.	13.0	9.7	4.1	8.6	14.0	17.7	10.1	17.8	21.6	14.0	9.9	18.6	3.6	4.8	18.6	5.4
45–64 yr.	14.0	13.5	3.2	9.2	21.7	21.3	13.4	18.3	16.7	9.9	8.0	25.4	4.1	3.6	14.8	3.1
65–84 yr.	20.3	15.7	13.8	16.8	35.1	17.3	16.6	17.0	21.7	15.6	16.0	44.3	5.5	5.6	33.2	5.0
Sex and age																
Women 20–24 yr.	23.2	19.8	20.2	23.9	18.0	27.5	24.1	22.7	27.9	12.3	28.8	26.8	12.6	23.3	20.8	18.1
25–44 yr.	14.1	11.3	4.4	9.8	14.6	18.1	10.5	19.0	23.4	15.3	10.1	19.4	2.8	4.3	20.7	5.7
45–64 yr.	14.4	13.5	3.6	9.5	23.0	21.4	13.6	18.4	16.2	9.5	9.2	27.8	3.1	2.9	15.7	3.7
65–84 yr.	21.6	17.3	15.3	17.7	36.4	17.5	18.0	18.1	25.7	17.6	16.1	44.7	8.0	7.0	36.5	6.6
Men 20–24 yr.	22.2	27.6	14.0	13.2	25.3	25.8	26.0	19.8	11.6	15.9	39.1	22.0	16.3	29.2	24.6	10.5
25–44 yr.	11.9	7.9	3.7	7.4	13.5	17.3	9.7	16.4	19.5	12.6	9.7	17.6	4.4	5.4	16.4	5.1
45–64 yr.	13.5	13.5	2.9	9.0	20.4	21.2	13.2	18.1	17.3	10.2	6.8	22.7	5.2	4.3	13.9	2.5
65–84 yr.	18.5	13.7	11.7	15.3	33.5	16.9	14.9	15.5	16.8	12.6	15.9	43.7	1.9	3.8	28.7	3.3
Household composition																
Single adult 65+ yr.	26.4	16.2	18.7	21.8	44.6	13.9	24.1	23.0	50.3	18.1	16.3	58.8	10.3	5.8	44.6	10.9
Single adult 30–64 yr.	15.1	12.0	4.5	13.4	18.4	20.9	15.4	16.6	35.7	14.9	5.7	38.4	8.6	4.1	23.2	10.0
Single adult –30 yr.	23.4	18.0	18.1	24.0	15.1	14.3	25.0	13.6	11.2	16.5	31.5	28.9	17.5	20.9	24.9	17.0
Single parent	24.6	16.0	6.9	24.8	19.0	22.5	18.9	19.0	34.6	—	26.7	30.3	5.5	14.8	38.8	8.5
Couple 65+ yr., no ch	18.7	18.1	9.5	13.1	40.8	23.6	15.1	12.9	9.8	17.4	17.0	54.1	1.2	0.9	30.2	2.2
Couple –65 yr., no ch	8.1	10.0	2.7	6.1	17.9	12.9	10.6	8.6	12.2	3.4	4.5	23.5	3.1	2.4	8.4	3.6

TABLE 5.3
Continued

	Nordic			Central							Southern					
	EU14	B	DK	D	GR	E	F	I	IRL	L	NL	P	FIN	S	UK	N
Couple with childr.	14.2	11.4	3.5	8.5	16.6	20.2	10.4	20.4	18.8	12.7	11.2	20.0	2.3	4.5	18.2	3.4
Other households	16.6	11.2	1.2	9.2	20.8	17.2	14.9	19.2	11.5	18.1	17.9	24.2	11.9	63.3	15.7	4.3
Type of family																
Couple w Ch	14.2	11.4	3.5	8.4	16.6	20.2	10.4	20.3	18.8	12.7	11.1	20.0	2.2	4.1	18.2	3.5
Couple no Ch	12.2	13.4	4.6	8.3	29.3	18.4	12.4	10.7	11.2	8.0	8.4	39.9	2.5	1.7	15.9	3.0
Single w Ch	24.6	15.3	7.1	25.2	18.2	22.0	19.0	18.1	34.6	—	26.9	29.9	4.5	14.9	38.9	9.0
Single no Ch	21.2	14.5	12.7	18.5	31.5	16.3	20.4	19.4	40.3	16.9	15.4	49.9	10.5	8.0	34.4	12.1
Other household type	16.6	11.2	1.2	9.2	20.8	17.2	14.9	19.2	11.5	18.1	17.9	24.2	11.9	63.3	15.7	4.3
No of children 0–17 yrs																
No childr.	14.4	12.3	7.4	11.0	23.4	16.5	14.4	15.1	16.1	9.2	10.4	30.5	5.7	6.2	18.5	5.2
1	14.3	12.5	3.0	8.6	17.5	19.1	11.1	19.2	16.0	17.1	12.6	16.2	2.6	3.1	20.1	2.4
2	17.0	12.1	3.8	12.6	19.5	24.5	10.3	23.4	20.5	18.5	13.3	26.3	2.1	4.0	21.7	5.4
3+	26.0	17.6	9.3	15.1	25.0	37.8	11.9	36.2	33.5	29.9	18.2	43.9	4.5	6.3	45.5	8.5
Parents of CH<16 yrs																
Mothers	15.8	12.3	4.0	10.6	16.8	20.5	11.6	20.1	22.0	13.4	13.5	21.3	2.1	5.5	22.5	4.6
Fathers	14.1	11.0	3.7	8.3	16.6	20.2	10.5	20.3	18.3	12.6	10.6	19.9	2.9	5.1	18.0	3.3
Single mothers	26.3	16.1	7.3	27.4	18.2	23.3	19.7	17.8	37.6	—	30.0	30.6	4.0	11.2	43.0	11.2
Parents of CH<7 yrs																
Mothers	17.6	13.5	6.3	12.9	14.4	22.6	11.3	20.8	29.1	21.9	14.9	21.3	1.5	4.9	31.1	9.7
Fathers	15.2	11.7	4.9	10.3	13.9	22.7	9.2	21.0	24.7	20.4	12.1	20.9	1.9	5.3	24.4	4.6
Education level																
3rd level	5.9	7.0	3.4	6.1	5.1	5.2	5.5	5.3	2.6	5.3	4.2	1.2	1.5	4.1	7.5	3.5
Post compulsory	10.7	11.0	5.4	9.8	9.9	11.8	9.5	9.6	11.1	7.3	10.8	9.3	3.9	7.2	15.7	5.5
Compulsory	19.7	16.4	5.0	11.4	26.0	24.7	18.1	22.7	30.0	16.9	15.1	25.3	4.9	4.9	23.8	4.8
Labour market position																
Self-employed	23.7	21.4	13.8	20.3	27.1	28.9	22.1	24.3	16.3	19.7	19.0	42.3	12.8	11.6	19.7	7.0
Employed	7.0	5.2	3.0	5.6	6.9	9.3	6.6	9.8	5.2	9.6	7.0	8.9	1.6	3.3	8.7	2.9
Unemployed	29.4	23.5	8.7	23.4	22.7	30.9	26.9	40.9	44.6	—	29.5	24.6	9.3	10.1	41.9	10.2
Retired	18.4	13.2	12.2	15.5	33.4	15.2	15.1	16.5	18.3	13.4	10.4	39.6	4.6	3.7	31.8	6.2
Doing housework	23.2	22.0	16.4	14.6	21.5	23.2	20.1	25.0	29.7	14.6	14.5	38.4	3.7	17.9	37.4	8.3

TABLE 5.3

Continued

	Nordic			Central							Southern					
	EU14	B	DK	D	GR	E	F	I	IRL	L	NL	P	FIN	S	UK	N
Working hours																
Men 30+ h/w	9.5	6.8	3.0	5.6	16.1	14.9	8.1	15.0	8.0	10.1	6.3	18.7	3.4	4.6	9.8	3.2
1–29 h/w	17.9	21.0	8.4	10.2	23.4	31.4	21.4	19.1	22.9	—	12.0	32.5	11.1	11.9	15.5	10.0
Women 30+ h/w	7.3	6.9	3.5	6.6	15.1	8.9	6.0	10.5	3.1	9.3	4.3	17.2	2.7	3.4	6.3	3.6
1–29 h/w	11.3	9.7	6.7	8.3	17.3	16.3	11.2	10.3	7.3	12.6	6.1	24.2	5.7	6.6	15.8	6.8
Total work load in households																
Couple, both full-time	5.9	6.3	2.1	4.0	15.5	7.3	5.0	9.0	2.9	7.1	3.2	15.5	0.2	1.9	5.4	2.1
Couple, full+part	8.5	8.2	3.7	5.6	17.9	14.9	7.6	11.1	5.5	14.7	4.2	16.7	0.9	3.5	12.5	3.7
Couple, full+non-act.	13.9	9.1	3.4	8.2	18.5	18.4	11.2	20.3	10.3	12.0	9.6	24.5	3.8	3.6	15.6	4.3
Couple, both part-time	9.2	7.8	5.3	5.3	15.0	13.7	8.4	9.0	5.1	9.1	5.0	17.3	0.0	13.0	13.5	0.0
Couple, part+non-act.	18.0	17.7	7.0	12.0	25.8	29.1	17.8	25.9	24.1	15.2	10.9	39.3	6.6	5.0	20.2	6.1
Couple, both non-act	20.1	18.2	8.0	13.0	26.1	24.2	16.3	21.0	27.3	14.2	15.3	36.8	3.9	3.3	31.3	3.8
Single, full-time	8.9	5.9	5.9	8.5	12.1	10.9	9.3	10.6	7.0	11.6	5.5	19.4	5.2	8.7	8.3	7.0
Single, part-time	24.1	17.1	17.2	26.1	20.9	27.1	25.6	13.6	20.3	—	10.1	50.1	15.6	17.2	33.3	22.4
Single, non-act.	27.2	18.4	15.7	24.9	30.6	19.1	24.9	23.0	37.8	19.3	22.8	45.3	11.0	13.2	42.9	11.3
Socio-economic group																
Upper non-man/empl.	10.6	9.6	2.9	7.4	12.6	15.9	8.4	17.7	5.4	4.7	4.8	21.8	5.1	6.6	9.9	—
Top managers	5.1	8.9	1.9	3.1	0.0	3.6	5.5	15.0	0.3	—	2.8	4.1	2.4	1.0	3.9	—
Professionals	4.2	4.4	1.5	4.8	2.9	1.6	2.6	5.9	1.0	3.0	3.3	2.2	2.0	3.4	5.2	—
Lower non-manual	5.6	4.7	3.7	5.3	3.1	4.4	5.1	5.6	3.1	3.1	4.1	4.9	1.6	3.2	8.8	—
Lower managers	17.1	13.5	6.7	14.2	14.7	26.3	18.7	22.8	9.5	—	13.2	24.2	10.6	10.1	16.2	—
All manual workers	10.1	5.7	2.1	6.9	11.9	14.7	9.6	15.5	9.3	19.5	10.0	14.0	1.9	4.6	10.9	—
Skilled man./foremen	8.4	3.8	1.5	5.3	12.5	11.5	8.8	11.9	4.9	17.6	9.7	13.7	1.6	4.2	9.6	—
Unskilled manual	11.9	7.0	2.6	9.3	11.3	17.9	10.4	19.7	12.4	21.1	10.3	14.2	2.1	5.0	12.1	—
Small farmers	35.6	43.9	27.8	—	42.4	39.6	38.1	32.0	19.9	—	24.6	55.3	9.0	—	15.4	—
Sector																
Private sector	11.1	9.1	4.3	7.1	20.4	16.6	9.5	16.4	9.2	13.3	7.2	22.1	4.4	3.6	10.9	3.7
Public sector	4.8	4.1	2.7	4.6	2.4	3.2	4.5	6.9	3.3	2.1	3.0	4.0	1.4	3.0	7.0	3.2

TABLE 5.4

Persons living in affluence, classified by adjusted disposable income over 150 of the national average. Persons aged 20-84 years, excluding full-time students and young adults living with their parents. Percent. Source: ECHP 1994/NSS

	Nordic			Central							Southern					
	EU14	B	DK	D	GR	E	F	I	IRL	L	NL	P	FIN	S	UK	N
All 16–84 years	15.5	14.0	9.1	14.9	16.5	16.5	16.7	15.7	16.5	16.1	15.7	15.9	10.3	12.6	15.9	8.6
Sex																
Men	16.9	15.0	10.1	17.5	17.6	17.0	17.5	16.6	17.3	17.6	16.2	16.9	11.3	13.8	17.5	9.5
Women	14.3	13.1	8.1	12.7	15.6	16.0	15.9	14.9	15.7	14.7	15.2	15.0	9.4	11.3	14.4	7.7
Age																
20–24 yr.	5.7	8.0	1.1	3.7	10.8	9.0	3.9	5.5	10.6	13.8	5.3	6.8	4.6	0.7	8.1	4.1
25–44 yr.	17.0	17.1	6.9	15.9	20.3	21.2	14.5	20.0	20.3	18.9	16.4	19.0	9.9	9.0	18.0	5.6
45–64 yr.	18.4	16.1	15.5	19.1	17.1	15.0	22.2	15.3	17.2	17.7	19.5	17.3	14.4	21.2	19.7	14.1
65–84 yr.	9.6	5.5	4.5	7.5	10.4	11.7	14.4	10.7	8.0	7.2	10.0	9.0	4.7	7.6	7.7	7.3
Sex add age																
Women 20–24 yr.	5.9	9.2	2.0	3.5	10.4	10.5	5.3	4.6	9.4	17.4	6.9	5.3	4.0	1.2	7.7	2.4
25–44 yr.	16.0	15.8	6.2	14.0	19.2	21.1	14.5	18.5	19.5	18.6	16.0	18.9	9.5	9.5	16.6	6.0
45–64 yr.	17.5	15.5	14.6	17.7	16.5	14.9	21.3	15.2	17.3	15.3	19.5	16.4	13.8	19.7	18.3	13.7
65–84 yr.	8.2	5.3	3.2	5.0	9.3	10.6	12.8	10.4	6.9	5.6	9.4	7.7	3.2	4.7	6.9	4.0
Men 16–24 yr.	5.4	5.7	0.0	4.2	11.6	7.1	1.6	6.7	13.0	7.1	2.7	8.8	5.2	0.0	8.5	5.8
25–44 yr.	18.0	18.5	7.6	17.9	21.4	21.4	14.5	21.6	21.1	19.2	16.7	19.2	10.2	8.6	19.4	5.2
45–64 yr.	19.2	16.7	16.4	20.5	17.7	15.1	23.1	15.4	17.1	19.9	19.5	18.4	15.0	22.7	21.0	14.5
65–84 yr.	11.6	5.7	6.3	11.6	11.7	13.1	16.5	11.1	9.4	9.6	11.0	10.7	7.0	11.3	8.8	11.1
Household composition																
Single adult 65+ yr.	6.3	3.1	3.1	5.5	6.7	7.7	10.1	8.4	4.1	3.9	8.7	2.7	1.3	4.3	4.3	2.6
Single adult 30–64 yr.	20.6	15.6	6.9	22.2	25.4	32.7	15.9	24.2	25.0	25.3	21.9	19.9	9.8	15.3	22.5	7.8
Single adult –30 yr.	8.9	12.9	0.8	7.3	11.4	28.7	8.8	25.6	25.1	6.1	2.8	7.4	7.9	3.0	12.6	0.9

TABLE 5.4
Continued

	Nordic			Central							Southern					
	EU14	B	DK	D	GR	E	F	I	IRL	L	NL	P	FIN	S	UK	N
Single parent	9.5	7.9	3.0	5.7	16.0	18.7	8.0	19.3	6.2	—	7.5	15.6	5.0	1.7	5.5	2.8
Couple 65+ yr., no ch	10.3	4.8	7.2	8.5	7.1	5.1	18.2	9.6	8.0	8.9	11.1	6.9	8.3	11.4	9.8	9.8
Couple –65 yr., no ch	27.9	25.3	18.9	26.4	26.1	29.9	26.8	31.6	45.0	28.1	32.7	23.6	20.6	30.2	28.9	20.0
Couple with childr.	13.9	14.1	6.5	12.6	18.7	17.7	15.0	14.6	14.7	15.0	7.6	19.2	8.8	7.3	12.5	7.0
Other households	12.0	14.8	14.3	8.1	13.6	12.0	11.1	11.0	15.1	10.6	8.8	11.3	6.0	0.0	17.7	8.0
Type of family																
Couple w Ch	13.9	14.1	6.5	12.6	18.6	17.7	15.0	14.6	14.7	15.0	7.4	19.3	9.0	7.4	12.5	7.2
Couple no Ch	21.0	16.5	15.6	20.7	16.7	17.1	23.4	20.7	29.5	21.8	25.2	14.7	16.6	22.2	22.4	15.0
Single w Ch	9.5	7.6	2.7	5.6	16.4	18.8	8.0	20.7	6.2	8.6	7.7	16.5	4.8	1.3	5.6	3.0
Single no Ch	12.5	10.3	4.2	12.7	14.0	18.0	12.5	16.1	14.8	13.6	12.6	8.9	6.5	8.4	12.1	4.5
Other type	12.0	14.8	14.3	8.1	13.6	12.0	11.1	11.0	15.1	10.6	8.8	11.3	6.0	0.0	17.7	8.0
No of children 0–17 yrs																
No childr.	17.8	15.1	11.0	17.4	17.0	17.2	19.2	17.6	21.9	18.6	19.9	17.1	11.7	15.3	18.9	11.6
1	13.6	14.3	4.8	12.1	17.7	16.8	14.8	15.4	16.9	13.1	6.1	16.7	10.6	9.1	10.5	5.7
2	10.4	10.4	3.6	6.6	15.3	14.9	12.5	10.6	11.5	11.8	5.3	13.0	6.8	5.9	10.7	3.1
3+	5.1	8.7	1.0	3.6	8.1	10.2	6.5	3.0	6.4	6.3	2.6	7.7	3.5	2.6	3.9	3.3
Parents of CH<16 yrs																
Mothers	13.2	13.2	6.0	11.4	18.2	17.8	14.0	15.0	13.4	14.1	7.4	18.7	8.5	6.7	11.1	7.4
Fathers	14.0	13.9	6.4	12.9	18.9	17.8	14.9	14.9	14.6	15.1	7.3	19.5	8.3	6.7	12.5	6.3
Single mothers	8.3	7.9	2.6	3.6	12.5	18.2	7.4	19.6	5.8	—	7.1	15.3	4.0	0.6	4.3	2.0
Education level																
3rd level	36.7	30.2	17.1	30.2	42.2	49.8	41.2	44.7	53.5	48.8	34.3	87.9	35.5	27.4	37.0	13.9
Post compulsory	16.5	14.3	8.1	14.2	22.8	27.5	13.4	26.7	23.1	20.0	14.1	38.6	14.8	10.9	15.8	7.5
Compulsory	9.1	6.9	4.4	10.7	7.9	8.4	8.3	9.9	5.8	7.5	7.5	8.9	7.7	11.3	9.2	8.0

TABLE 5.4

Continued

	Nordic			Central							Southern					
	EU14	B	DK	D	GR	E	F	I	IRL	L	NL	P	FIN	S	UK	N
Labour market position																
Self-employed	17.8	20.4	14.4	18.7	16.2	14.1	21.3	17.1	20.3	25.4	23.4	10.8	12.5	16.8	21.6	17.6
Employed	21.3	21.5	11.4	20.1	26.4	29.2	19.8	24.7	29.7	21.9	20.0	24.2	15.8	14.7	21.2	9.8
Unemployed	7.4	5.6	6.1	5.3	10.2	6.6	8.6	5.0	4.0	—	9.4	10.2	3.2	8.0	10.6	3.1
Retired	10.1	6.3	3.9	7.3	12.3	13.3	15.5	11.1	10.3	9.6	20.0	9.9	4.8	10.1	7.3	5.1
Doing housework	9.4	5.7	7.5	11.6	11.1	10.0	9.5	8.1	7.2	8.8	8.1	10.3	3.9	9.0	8.6	0.0
Socio-economic group																
Upper non-man/empl.	33.9	29.6	25.3	36.0	31.2	39.2	42.9	26.8	43.9	44.5	32.5	36.5	27.0	28.8	32.1	—
Top managers	43.1	40.0	38.6	32.1	80.6	65.7	57.1	44.5	56.6	65.1	29.5	80.4	42.6	39.5	43.1	—
Professionals	43.9	32.6	24.8	42.6	52.8	71.2	53.3	41.7	60.0	47.5	35.4	86.8	26.9	26.9	40.0	—
Lower non-manual	21.6	23.4	9.5	19.7	28.4	34.7	18.8	31.6	30.9	25.4	22.5	31.9	11.9	17.2	17.2	—
Lower managers	21.4	23.2	8.8	24.2	26.0	19.3	18.4	37.8	23.9	37.6	28.7	26.4	33.7	20.5	16.7	—
All manual workers	7.8	9.0	4.4	6.2	12.1	9.8	5.9	11.2	12.2	4.8	6.3	5.1	7.1	5.2	9.8	—
Skilled man./foremen	9.1	10.9	5.1	7.6	13.7	10.9	6.6	12.8	15.3	6.2	9.0	5.9	6.7	6.1	11.3	—
Unskilled manual	6.5	7.6	3.8	3.9	10.3	8.8	5.2	9.3	10.1	3.7	3.2	4.3	7.4	3.5	8.5	—
Small farmers	7.6	1.4	—	9.9	5.4	6.9	5.2	3.1	13.5	—	25.1	2.5	6.1	—	28.5	—
Sector																
Private sector	19.3	21.1	13.2	19.0	18.2	20.2	18.0	20.7	23.7	17.5	21.4	14.1	13.5	15.5	20.7	11.6
Public sector	25.4	23.2	9.8	23.4	33.3	47.1	24.6	27.4	38.3	36.4	24.2	46.3	13.6	14.3	24.3	9.1

TABLE 6.1

Subjective general health is rated as "good". Adults 16–84 yrs. Percent. Source ECHP/NSS

	Nordic			Central							Southern				
	EU14	FIN	S	DK	B	D	F	IRL	UK	L	NL	GR	E	I	P
All 16–84 years	66.1	62.5	74.8	78.3	71.8	66.8	63.1	79.7	73.4	66.9	74.0	72.7	63.8	57.7	52.4
Sex Men	69.6	63.2	77.9	80.3	76.3	70.2	66.8	81.6	75.6	70.4	78.2	76.0	67.7	62.2	58.6
Women	62.8	61.8	71.8	76.4	67.6	63.7	59.6	78.0	71.4	63.6	70.0	69.7	60.2	53.6	46.8
Sex and age															
Women 16–24 yr.	87.9	88.5	86.3	95.0	88.4	90.9	81.8	93.3	86.6	83.2	86.5	97.5	90.6	88.2	84.5
25–44 yr.	78.5	80.8	84.8	88.7	80.6	84.1	72.2	86.4	81.9	81.0	80.3	91.2	79.8	69.0	64.0
45–64 yr.	53.0	49.3	67.0	72.1	61.5	52.7	52.3	75.0	68.0	49.9	64.4	59.2	43.6	40.3	29.3
65–84 yr.	32.7	26.9	49.2	49.4	40.6	33.9	30.0	47.9	48.2	32.1	44.8	28.6	22.6	19.6	9.9
Men 16–24 yr.	90.0	90.4	90.9	93.9	92.3	92.7	84.3	93.6	89.1	89.2	90.7	97.8	92.3	89.9	87.1
25–44 yr.	81.7	77.2	87.2	89.8	85.9	85.2	77.5	90.0	84.8	81.6	87.1	93.2	81.2	73.7	71.5
45–64 yr.	60.1	47.9	72.2	75.5	70.3	58.2	58.9	75.4	71.6	61.3	71.1	69.0	53.5	50.7	45.7
65–84 yr.	39.0	29.4	57.7	54.4	52.0	40.4	38.0	56.8	48.9	37.2	51.2	35.0	32.3	26.4	17.6
Disp.income, nat.stand.															
More than 1,5*average	76.0	72.1	82.2	89.1	81.1	76.5	68.0	91.8	85.6	80.2	78.9	84.3	77.8	66.3	69.9
Intermediate	65.5	60.0	72.1	77.7	71.1	66.4	62.5	80.3	74.6	66.5	73.5	74.2	61.5	55.7	53.1
Less than 0,5*average	57.0	64.8	84.8	70.2	65.2	56.9	54.8	67.7	62.3	55.8	68.4	58.0	56.2	51.3	35.2
Disp.income, eu.stand.															
More than 1,5*average	77.4	73.1	83.2	89.9	81.1	76.0	68.5	92.6	85.5	71.3	79.4	85.9	80.6	67.8	68.7
Intermediate	65.9	60.2	72.4	77.1	69.8	66.0	62.6	82.6	73.1	59.6	73.6	78.4	64.8	56.8	56.7
Less than 0,5*average	56.0	62.1	83.4	74.0	70.5	55.5	54.6	67.2	63.4	80.5	67.2	61.6	54.4	51.1	40.7
Socio-economic group															
Upper non-man/empl.	80.7	77.3	86.7	92.7	84.8	84.4	75.1	93.5	88.0	85.6	86.0	88.1	79.0	67.3	64.5
Lower non-manual	80.0	73.8	87.2	90.3	85.9	80.9	73.0	93.2	85.9	83.8	85.2	92.7	84.3	70.6	71.1
All manual workers	74.7	67.8	80.3	86.4	83.6	74.1	73.3	90.0	81.7	68.9	81.8	84.4	73.7	65.9	66.8
Skilled man./foremen	76.8	68.8	83.1	88.5	87.0	77.4	74.4	91.1	84.0	74.1	84.6	88.8	74.2	68.1	70.6
Unskilled manual	72.4	67.0	78.7	85.0	81.3	68.0	72.3	89.3	79.6	64.2	78.8	79.4	73.3	63.2	62.2
Small farmers	67.2	56.1	55.0	70.4	77.9	80.7	69.5	80.0	81.4	91.0	80.9	74.9	59.4	62.4	45.7

TABLE 6.2

Subjective general health is rated "bad". 16'-84 years. Percent. Source: ECHP/NSS

	Nordic			Central							Southern				
	EU14	FIN	S	DK	B	D	F	IRL	UK	L	NL	GR	E	I	P
All 16–84 years	9.2	7.6	5.5	6.3	6.3	8.0	7.9	3.6	6.5	7.6	4.8	12.4	10.4	13.7	20.1
Sex															
Men	8.0	7.8	4.9	5.5	5.2	7.2	6.8	3.3	6.2	6.2	3.8	10.6	9.2	11.1	16.7
Women	10.3	7.4	6.2	7.1	7.3	8.8	8.8	4.0	6.8	9.0	5.8	14.1	11.6	16.0	23.2
Sex and age															
Women 16–24 yr.	1.4	0.9	0.9	0.8	1.3	1.4	2.3	0.8	1.1	3.6	2.0	1.1	0.4	1.0	2.4
25–44 yr.	3.5	2.2	2.4	1.9	3.3	3.1	4.1	2.4	3.3	3.9	3.6	3.4	1.8	4.1	7.8
45–64 yr.	12.6	8.1	8.0	8.3	7.6	8.7	11.3	4.3	8.0	12.6	7.2	17.3	14.4	23.3	31.7
65–84 yr.	25.0	20.8	12.8	18.6	17.6	21.7	18.9	10.3	14.6	18.5	11.5	38.4	32.4	40.6	56.0
Men 16–24 yr.	1.1	0.7	0.9	0.9	1.2	0.4	1.0	0.2	1.4	1.9	0.7	1.5	0.8	1.3	2.9
25–44 yr.	3.1	3.2	2.4	2.0	2.5	2.4	4.1	1.2	2.8	4.3	2.1	3.5	1.8	3.4	8.1
45–64 yr.	10.8	9.8	6.1	7.1	7.4	10.8	8.9	4.9	8.0	7.7	4.8	13.0	10.7	17.4	21.5
65–84 yr.	20.9	23.9	11.5	15.0	10.9	16.6	15.3	9.3	15.5	13.0	10.2	33.4	29.0	30.0	45.4
Education level															
3rd level	2.4	2.7	1.7	1.6	2.8	3.6	2.4	0.6	2.2	0.9	2.9	2.0	1.2	1.2	1.6
Post compulsory	3.4	1.1	1.8	2.9	3.3	4.5	4.2	1.2	3.1	3.2	2.4	2.6	1.2	2.1	1.9
Compulsory	8.3	6.3	6.9	7.8	6.3	6.3	9.3	3.7	6.4	8.5	7.4	8.0	7.4	11.1	14.5
Disp.income, nat.stand.															
More than 1,5*average	4.1	5.1	3.7	2.5	1.9	4.1	4.2	0.7	1.7	2.9	1.7	5.6	4.4	5.5	7.8
Intermediate	9.0	8.1	6.2	6.3	6.3	7.9	7.9	3.8	6.0	7.5	4.8	12.8	9.3	14.2	17.9
Less than 0,5*average	14.8	9.9	4.1	10.5	9.9	12.6	12.0	5.3	10.7	12.5	8.0	17.3	18.9	19.5	35.5
Socio-economic group															
Upper non-man/empl.	2.5	2.2	1.8	0.8	1.9	1.9	2.4	0.3	1.1	1.5	1.4	4.4	2.6	3.7	8.7
Lower non-manual	2.3	2.5	1.9	1.4	1.7	3.0	2.6	0.4	1.3	1.9	1.6	2.6	0.9	2.2	3.8
All manual workers	4.0	3.7	2.4	2.3	2.1	4.5	4.3	1.0	1.7	6.4	1.8	5.5	2.7	4.8	7.6
Skilled man./foremen	3.5	2.1	1.7	2.9	0.8	3.8	3.8	0.8	1.5	4.4	1.3	4.6	1.5	4.7	6.4
Unskilled manual	4.6	4.8	2.9	1.9	3.0	5.7	4.8	1.1	1.9	8.2	2.3	6.6	4.1	5.0	9.1
Small farmers	7.6	5.1	16.1	7.4	1.3	0.0	3.8	1.0	0.0	0.0	0.0	8.9	5.2	14.2	20.4

TABLE 6.3

Persons reporting being "severely hampered in daily activities". 16–84 yrs. Percent. Source: ECHP/NSS

	Nordic			Central							Southern					
	EU14	FIN	S	DK	N	B	D	F	IRL	UK	L	NL	GR	E	I	P
All 16–84 years	7.5	15.1	11.7	5.1	10.3	6.8	7.1	10.4	3.9	5.6	4.5	6.8	6.9	6.1	7.2	8.9
Sex																
Men	7.1	15.3	10.5	4.5	8.2	6.3	7.5	10.0	3.8	5.4	4.8	5.9	6.5	5.7	6.1	8.6
Women	7.8	14.9	12.9	5.7	12.5	7.3	6.7	10.9	3.9	5.8	4.2	7.8	7.3	6.5	8.2	9.2
Sex and age																
Women 16–24 yr.	1.3	5.4	1.5	1.7	5.7	1.1	0.8	3.1	0.5	0.8	0.0	1.4	1.5	0.0	1.0	2.2
25–44 yr.	2.7	5.5	6.5	1.6	6.7	3.6	2.3	4.2	2.7	1.8	1.9	4.3	2.1	2.0	2.2	3.6
45–64 yr.	8.5	13.2	16.8	5.8	16.2	8.0	6.2	13.2	4.1	5.8	6.8	8.2	9.4	8.2	8.8	12.2
65–84 yr.	19.8	30.8	24.5	15.4	24.7	16.8	17.6	25.8	9.8	15.5	8.2	19.0	17.6	17.9	23.8	20.8
Men 16–24 yr.	1.5	1.6	1.5	1.5	1.6	1.4	1.2	2.4	0.8	1.1	1.0	2.0	2.2	1.1	1.4	2.1
25–44 yr.	2.9	7.0	4.6	1.3	3.5	2.5	2.0	5.8	1.5	2.1	3.0	2.7	2.1	2.6	2.2	5.4
45–64 yr.	9.3	16.9	15.1	5.8	11.5	8.1	10.2	12.1	5.4	6.4	7.0	8.3	8.0	9.3	7.3	11.4
65–84 yr.	18.5	31.5	22.1	12.6	20.2	15.8	21.1	24.2	10.6	14.5	9.5	15.0	16.7	12.0	18.7	19.0
Disp.income, nat.stand.																
More than 1,5*average	3.4	6.8	7.5	2.0	4.6	2.1	3.5	6.3	1.1	1.2	2.8	3.0	3.1	2.3	3.9	4.8
Intermediate	7.5	15.6	13.1	5.1	11.0	7.1	6.9	10.5	3.8	5.4	4.6	7.0	6.2	6.6	7.3	8.2
Less than 0,5*average	10.7	18.1	9.2	8.8	11.2	9.3	12.2	15.1	6.5	8.8	5.9	10.0	11.9	8.0	10.4	14.4
Socio-economic group																
Upper non-man/empl.	1.9	4.3	3.1	0.3	—	2.3	2.0	2.9	0.3	0.7	1.2	1.5	2.0	1.1	2.4	4.5
Lower non-manual	2.1	4.9	2.8	0.8	—	2.2	1.9	4.2	0.8	0.9	1.3	2.2	0.7	1.1	1.7	2.3
All manual workers	3.0	6.0	6.6	1.7	—	2.0	3.1	6.2	0.9	0.7	2.4	2.9	1.8	1.6	2.5	2.8
Skilled man./foremen	2.4	6.0	4.8	1.5	—	2.1	2.4	5.6	0.7	0.4	1.0	2.4	1.9	1.3	1.8	2.1
Unskilled manual	3.7	6.0	8.3	1.8	—	1.9	4.4	6.8	1.1	1.1	3.6	3.3	1.7	1.8	3.4	3.7
Small farmers	4.6	12.6	7.5	3.9	—	1.2	1.2	7.1	0.8	1.9	0.0	6.6	3.2	5.9	5.6	5.7